Rome's Audacious Claim

Should Every Christian Be Subject to the Pope?

by Paul F. Pavao

Greatest Stories Ever Told® • Selmer, Tennessee

ROME'S AUDACIOUS CLAIM

by Paul F. Pavao

ISBN, paperback edition: 978-0-9960559-9-4

Published by:

Greatest Stories Ever Told®
P.O. Box 307
Selmer, TN 38375
admin@Christian-History.org
http://www.RebuildingTheFoundations.org

History is, by definition, the most exciting stories and interesting facts of all time.

Copyright 2019 © by Paul F. Pavao. All rights reserved.

Important Notes

References

My reference style is based on APA style, but adapted to make the references easier to follow for the average reader. Partial references are in the footnote, with full references in the bibliography.

New American Bible, Revised Edition

The New American Bible, Revised Edition (NABRE) is used throughout *Rome's Audacious Claim* unless otherwise noted. It is an approved translation of the United States Council of Catholic Bishops. Its copyright notice is: New American Bible, revised edition © 2010, 1991, 1986, 1970 Confraternity of Christian Doctrine, Inc., Washington, D.C. All Rights Reserved.

The Early Church Fathers

Quotes from the early church fathers are taken from *The Ante-Nicene Fathers* and *The Nicene and Post-Nicene Fathers* unless otherwise noted. Those series are in the public domain and are currently in print from William B. Eerdmans Publishing Company (Grand Rapids, MI), Hendrickson Publishers (Peabody, MA), and the Christian Classic Ethereal Library (CCEL). CCEL has rendered the aforementioned series into PDF form, and I have used their PDF version for citations. All the passages I reference can be read online at http://www.ccel.org/fathers.html and at http://www.earlychristianwritings.com. Both web sites are functional as of the publication date of this book.

Catechism of the Catholic Church

The *Catechism of the Catholic Church* is used throughout the book as a reference for Roman Catholic dogma. It bears the "Apostolic Authority" of Pope John Paul II, who wrote:

> The Catechism of the Catholic Church, which I approved June 25th last and the publication of which I today order by virtue of my Apostolic Authority, is a statement of the Church's faith and of catholic doctrine, attested to or illumined by Sacred Scripture, the Apostolic Tradition, and the Church's Magisterium. I declare it to be a sure norm for teaching the faith and thus a valid and legitimate instrument for ecclesial communion. (*Catechism of the Catholic Church*, 1995, par. 3)

Capitalization of Church

I have chosen to capitalize Church where it refers to the Church universal or to a collection of churches. I use the small "church" to reference individual churches. When citing the fathers, I have applied that distinction according to my best judgment. When citing other authors, I did not change their capitalization.

Contents

Important Notes iii
Preface ix
Dedication xi

Part I: What is Rome's Audacious Claim 1

What is Rome's Audacious Claim? 1
Chapter 1: Rome's Audacious Claim 3
Vatican II 4
Chapter 2: First-Round Knockout 9
Chapter 3: The Development of the Papacy 17

Part II: Peter in Roman Catholic Doctrine 25

Peter in Roman Catholic Doctrine 25
Chapter 4: Matthew 16:15-19 27
Peter as the Rock 28
The Gates of Hades Will Not Prevail against the Church ... 29
Keys of the Kingdom of God 30
Isaiah 22:15-25 32
The Keys of the Kingdom in the Early Church Fathers 33
Binding and Loosing 40
Chapter 5: John 21:15-17 43

Part III: New Testament History 47
Chapter 6: Popes, Patriarchs, and the Episcopacy 49
One Holy, Catholic, and Apostolic Church 53
Protestants and Apostolic Churches 54
Chapter 7: Peter the Presbyter 59
Peter and James 61
Hypocrisy in Antioch: Who Was Submitting to Whom? 63
Chapter 8: Paul and Peter 65

Part IV: The Apostolic Fathers 69

Chapter 9: Clement of Rome 71
   Clement as Messenger 73
   Answers to Roman Catholic Apologist Arguments 75
Chapter 10: The Origin of Monarchial Bishops 79
Chapter 11: Ignatius of Antioch 83
   Answers to Roman Catholic Arguments 85
Chapter 12: Polycarp of Smyrna 89
Chapter 13: The Didache and Other Early Works 90

Part V: The Apologists 91
  Chapter 14: The Apologists 93
  Chapter 15: Irenaeus 97
   Introduction to *Against Heresies* 98
   Apostolic Tradition 98
   Apostolic Succession 102
  Chapter 16: Tertullian 113
   The Keys of the Kingdom 116
   Scorpiace 118
   The Montanists Appeal to the Bishop of Rome 119
  Chapter 17: Victor 123

Part VI: The Third Century 129
  Chapter 18: Hippolytus 131
  Chapter 19: Origen 133
   Origen's Commentary on Matthew 136
  Chapter 20: Cyprian 141
   Rome Was the Nearest Apostolic Church to Carthage 141
   Cyprian, Peter, and Matthew 16 142
   The Seventh Council of Carthage 145
   Misuse of Cyprian's Writings by Catholic Apologists 151
   Initial Conclusions and Summary 155
  Chapter 21: Cyprian's Epistles and Treatises 157
   On the Unity of the Church 189
   The Remainder of Cyprian's Treatises 190
  Chapter 22: Other Third-Century Writers 191
   Dionysius of Rome and Dionysius of Alexandria 191
   Paul of Samosata 193
   The Letter of Clement to James 194
   Pseudo-Tertullian: Poem against the Marcionites 195

    Conclusion 196
Part VII: The Fourth Century and Afterward 197
    Chapter 23: The Fourth Century 199
        The Council of Nicea 199
    Chapter 24: Rome Makes Its Audacious Claim 207
    Chapter 25: The Papacy After Leo I 213
        The Great Schism 218
        Conclusion 218
Part VIII: Arguments 219
    Chapter 26: Is Papal Primacy a Divine Development? 221
    Chapter 27: Rome's Corrupt Succession 229
        Corruption 229
        The Popes of the Tenth and Eleventh Century 231
        Breaks in the Succession 241
    Chapter 28: Apostolic Tradition Preserved in Rome? 243
        True Roman Catholic Doctrines 243
        The Papacy 246
        A New Priesthood 246
        Indulgences 246
        Foreign Language Bibles and Liturgies 249
        State Churches 250
        Idolatry and the Ten Commandments 252
        The Peak of Idolatry: The Virgin Mary 256
        Conclusion: The Fruit of Papal Primacy 257
    Chapter 29: A Call to Action 259
        Build on the Right Rock 259
        Salvation by Faith Alone 260
        The Final Judgment 261
        The Atonement 264
    Bibliography: 271
    Index 291

Preface

Honesty was the biggest difficulty I faced in writing this book. My primary argument was easy enough to prove. The pope's audacious claim to full, supreme, and universal power over the whole Church did not come from Jesus or Peter, but from centuries later. A thorough treatment of history demands that conclusion, and authorities in the Roman Catholic Church have recently been admitting it. The details, though, were not so easy.

For example, I was caught off guard by Scott Hahn's use of Isaiah 22. I found his argument after I was well into the book. I found a dismissive answer right away, but I hated it. It was the kind of argument that sweeps a Scripture under the rug rather than dealing with it. It would have sufficed, but I did not use it. You can read the research I chose to do instead in chapter 4.

To an unbiased historian, it is obvious that neither Peter nor the churches of the second century believed there was or would be a supreme authority in Rome. The average Christian, though, has no way to know that. Defenders of Rome's Audacious Claim take advantage of this ignorance and create an unhistorical story bolstered by small details taken out of historical context.

The temptation to dishonesty was strongest in refuting those details. As God is my witness, I did not give in to it. I am human, and I assume that some bias has leaked out on these pages. My conscience is clear, however, that I have presented my opponents' arguments fairly and fully.

As a result, I am absolutely confident that the story told across these 270 pages is accurate and will stand the test of time and the assaults of its opponents.

Paul Pavao
November 7, 2019

Dedication

To all the Roman Catholics who have argued with me without regard to my responses, thank you. Without you, I probably would not have written this book. They say necessity is the mother of invention, but sometimes irritation is.

I definitely could not have written this without God. The times I prayed for direction and found it are too numerable to recount.

To God and my parents, who taught me not to lie: you put most of the value in this book. When one is writing a polemic, the temptations to be dishonest are severe. The comfort of the Holy Spirit and confidence that Jesus, who is the Truth, is always good are the only reasons I could overcome.

To my wife, who not only allowed me the time to write this book, but encouraged, supported, and helped me: I cannot imagine life without you.

To the Patristics for Protestants Facebook group: your advice, arguments, and interest were invaluable.

To my daughter-in-law, Esther Pavao: I never get nervous about ending the book because I know you will wrap up all the final details with patience and skill.

To my six children: I love you and am proud of you! You are fighters. You deserve to be in all my book dedications.

To David Noah Taylor, Glenn Roseberry, J.T. Tancock, David Servant, and K.V. Daniel: that I have your praise leaves me surprised and honored. You are my living heroes in the faith.

To Bruce Patterson: your free proofreading and several objections were invaluable.

To Matthew Bryan: thank you for reminding me there were churches outside the Roman Empire! You proofed the text, too, but mostly you are a true friend.

Part I

What is Rome's Audacious Claim?

Rome's Audacious Claim

Chapter 1: Rome's Audacious Claim

The Roman Catholic Church claims authority over you and every other Christian and church on the face of the earth. I find that claim "audacious."

Rome's Audacious Claim is known to theologians as "Papal Primacy."[1] Father John Trigilio, Jr., the president of the Confraternity of Catholic Clergy and a noted Roman Catholic apologist, quotes the First Vatican Council in defining Papal Primacy:

> All the faithful of Christ must believe that the Apostolic See and the Roman Pontiff hold primacy over the whole world, and that the Pontiff of Rome himself is the successor of the blessed Peter, the chief of the apostles, and is the true Vicar of Christ and head of the whole Church and faith, and teacher of all Christians.[2]

With these words, the Catholic Church claims that the Pope ("the Pontiff of Rome") is the head of your church and your faith and is your teacher.

Most non-Catholic Christians find this claim ludicrous, so they simply dismiss it. They go about the business of following Jesus and participating in their particular Christian tradition without a further thought.

Times are changing, though. The Information Age is upon us, and Christians are lapping up information like never before. Some of that information is the argument of Roman Catholic apologists that they can trace the universal authority of the bishop of Rome through history back to the apostles and even to Jesus himself.

There is a whole industry devoted to converting evangelicals to Catholicism. Scott Hahn is surely the champion of these apologists. His ministry's website, Coming Home, draws at least several hundred visitors every day.[3] His book *Rome Sweet Home* has 697 reviews on

---

[1] I will be capitalizing both "Papal Primacy" and "Rome's Audacious Claim" throughout this book.
[2] Trigilio, 2013, "What Is Papal Primacy," par. 5
[3] Catholics Come Home, 2008-2019. I base my traffic estimate on the site's Alexa rating (Alexa.com), which was 260,719 in the U.S. on December 8, 2016. My own

Amazon, 92 percent of which have four or five stars.[4] To get an idea of how many that is, the popular Protestant apologist Hank Hanegraaff, radio's "Bible Answer Man," has had just 135 reviews for his *The Complete Bible Answer Book*.[5]

On a personal note, I am among the most proselytized non-Catholics on earth. My website, Christian History for Everyman,[6] apparently causes Roman Catholics to marvel that I am not Roman Catholic with them. They are certain that early Christian history testifies against Protestantism so strongly that anyone who studies the early church fathers will become Roman Catholic.

Admittedly, early Christian history does testify against many Protestant doctrines, but the earliest church fathers also witness against many Roman Catholic doctrines. Perhaps the most important of those is Papal Primacy.

Perhaps that is why, despite their efforts and audience, these apologists have had little success. The exodus of Catholics to Protestantism is far greater than the conversion of Protestants to Catholicism. Fifteen percent of those raised Catholic are now Protestant,[7] whereas only three percent of those raised Protestant are now Catholic.[8]

Vatican II

Papal Primacy is not just a relic of the past; it is still Roman Catholic dogma. From 1962 to 1965, the Roman Catholic Church held a Second Vatican Council to "make the message of faith more relevant to people in the twentieth century."[9] It is the most authoritative source for the current beliefs of the Roman Catholic Church. In 2016, Bishop

---

site, www.christian-history.org, is ranked similarly (228,130 on the same day) and draws just over 1,000 unique visitors per day.

[4] Amazon.com, inc., 1996-2019, "Rome Sweet Home." Review count as of December 8, 2016.

[5] Amazon.com inc. 1996-2019, "The Complete Bible Answer Book." Review count as of December 8, 2016.

[6] Pavao, 2009-2019

[7] Pew Research Center, 2011, "Leaving Catholicism"

[8] Pew Research Center, 2011, "Changing Within Protestantism"

[9] Butler, 2016, "The Need for Vatican II," par. 1

Part I | Chapter 1: Rome's Audacious Claim

Christopher Butler wrote, "The Second Vatican Council expresses the mind of the Church for today."[10]

The council softened many Roman Catholic doctrines; so much so that Vatican II prompted its own exodus of long-time Roman Catholics.[11] My own father left the Roman Catholic Church some years after Vatican II as the changes decreed there began to take effect in local parishes.

Papal Primacy, however, was not softened at all. Toward the end of the council, Pope Paul VI issued the "Dogmatic Constitution of the Church," better known by its Latin title: *Lumen Gentium*.[12] In it, he told the world:

> The pope's power of primacy over all, both pastors and faithful, remains whole and intact. In virtue of his office, that is as Vicar of Christ and pastor of the whole Church, the Roman Pontiff has full, supreme and universal power over the Church. And he is always free to exercise this power.[13]

Vatican II expressly confirmed Papal Primacy without retreat. The pope's primacy is over all, leaders and congregations alike, and it remains whole and intact, at least in the eyes of the Roman Catholic Church. To this day, the *Catechism of the Catholic Church* includes the wording of *Lumen Gentium* almost verbatim.[14]

Obviously, the pope and the Roman Catholic Church are aware that most of the world's Christians reject his authority. As a result, Vatican II had to provide guidelines to determine which of those who reject the pope's authority are to be called "Christian" and "brothers."[15]

Allowing that *any* of those who deny the pope's authority are to be considered Christian was a new attitude for the Roman Catholic Church. Vatican I, held from 1869-1870, was not nearly so gracious:

> If then, any should deny that it is by the institution of Christ the Lord and by Divine right, that Blessed Peter should have a perpetual line of successors in the Primacy over the Universal

---

[10] Butler, 2016, "The Need for Vatican II," par. 4
[11] Cunningham & editors, 2017, "The Church Since Vatican II"
[12] *Lumen Gentium* means "Light of the Nations."
[13] Pope Paul VI, 1964, "Dogmatic Constitution," ch. 3, sec. 22
[14] *Catechism of the Catholic Church*, 1995, par. 882
[15] *Unitatis Redintegratio*, 1964, ch. 1, sec. 3

Rome's Audacious Claim

Church, or that the Roman Pontiff is the successor of Blessed Peter in this primacy; let him be anathema.[16]

We will not address papal infallibility in this book. Once we establish that the doctrine of Papal Primacy was neither early nor ever universally accepted, the doctrine of infallibility disappears with it. In fact, it crumbles upon itself already. All councils that the Roman Catholic Church defines as "ecumenical" are infallible.[17] Vatican Councils I and II are both ecumenical,[18] and they contradict each other on this matter. Are those who reject Rome's Audacious Claim anathema, or are they brothers?[19]

Of course, the contradiction between Vatican I and Vatican II is apparent to Roman Catholics as well. The Eternal Word Television Network argues that there is no contradiction, but they fail to compare Vatican I's anathematization of those who reject Papal Primacy with the term "separated brethren" used at Vatican II.[20]

CatholicApologetics.info denies the infallibility of Vatican II because it was a "pastoral" council rather than a "doctrinal one."[21] This ignores the fact that any council deemed "ecumenical" by the Roman Catholic Church is, by definition, infallible.[22] Because CatholicApologetics.info is not the only Roman Catholic group that denies the infallibility of Vatican II,[23] the "Most Holy Family Monastery" gives translations of Pope John XXIII's opening speech to establish that he fully intended for Vatican II to be infallible.[24]

---

[16] Conte, n.d., "First Vatican Council," ch. II, par. 4. Definitions of "anathema" vary, but it certainly involves excommunicating the anathematized persons.

[17] Catholic Answers, 2018, "Infallibility," sec. "Ecumenical Councils," par. 2

[18] Keating, 1993, "The 21 Ecumenical Councils"

[19] *Unitatis Redintegratio*, 1964, introduction

[20] Eternal Word Television Network, n.d., "Questions and Answers"

[21] Catholic Apologetics, n.d., "Vatican II: Renewal or a New Religion?"

[22] Catholic Answers, 2018, "Infallibility," sec. "Ecumenical Councils," par. 2

[23] e.g., Society of St. Pius X, 2003, "The Errors of Vatican II: Part I. The fact that the Most Holy Family Monastery wrote the article "Was Vatican II infallible" (see next footnote) shows how many Roman Catholic organizations deny its infallibility.

[24] Most Holy Family Monastery, 2014, "Was Vatican II Infallible." Unfortunately, the Vatican website (John XXIII, 1962, "Speeches 1962") does not give an English translation of the speech cited by the Most Holy Family Monastery, so I am forced to rely on this secondary source.

Part I | Chapter 1: Rome's Audacious Claim

In this book we will try to spare the Roman Church the difficult determination of which Vatican Councils are infallible and which non-Roman Catholics are brethren. Once we establish that Jesus did not give supreme authority to Peter and that Peter did not pass supreme authority on to the bishop of Rome, the doctrine of infallibility will fall with the doctrine of Papal Primacy.

We will resort to both Scripture and history to refute their claim, because Roman Catholic apologists argue from both sources. Many of my readers will be familiar with the Scriptures, but most will not be familiar with early Christian history.

Therefore, we will begin by telling the story of how the Roman Catholic Church rose to power, how the Roman bishop became known as the pope, and how he came to claim supreme authority over every Christian on earth. To make such a claim requires great audacity because all other churches descended from apostolic times have consistently rejected Rome's claim to "full, supreme, and universal power." This includes all the churches mentioned in the New Testament, most of whom are part of what are now known as the Eastern Orthodox Churches. We will also touch on the churches descended from apostolic times that exist in Persia, India, Egypt, and Ethiopia, many of which never heard of Rome's Audacious Claim until this millennium.

We will establish exactly when that claim was first asserted and how other churches reacted at that time. First, though, we need to look at an astonishing fact I discovered during my research for this book: the Roman Catholic Church has been fighting, and losing, the battle for Papal Primacy in back rooms, out of the public eye.

Rome's Audacious Claim

Chapter 2: First-Round Knockout

When I began this work, I intended it to be a battle with the more well-known Roman Catholic apologists. I was angry with the deceitful things I had heard from them, and I wanted to set the record straight: my history against their history, my evidence against their evidence, my arguments against their arguments. Toe to toe, I expected to trade blows with them. I would lay out their evidence, and I would expose that evidence as misrepresented or misinterpreted.

Research revealed I do not have to do this! I will knock them off their feet, never to get back up, right here at the beginning. It turns out that the Vatican, the U.S. Conference of Catholic Bishops, and many of the Roman Catholic Church's own scholars have given up the battle for Rome's Audacious Claim, as it is impossible to win.

The Roman Catholic Church has attempted to restore unity with other large Churches, primarily the Eastern Orthodox Churches, and the U.S. Conference of Catholic Bishops has parlayed with the Lutherans as well.[25] When such large organizations meet, they choose not only high-ranking officials as representatives, but also well-educated ones. As a result, the representatives of Rome cannot play fast and loose with the facts of history like apologists do.

For example, a couple days ago I was reading Dave Armstrong's *Catholic Church Fathers*. I have the Kindle edition, and at location 3163, he writes:

> About the year 190 the question regarding the proper day for celebrating Easter was agitated in the East, and referred to Pope St. Victor I ... St. Victor directs the Eastern churches, for the sake of uniformity, to conform to the practice of the West, and his instructions are universally followed ...[26]

This claim is false. The only reason we know about Victor's directive at all is because Eusebius tells the story in his *Church History*.[27] He tells us that there was a controversy about the day on

---

[25] United States Conference of Catholic Bishops, 1973, "Differing Attitudes Toward Papal Primacy"
[26] Armstrong, 2013, *Catholic Church Fathers*, Kindle location 3163, ellipses in original
[27] Eusebius, *Church History*, Bk. V, ch. 23

Rome's Audacious Claim

which to celebrate *Pascha*. This is the Greek word for "Passover," but English speakers call it "Easter." In the second century, individual churches fasted between two and forty days, then broke the fast on Passover.[28]

The problem was that some churches celebrated Passover on the same day as the Jews, Nisan 14 by the Jewish calendars, no matter which day of the week it fell on. Most churches, though, including Rome, where Victor presided as bishop, celebrated the Passover on the Sunday after Nisan 14.

Eusebius tells us that churches all over the empire held synods (meetings of bishops) and decided to only celebrate Passover on Sunday. He ends that chapter by saying this "was their unanimous decision."[29]

The next chapter, however, begins with, "But the bishops of Asia[30] led by Polycrates, decided to hold to the old custom handed down to them." Eusebius then gives the text from a letter Polycrates, the bishop of Ephesus, sent to Victor in Rome. We can determine from his letter that Victor must have written first, threatening the church at Ephesus, probably with excommunication. In response, Polycrates writes:

> I, therefore, brethren, who have lived sixty-five years in the Lord, have met with brethren throughout the world, and have gone through every holy Scripture, am not frightened by terrifying words. For those greater than I have said, "We ought to obey God rather than man." [Acts 5:29].[31]

Once Victor got the letter, he immediately "attempted to cut off" the churches in Asia from what Eusebius calls "the common unity." He sent letters declaring them "wholly excommunicate."[32]

Dave Armstrong tells us that Victor's instructions were "universally followed."[33] This is just false. The churches of Asia rejected his instructions. Worse, once those letters of

---

[28] Today we call the fast "Lent." It was mandated to be forty days long at the First Council of Nicea in 325.
[29] Eusebius, *Church History*, Bk. V, ch. 23, par. 3
[30] Asia Minor, modern Turkey; Ephesus was the central city there.
[31] Eusebius, *Church History*, Bk. V, ch. 24, par. 7, brackets mine
[32] Eusebius, *Church History*, Bk. V, ch. 23, par. 9
[33] Armstrong, 2013, *Catholic Church Fathers*, Kindle location 3163

excommunication went out from Rome, "This did not please all the bishops.... words of theirs are extant, sharply rebuking Victor."[34]

Did Dave Armstrong not know about the response of the churches? Ignorance is not a good basis for a book, especially a polemical one.[35] Did he know, but then hide it from his readers? Deceit is an even worse basis for a book.

The end of this story is that Irenaeus of Lyons, whom we will cover in chapter 17, wrote a letter to Victor reminding him that his predecessors had had peaceful dealings with the Asian churches over the celebration of *Pascha*. He "admonished" Victor that "he should not cut off whole churches of God which observed the tradition of ancient custom."[36]

Mr. Armstrong was able to publish a book, though it was self-published through Lulu Press, with errors like this one because no scholars were going to review his books in scholarly publications. Apologists can get away with errors and intellectual dishonesty. If representatives of the Roman Catholic Church did this with the Orthodox or Lutherans, their meeting would come to an abrupt end.

Roman Catholic scholars must meet a similar standard. Just as Orthodox and Lutheran representatives require intellectual honesty of Roman Catholic legates, so Roman Catholic scholars must justify their history and their claims to other scholars.

An apologist writes for the populace. He is trying to convince the average person about his subject. Since an apologist's readers generally know little of his subject, he can get away with the kind of misinformation we just saw in *Catholic Church Fathers*. Scholars, on the other hand, typically write for other scholars. Their books and articles explore a subject thoroughly, and other scholars scrutinize it. There is much more pressure for a scholar to be accurate in what he writes than there is for an apologist.

Knowing this, I looked for scholars who would deal more honestly with the subject of the pope's authority. Scholars would have to cover

---

[34] Eusebius, Church History, Bk. V, ch. 23, par. 10
[35] Polemical: disputatious, argumentative
[36] Eusebius, *Church History*, Bk. V, ch. 23, par. 11-18. The controversy was eventually put to rest at the Council of Nicea, where all the churches of the Roman Empire agreed to celebrate Passover on Sunday. In English, we now call it Easter, and many Christians have forgotten Easter used to be Passover.

all the evidence, not just the parts they like. The evidence the apologists—and not just Dave Armstrong—presented looked sloppy, inaccurate, and even deceitful to me. Surely Roman Catholic scholars could not get away with the sloppy scholarship of the apologists?

As it turned out, Rome's scholars are as honest as I expected. The result, however, was not that they had stronger arguments. Instead, they gave up the fight at the outset!

The first scholarly book I ran across was by pure happenstance at a McKay's used bookstore. The book was *The Church: The Evolution of Catholicism* by Father Richard McBrien.[37] Father McBrien, who died in January 2015, had been president of the Catholic Theological Society of America and was Crowley-O'Brien Professor of Theology at Notre Dame when he wrote the book.

The concessions in his book made me think I might not need to write mine! He wrote things like: "By the late second or early third centuries ... Peter did become identified in tradition as the first bishop of Rome. But tradition is not a fact factory. It cannot make something into historical fact when it is not."[38]

Later, I went searching for more books. One I found was *Papal Primacy: From Its Origins to the Present* by Dr. Klaus Schatz. Dr. Schatz received a doctorate from Rome's Gregorian University and teaches Church history at Sankt Georgen School of Philosophy and Theology in Frankfurt, Germany. He is still Roman Catholic, and his book defends Rome's Audacious Claim, but from a different perspective. He begins the book by dispensing with the claims of the apologists. On page 3, he writes:

> If one had asked a Christian in the year 100, 200, or even 300 whether the bishop of Rome was the head of all Christians, or whether there was a supreme bishop over all the other bishops and having the last word in questions affecting the whole Church, he or she would certainly have said no.[39]

Dr. Schatz does not even attempt to defend the position of Vatican II and the *Catechism of the Catholic Church*. He knows it is futile to try to prove that the bishop of Rome had "full, supreme, and universal

---

[37] 2008, HarperOne
[38] McBrien, 2008, *The Church*, p. 96
[39] Schatz, 1996, *Papal Primacy*, p. 3

Part I | Chapter 2: First Round Knockout

power over the whole Church" in the early centuries of the Church. Instead, he turns his attention to arguing that God supported the increasing authority of the bishop of Rome over the centuries. (I will devote a separate chapter later to addressing Schatz's arguments.)[40]

Finally, I was thrilled to run across a book by Hans Küng, who participated in the Vatican II Council. Since then, he has gone too far in rejecting the promulgation of the council in which he took part, and he has been sanctioned by the Roman Catholic Church. He has not been excommunicated, but he is not allowed to call himself a Catholic theologian.[41]

In his book, *The Catholic Church: A Short History*, he writes:

> But there could be no question of a legal primacy—or even of a preeminence based on the Bible—of the Roman community or even of the bishop of Rome in the first centuries. ... The promise to Peter from the gospel of Matthew (16:18), "You are Peter, and upon this rock I will build my church," which is so central for today's bishops of Rome and which now adorns the interior of St. Peter's in gigantic black letters on a gilt background, is not once quoted in full in any Christian literature of the first centuries—apart from a text in Tertullian, and this does not quote the passage in connection with Rome, but in connection with Peter.[42]

These three scholars have dismissed the idea that the bishop of Rome held supreme authority in the early centuries of the Church. Their word, however, is overshadowed by two greater authorities who have also given up the fight for an early origin of Papal Primacy: the Vatican and the United States Conference of Catholic Bishops.

The Roman Catholic Church has engaged in several attempts to reconcile with other churches over the last century. These reconciliation attempts have produced documents that undercut the claims of Vatican II and the *Catechism of the Catholic Church*.

In 2016, the Roman Catholic and the Orthodox Churches made some concessions to one another in a document called "The Chieti Agreement." One of the Roman concessions is:

---

[40] Chapter 26
[41] canonlawmadeeasy, 2012, "Was Theologian Hans Küng ever excommunicated"
[42] Küng, 2001, *The Catholic Church*, pp. 41-42, parentheses in original

Rome's Audacious Claim

> In the West, the primacy of the see of Rome was understood, *particularly from the fourth century onwards*, with reference to Peter's role among the Apostles. The primacy of the bishop of Rome among the bishops was *gradually* interpreted as a prerogative that was his because he was successor of Peter, the first of the apostles. This understanding was not adopted in the East, which had a different interpretation of the Scriptures and the Fathers on this point.[43]

In this paragraph, the Vatican acknowledges that Rome's Audacious Claim developed gradually, that it was not fully put forth until at least the fourth century, and that it was never accepted in the East.

In an agreement with the Lutherans in 1973, the U.S. Conference of Catholic Bishops (USCCB) conceded:

> Any biblical and historical scholar today would consider anachronistic the question whether Jesus constituted Peter the first pope, since this question derives from a later model of the papacy which it projects back into the New Testament.[44]

The USCCB speaks here not just for itself, but for "any biblical and historical scholar today," a sweeping rejection of the claims of Roman Catholic apologists like Patrick Madrid, Jimmy Akin, Stephen Ray, and Scott Hahn. It disqualifies all of them as scholars! They all claim Jesus constituted Peter the first pope and transmitted his primacy to the bishop of Rome.[45]

The USCCB gives a time frame for the first time Rome issued its Audacious Claim, saying, "With Leo I the correlation between the bishop of the Roman church and the image of Peter, which had already

---

[43] Joint International Commission, 2016, "Synodality and Primacy," par. 16, emphasis mine

[44] United States Conference of Catholic Bishops, 1973, "Differing Attitudes Toward Papal Primacy," par. 9

[45] Madrid, 2016, "Pope Fiction," Kindle Location 117; Akin, 207, "What is the Evidence for Papal Primacy?," 5:30-6:45; Ray, 2009, *Upon This Rock*, Kindle location 2125; Hahn, 2007, *Reasons to Believe*, Kindle location 1137

been suggested by some of his predecessors, became fully explicit."[46] Pope Leo the Great began his episcopate[47] in 440.

Throughout this book, I will distinguish between Roman Catholic "scholars" and "apologists." The two are not the same. Rome's scholars agree with the arguments made in this book; their apologists are obligated to defend the claims of Vatican II, even while the Vatican itself is backing off from it. Laurent Cleenewerck, an Orthodox scholar, was also careful to separate scholars from apologists in *His Broken Body*, a book calling for reconciliation between Rome and the Orthodox Churches. He refers to the popular apologetic books *Upon This Rock*[48] and *Jesus, Peter, and the Keys*[49] as "popular evidence" and calls Dr. and Archbishop J. Michael Miller's more scholarly tome, *The Shepherd and the Rock*, a "more balanced presentation."

> It is important to emphasize that we will be reviewing what can be called 'popular evidence' for the Papacy, not academic studies. The simple reason is that lay Roman Catholics are much more likely to read [*Upon This Rock* and *Jesus, Peter and the Keys*] than *The Shepherd and the Rock* which happens to be a more balanced presentation.[50]

Like the other scholarly works I have cited and will cite in this book, *The Shepherd and the Rock* concedes that there was no monarchial (single) bishop in Rome until the second century.[51]

Roman Catholic scholars, the U.S. Conference of Catholic Bishops, and the Vatican itself have given up the claim that Jesus had the bishop of Rome in mind when he gave Peter the "keys to the kingdom of Heaven." That makes my job in this book much easier. I do not have to prove Rome's Audacious Claim wrong. I need only explain how that claim made it into the documents of the Vatican I and

---

[46] United States Conference of Catholic Bishops, 1973, "Differing Attitudes Toward Papal Primacy," par. 18
[47] "Episcopate" is the office or term of office of a bishop.
[48] Ray, 2009, Ignatius Press
[49] Butler, Dahlgren, & Hess, 1996, Queenship Publishing Co.
[50] Cleenewerck, 2007, *His Broken Body*, p. 258
[51] Miller, 1995, The Shepherd and the Rock, p. 62

Vatican II Councils, and from there into the *Catechism of the Catholic Church*.

Chapter 3: The Development of the Papacy

The Roman Catholic version of the story of the papacy is short. In Matthew 16:13-19, Jesus made Peter "the rock" and the chief over all the apostles. He alone received the keys to the kingdom of God, which represent his authority to rule on behalf of Christ.[52] He also received the authority to "bind and loose," which has to do with retaining or remitting sins. Rome acknowledges the power to bind and loose was also given to the other apostles in John 20:22-23.[53]

Later, Peter denied Jesus three times. Jesus restored him as universal shepherd with a threefold affirmation in John 21:15-17. Peter led the whole Church as it spread through Judea, and later he went to Rome to become its first bishop. Before he was martyred, he appointed Linus to replace him both as Rome's bishop and as chief shepherd and supreme authority over the whole church.

This succession continues to this day in so real a way that Peter "lives, presides, and judges" through his successors, the bishops of Rome.[54]

That is the story of the papacy the Roman Catholic Church teaches. Two ecumenical councils, Vatican I and Vatican II, tell this story, supposedly infallibly. Nonetheless, we have seen that neither the USCCB nor the Vatican stand by that story when seated across from scholars from other traditions.[55] Instead, the Vatican now admits that "the primacy of the bishop of Rome ... was *gradually* interpreted as a prerogative that was his because he was a successor of Peter."[56]

Here is the real story, which we will prove through the rest of this book.

There is no doubt that Peter was in some sense the leader of the apostles. Though sometimes he was the first to put his foot in his mouth, he was typically first in all things apostolic. He was the first to make the confession that Jesus is "the Messiah, the Son of the living God" (Matt. 16:16-17; Jn. 20:31); he was the first to preach the Gospel

---

[52] The keys of the kingdom are not physical keys; they are spiritual.
[53] *Catechism of the Catholic Church*, 1995, par. 881
[54] Pope Pius IX, 1870, "First Dogmatic Constitution," ch. 2
[55] See chapter 2, "First Round Knockout."
[56] Joint International Commission, 2016, "Synodality and Primacy," par. 16

and obtain converts (Acts 2); and he brought the Gentiles into the Church (Acts 10).

By the Council of Jerusalem, described in Acts 15, James seems to have the presidency in Jerusalem. Paul tells us in Galatians 2 that emissaries from James caused Peter to act "hypocritically" out of fear (vv. 12-13).

Peter did eventually go to Rome. His greeting from "the chosen one at Babylon" (1 Pet. 5:13) is an almost certain reference to Rome. In Christian writings after New Testament times, Peter is often and consistently said to have been martyred in Rome.[57]

Peter was a bishop in Rome, but not the only bishop. He calls himself a "fellow presbyter" in 1 Peter 5:1. In 1 Peter 5:2, he charges the presbyters to whom he is writing with "overseeing" the flock of God. The word "overseeing" is the verb form of the noun typically translated "bishop." Peter, like Paul, set up churches governed by a college of elders, all called bishops, and all charged with shepherding the church of God. In other words, "bishop," "overseer," "presbyter," "elder," "pastor," and "shepherd" are all equivalent in the New Testament.[58]

By the time Peter died, Rome's faith was already "heralded throughout the world" (Rom. 1:8). Thirty years later, the church in Rome sent a letter to the church in Corinth, which almost became a part of our New Testament.[59] It chided Corinth for lapsing back into conflict and division after repenting at the admonition of the apostle Paul in the letter we know as 1 Corinthians.

The fame of the Roman church only grew. Its prestige was based on the presence of the two most famous apostles in their city, its faithfulness, the blood of many martyrs shed there, and its generosity to other churches.[60]

As a result, when the famous bishop Irenaeus wrote his five-volume tome against gnosticism around the year 185, he appealed to Rome as "very great" and used that church as a prime example of the

---

[57] Tertullian, c. 205, *Scorpiace*, ch. 15; Peter of Alexandria, 300-311, "The Canonical Epistle," Canon IX, par. 1; Eusebius, 323, *Church History*, Bk. III, ch. 1, par. 2

[58] Chapter 6 explains these church offices and those that developed later.

[59] The letter is known as "1 Clement." I will address it in the chapter on Clement of Rome (chapter 9).

[60] United States Conference of Catholic Bishops, 1973, "Differing Attitudes," par. 16

Part I | Chapter 3: The Development of the Papacy

preservation of apostolic truth. He even called Rome the "preeminent authority" on the teaching of the apostles.[61]

Only a few years later, we see the first example of a Roman bishop trying to exercise authority over other churches. As noted in the previous chapter, Victor, who led the Roman church from 189 to 199, tried to force churches in Asia Minor to celebrate Passover on Sunday rather than on the same day the Jews celebrated it. Those churches refused, and Victor excommunicated them. Other churches "sharply rebuked" Victor for this, and a letter from Irenaeus persuaded Victor to back off for the sake of peace.[62]

In the third century, things did not continue as well for Rome as they had in the second. In 218, the well-known church father Hippolytus split the church in Rome. He had himself elected bishop in the place of Callistus, Rome's legitimately elected bishop. Almost twenty years later, Hippolytus reconciled to the church while imprisoned in the mines alongside Pontianus, who had been elected in 230.[63]

In 251, Novatian split the Roman church again, having himself elected bishop against Cornelius. Bishops across the Roman Empire supported Cornelius, but this did not dissuade Novatian. His faction continued for centuries. Its adherents are generally known as Novatians, but they eventually came to call themselves *Cathari*.[64] They gained followers all over the empire and lasted until at least 600.[65]

Cornelius was martyred and replaced by Lucius. Lucius was also martyred, then followed by Stephen. Stephen became the first bishop of Rome we know to have claimed authority over other churches based on his descent from Peter.[66]

Oddly enough, it was a defense of Novatian baptism that prompted his claim. When Novatian converts repented and returned to the church in Rome, Stephen did not rebaptize them. He accepted

---

[61] Irenaeus, *Against Heresies*, Bk. III, ch. 3, par. 2
[62] Eusebius, *Church History*, Bk. V. chs. 23-24
[63] Kirsch, 1910, "St. Hippolytus of Rome"
[64] "The Pure"
[65] Chapman, 1911, "Novatian and Novatianism," last paragraph
[66] How we know this is discussed in chapters 20 and 21.

Rome's Audacious Claim

Novatian baptism, even though Novatian himself had split the Roman church. Many other churches, though, rebaptized Novatian converts.

Apparently, Rome had accepted the baptism of heretics during the second century, and Stephen felt that all churches should follow Roman tradition. He tried to excommunicate the churches that did not; but once again, this was not received well by anyone.[67]

Stephen's action is an important step in the history of Rome's Audacious Claim. Cyprian, bishop of Carthage, wrote many letters against Stephen, and even called a council of eighty-seven North African bishops to refute him. From Cyprian's letters, and from letters returned to him by other bishops, we learn that Peter had become a central part of the third-century ecclesiology of all churches.[68] While Cyprian taught that all bishops together were the descendants of Peter and the foundation of unity, Stephen saw himself as the primary representative of Peter.

Stephen, though, was soon martyred, and the controversy died with him.[69]

The next important event in papal history was the Council of Nicea, held in 325.[70] After "The Great Persecution" that lasted from 303 to 311, the Emperor Constantine I began showing favor to Christians and their churches. As his favor towards the Christians grew, many Roman citizens converted to Christianity. At that inopportune time, a controversy arose over the exact relationship between God and his Son.

This conflict is known as the Arian Controversy, after an Egyptian elder named Arius. It was a bishop, however, Eusebius of Nicomedia, who took up Arius's cause and heated the conflict to a fever pitch. The timing was unfortunate. Emperor Constantine had just brought the Roman Empire under his own control by defeating his co-emperor, Licinius, in battle. When word reached him, he feared the religion he was supporting would destroy the empire's unity.

Constantine called the bishops of the empire to the imperial resort city of Nicea to resolve the issue. Eusebius and his supporters had to defend themselves before more than 250 bishops. In a quirk of history,

---

[67] Eusebius, *Church History*, Bk. VII, chs. 3-5
[68] Ecclesiology is the study of the nature and structure of the church.
[69] Eusebius, *Church History*, Bk VII, ch. 5
[70] Also called "Nicaea."

Part I | Chapter 3: The Development of the Papacy

the famous historian Eusebius, bishop of Caesarea, led the council at which the heretical Eusebius, bishop of Nicomedia, was condemned and banished from the empire.[71]

The Council of Nicea sided with the early tradition of the churches, issuing a creed that included "begotten, not made." The trouble was hardly over, however. Eusebius returned to Nicomedia after signing a retraction for Emperor Constantine. When Constantine died, Eusebius convinced his son, Constantius II, to oppose the decisions of Nicea. Constantius began replacing Nicene bishops in the Eastern empire with Arian ones, and the controversy became greater than it had been before the council.

The Western churches enjoyed relative peace during this time because Constantius's brothers ruled in the Western empire. Julius, the bishop of Rome, became the place to go for Eastern bishops deposed by Constantius. This increased the prestige of Rome, even though Constantius eventually ruled the whole empire and forced Liberius, the bishop of Rome from 352 to 356, to deny the Nicene Creed.[72]

The Council of Nicea set a precedent for general councils being called by Roman emperors. During the fourth such council, in Chalcedon in 451, Leo was bishop of Rome. Not only did Leo declare that Peter was still "fully and effectually" at the helm of the Church through himself,[73] but after his letter was read at the Council of Chalcedon, the bishops cried out, "Peter has spoken through Leo."[74]

Because of this, many historians regard Pope Leo "the Great" as the first pope, and the first to make Rome's Audacious Claim.

Although Leo made the claim, and despite what they said at the Council of Chalcedon, the Roman Empire's Eastern bishops did not simply agree to his authority. As Roman Catholic Archbishop J. Michael Miller puts it:

> Not all of Leo's views on papal-episcopal relations were accepted. When his legates at the Council of Chalcedon suggested that the pope was the "bishop of all the churches" or

---

[71] Pavao, 2014, *Decoding Nicea*, chs. 4-5
[72] The Nicene Creed is the name of the creed decided upon by the Council of Nicea.
[73] Leo I, 443, "Sermons," Sermon III
[74] "The Fourth Ecumenical Council," sec. "Extracts from the Acts. Session II. (Continued)." There are two sections with this title; this reference is in the second.

Rome's Audacious Claim

the "bishop of the universal Church," a kind of "universal bishop," the Fathers rejected this.[75]

He adds:

> Later, Gregory the Great (590-604) explicitly repudiated all titles which could easily have led to infringing the rights of the bishops. After the example of Christ, he preferred the title "servant of the servants of God."[76]

From the fifth century on, and perhaps even earlier, the empire's Eastern churches granted the Roman church and its bishop a "primacy of honor," though this was often contested by the bishop of Constantinople.[77]

Rome's Audacious Claim, however, is not a primacy of honor, but a primacy of jurisdiction and authority. As the Vatican I Council put it:

> If anyone, therefore, shall say that the Blessed Peter the Apostle ... received from the same, our Lord Jesus Christ, a primacy of honor only, and not of true and proper jurisdiction; let him be anathema.[78]

The conflict between the primacy of honor granted by the East and the primacy of jurisdiction demanded by Rome eventually split the churches in the Roman Empire permanently. Rome and Constantine excommunicated each other in 1054, but the schism took centuries to develop and centuries to settle into the consciousness of the churches.

Today, the Roman Empire's Eastern churches call themselves "Orthodox" rather than "Catholic."[79] This makes sense because

---

[75] Miller, 1995, The Shepherd and the Rock, p. 87
[76] Miller, 1995, The Shepherd and the Rock, p. 87
[77] A "primacy of honor" granted the Roman bishop the status of "first among equals." In the fifth century, his equals would be the bishops of Alexandria, Antioch, Constantinople, and Jerusalem. Today, at least the bishop of Moscow would be added to those. In theory, if the pope were to retract his claim to "full, supreme, and universal power" and repeal the decrees and dogmas popes have issued on their own authority the last 1500 years, then the Eastern Orthodox bishops would reunite and again grant him a primacy of honor, first among equals.
[78] Pope Pius IX, 1870, "First Dogmatic Constitution," ch. 1, par. 5
[79] The *Encyclopedia Britannica* has an article by John Meyendorff, a prominent Orthodox scholar, saying that the official name of the Eastern Orthodox Churches is

Part I | Chapter 3: The Development of the Papacy

"catholic" means "universal." Thus, the "one holy, catholic, and apostolic Church" mentioned in the great creeds refers, by definition, to all the churches descended from the apostles as long as they are united. Although the Great Schism between Rome and the other apostolic churches of the Roman Empire is more well-known, the Church has not been one or catholic since the fifth century. The "ecumenical" councils of the fifth century separated "vast parts of Asia and Africa" from the catholic Church.[80]

Once the Church is no longer universal, neither is it catholic. The "Roman Catholic Church" consists only of those churches who submit to the authority of the bishop of Rome (the pope). It may call itself "the Catholic Church," but it is, by definition, no longer "catholic."

With the empire's Eastern churches out of the way, the politics and historical circumstances that made the Roman bishop the supreme religious figure in Europe also gave him "full, supreme, and universal power" over the European churches without opposition. It is said that absolute power corrupts absolutely, and that is exactly what happened to both the Roman bishop (the pope) and the Roman church. It eventually got so bad that much of Europe left the Roman Catholic Church in the fifteenth and sixteenth centuries, an event known as the Protestant Reformation.

That is the history of the Roman Catholic Church, and we will spend the rest of this book verifying this history against the distorted history portrayed in books, articles, and videos by Roman Catholic apologists. We will be going through their arguments in chronological order.

It is always good to begin at the beginning, and, for us, the beginning is Peter.

"Orthodox Catholic Church" (Meyendorff, 2019, "Eastern Orthodoxy," par. 1). In articles, books, and conversations, however, no one uses that name. Both individuals and official sources refer to them as "Eastern Orthodox Church" (or "Churches"), or "Eastern Orthodoxy," or "The Orthodox Church." Even the synod between the Roman Catholic and Eastern Orthodox Churches titled itself the "Joint International Commission for Theological Dialogue between the Roman Catholic Church and the Orthodox Church" (Joint International Commission, 2016, "Synodality and Primacy During the First Millennium").

[80] Moffett, 1998, *A History of Christianity in Asia*, Kindle location 4150-4155

Rome's Audacious Claim

Part II

Peter in Roman Catholic Doctrine

Rome's Audacious Claim

Part II | Chapter 4: Matthew 16:15-19

Chapter 4: Matthew 16:15-19

Peter could not have passed on "full, supreme, and universal power over the whole Church" to the Roman bishop unless he had it himself. He could not lay hands on a Roman bishop to make him "shepherd of the whole flock" unless he was that shepherd himself.

The Roman Catholic Church bases their claim that Jesus gave Peter the authority to govern the whole Church on Matthew 16:15-19. It bases its claim that Peter is "shepherd of the whole flock" on John 21:15-17. Let us begin our refutation of Rome's Audacious Claim by examining those two passages.

We will use the New American Bible Revised Edition (NABRE) for all Scripture quotes. It is the official translation of the U.S. Conference of Catholic Bishops. We do not need a Protestant translation to show that the Catholic magisterium[81] misinterpreted the Bible at Vatican II and in the *Catechism of the Catholic Church*. As we have seen, even the Vatican retreats from those claims when challenged by those who know history. Matthew 16:15-19 reads as follows in the NABRE:

> [Jesus] said to [his disciples], "But who do you say that I am?" Simon Peter said in reply, "You are the Messiah, the Son of the living God." Jesus said to him in reply, "Blessed are you, Simon son of Jonah. For flesh and blood has not revealed this to you, but my heavenly Father. And so I say to you, you are Peter, and upon this rock I will build my church, and the gates of the netherworld shall not prevail against it. I will give you the keys to the kingdom of heaven. Whatever you bind on earth shall be bound in heaven; and whatever you loose on earth shall be loosed in heaven."

Jesus promises Simon four things:
1. His name will be Peter (Rock), and Jesus will build his church on "this rock."
2. The gates of Hades will not prevail against Jesus's Church.

---

[81] "Magisterium" is the teaching authority of the Roman Catholic Church and does not necessarily refer to a specific person or persons.

3. Jesus will give Peter the keys to the kingdom of God.[82]
4. Peter will be able to "bind" and "loose" on earth, and heaven will support him when he does.

Obviously, none of these say, "Peter, you shall have full, supreme, and universal power over the whole Church," but are any of them close enough that they suggest that role for Peter?

Peter as the Rock

Although Protestants will not like this, we can and must grant the Roman Catholic Church their assertion that Peter is the rock on which Jesus will build the church. First, it is the most natural reading of the verse. Second, it is almost irrelevant to the argument that the pope has "full, supreme, and universal authority over the whole Church."

Even Protestants have to admit that the most natural reading of Matthew 16:18 is that Simon was named "Rock" because he was the rock on which Jesus would build his Church. What most do not realize is this natural reading causes Protestants no problem.

Peter is not the "foundation" of the Church. As the apostle Paul points out, "No one can lay a foundation other than the one that is there, namely, Jesus Christ" (1 Cor. 3:11). Nonetheless, rocks are built upon that foundation. God builds his house with "living stones" (1 Pet. 2:5). All Jesus was saying is that Peter was the first of these stones.[83]

Admitting this grants nothing to the argument that the pope has "full, supreme, and universal power over the whole Church." Peter was the first to confess that Jesus is the Christ, the Son of the living God. No one, not the pope, nor you, me, or any of the apostles can inherit

---

[82] The Gospel of Matthew is the only book in the Bible that uses the phrase "kingdom of Heaven." Jews were reluctant to pronounce YHWH (the divine name as given in Hebrew) or even say "God" because of the third commandment, which says that we are not to use the Lord's name in vain. Because of this they often substituted "heaven" for "God." Matthew wrote his Gospel primarily to the Jews, so he used "kingdom of Heaven" rather than "kingdom of God." The rest of the New Testament uses "kingdom of God." I will use "kingdom of God" throughout this book.

[83] The common Protestant argument that Peter (Gr. *Petros*) cannot be "the rock" (Gr. *Petra*) because *petros* means "pebble" and *petra* means "boulder" is not true. *Petros* does not necessarily mean pebble, nor necessarily differ from *Petra*. Peter could not have been called *Petra*, because *Petra* is feminine. Finally, Jesus was almost certainly speaking in Aramaic, where both words would have been *Kephas*. See the Protestant commentaries at https://biblehub.com/commentaries/matthew/16-18.htm.

Part II | Chapter 4: Matthew 16:15-19

that from Peter. We can all make the same confession. We also become living stones when we make that confession (Jn. 20:31), but none of us can be the first to make it.

Roman Catholics agree that the rock is not only Peter, but also Peter's confession. The *Catechism of the Catholic Church* says:

> Moved by the grace of the Holy Spirit and drawn by the Father, we believe in Jesus and confess: "You are the Christ, the Son of the living God." On the rock of this faith confessed by St. Peter, Christ built his Church.[84]

Even Roman Catholic apologist Jimmy Akin is careful to point this out. In a radio discussion on *Catholic Answers*, he tells us that just as the seven heads of the beast in Revelation 17 are both seven mountains and seven kings, so the rock in Matthew 16 can be both Peter and his confession.[85]

Because the rock on which Jesus will build his Church is Peter's confession, it follows that in naming Peter "Rock," Jesus has simply acknowledged that Peter was the first to make that confession.

The picture Jesus paints with his words is a bottom-up picture. Peter is the support, the first of what comes after him and will be built upon him. The argument of the Roman Catholics, that he had authority over every Christian who comes after him, is a top-down picture. If Jesus were talking about supreme authority over the whole church, he could have said that Peter would sit on a throne ruling the churches. It would not have been strange for Jesus to say such a thing. He told all the apostles that they would sit on thrones judging the twelve tribes of Israel (Luke 22:30). If Jesus meant for Peter to have supreme authority over all the churches, he could have expressed it much more clearly.

The Gates of Hades Will Not Prevail against the Church

The second thing Jesus said to Peter is that the gates of Hades would not prevail against the Church. This statement is not about Peter, but about the Church as a whole. As a result, the statement is irrelevant to the purpose of this book. The Roman Catholic

---

[84] *Catechism of the Catholic Church*, 1995, par. 424
[85] Akin, 2017, "What Is the Evidence for Papal Primacy?," 8:10-9:05

magisterium does not use it to argue for the authority of the bishop of Rome.

On the other hand, it *does* use this promise to argue that the Roman Catholic organization could not and cannot fall. The answer to this argument is that the Roman Catholic Church not only could fall—it *did* fall.

Interpreting a verse to say something could not have happened does not change the fact that it did happen. As Catholic theologian Richard McBrien puts it, "Faith is not a fact factory."[86] Instead, it proves that the interpretation of the verse was wrong. In the book of Revelation, Jesus said that he would spew the church of Laodicea out of his mouth. Had he done so, this would not mean that the gates of Hades triumphed over the Church as a whole.

In the same way, when the church in Rome led almost all of Europe into superstition, idolatry, worldliness, and lusts in the late medieval period, this did not void Jesus's promise.[87] As God pointed out to Elijah, he always has his seven thousand who have not bowed their knee to the enemy (1 Kings 19:18). God did not let the corruption continue, but raised up Reformers who brought light to Europe once again. The triumphant Church promised in Matthew 16:18 is not the Roman church, nor any other church in particular, but God's chosen wherever they might be. The gates of Hades can never withstand their onslaught.

Keys of the Kingdom of God

Scripture mentions the keys of the kingdom of Heaven only once, in Matthew 16:19. They do not appear anywhere else in the Bible. The Roman Catholic Church argues that these keys represent "the authority to govern the house of God."[88]

Three other spiritual keys are mentioned in the Bible: the key of knowledge, the keys of Hades and death, and the key of David. The scribes possessed the key of knowledge (Luke 11:52), and Revelation 1:18 and 3:7 tell us that Jesus has the keys of Hades and death and the key of David. He obtained the keys of Hades and death during his time

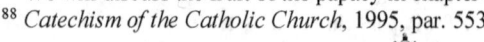

[86] McBrien, 2008, *The Church*, p. 96
[87] We will discuss the fruit of the papacy in chapter 27.
[88] *Catechism of the Catholic Church*, 1995, par. 553

Part II | Chapter 4: Matthew 16:15-19

in Hades (Acts 2:31) and took them with him when he rose from the dead.

Jesus gives us a hint of what the keys to the kingdom might be in Luke 11:52. There he upbraids the scribes, saying, "Woe to you, scholars of the law! You have taken away the key of knowledge. You yourselves did not enter and you stopped those trying to enter."

This gives us a good working definition of "keys." Keys are for entering and exiting. The scribes possessed figurative "keys" that would allow others to come into knowledge, but they did not even enter themselves. Their opposition to Jesus prevented both others and themselves from receiving the knowledge that he was bringing.

The two other passages that address keys also remind us that keys are for opening and closing doors. Servants opened the doors of King Ehud's chambers after Japheth killed him (Judg. 3:25), and a messenger (or angel) uses a key to open the bottomless pit in Revelation 9:1-2 and to lock it shut in Revelation 20:1-3.

Since keys, in the Bible, are used for opening and closing, the most likely interpretation of the keys of the kingdom is that Peter had authority to preach the gospel and thus open God's kingdom to those who believe that Jesus is the Christ, the Son of God. While all preachers of the gospel have the power to bring hearers into the kingdom of God, Peter was the first to open the doors of the kingdom of God when he preached the gospel on the day of Pentecost, bringing people into the Church for the first time (Acts 2).

Peter also opened the door to the Gentiles, something that required divine intervention (Acts 10). Even more importantly, his presence was needed to bring the Samaritans fully into Christ. Philip was able to baptize the Samaritans, but they did not receive the Holy Spirit until Peter and John showed up to lay hands on them. The likely reason for this is Jesus's promise to Peter that he would open the doors of the kingdom of God.

This interpretation of the keys of the kingdom lines up with everything we have seen in Scripture about the kingdom.

It is not the only interpretation that is possible, though. Roman Catholic apologist Scott Hahn has a card up his sleeve by way of a passage from Isaiah 22. Remarkably, Protestant scholars agree with him!

Isaiah 22:15-25

Catholic apologist Scott Hahn appeals to Isaiah 22:15-22 to argue that Peter's keys are not about opening the door to the kingdom of God by preaching, but they are about being a chief steward of the house of God. He points out that even Protestant commentators apply Isaiah 22 to the keys Peter received. I do not have access to Albright's commentary, to which Hahn appeals,[89] but BibleHub.com provides several Protestant commentaries that all agree Isaiah 22:22 is the context for Matthew 16:19 and the keys of the kingdom.[90]

The common idea of those commentaries is that Jesus was making Peter a "chief steward." *Meyer's NT Commentary*, for instance, calls Peter a "house-steward, who is empowered to determine who are to belong and who are not to belong to the household over which his master has commissioned him to preside."[91]

Oddly, these Protestant commentaries also deny that binding and loosing, which we have not gotten to yet, has anything to do with the forgiveness of sins. *Ellicott's Commentary for English Readers* suggests that binding and loosing gives Peter the right to declare, as a scribe, what is binding on the Christian conscience. Ellicott does point out that this authority is given to the other apostles and the church in Matthew 18:18.[92]

Meyer's NT Commentary is similar, saying that Jesus gave Peter the right to determine which behaviors would keep a person out of the kingdom and which would qualify them for it.[93]

This is not as strange as it might seem. The primary reason the writings of the New Testament are in our Bibles is that they were written, or approved, by apostles. Luke and Mark were not apostles, but Luke was a companion of Paul, and Mark was a companion of Peter.[94] As Bible believers, Protestants and Catholics alike believe that what the apostles wrote in the New Testament marks who can be in and who is out of the kingdom of God.

---

[89] Hahn, n.d., "Scott Hahn on the Papacy," sec. 2, par. 19-27
[90] Bible Hub, 2004-2018, "Matthew 16:19"
[91] Bible Hub, 2004-2018, "Matthew 16:19," right column, par. 2
[92] Bible Hub, 2004-2018, "Matthew 16:19," left column, par. 1
[93] Bible Hub, 2004-2018, "Matthew 16:19," right column, par. 4
[94] Col. 4:14; Eusebius, *Church History*, Bk. II, ch. 15, par. 1

Part II | Chapter 4: Matthew 16:15-19

Dr. Hahn points out that in Isaiah 22:15-22, the role of steward was passed on. It was passed from Shebna, who was unworthy, to Eliakim, who presumably was worthy. Therefore, Hahn concludes, Peter was receiving a dynastic stewardship as well, which would be transferred to successors. And, of course, he believes those successors to be the bishops of Rome.[95]

Isaiah 22:15-25 is actually a terrible example of succession. In verse 23, Eliakim was a "peg in a firm place," but in verse 25, the "peg fixed in a firm place" will "break off and fall," and everything hung on it shall be "done away with."

It is true that the churches that came after Peter believed the promises made to him were passed down. They did not believe, however, that they went to the bishop of Rome.

The Keys of the Kingdom in the Early Church Fathers

Tertullian, a prolific writer from Carthage, is the earliest known writer to mention the keys of the kingdom, and he does not do so until around the year 205. That is at least 170 years after Jesus gave those promises to Peter. How important can those keys be when there are 170 years of silence regarding them?

Here is what Tertullian has to say about those keys:

> For though you [gnostics] think heaven still shut, remember that the Lord left here to Peter and through him to the Church, the keys of it, which everyone who has been here put to the question, and also made confession, will carry with him.[96]

Here Tertullian says the keys were left to "the Church." All martyrs ("everyone who has been here put to the question, and also made confession") could use them to enter heaven.

Oddly, Catholic apologist Jimmy Akin cites this passage, without explanation, on behalf of Papal Primacy.[97] Why he would do this is puzzling. Tertullian did not say that Peter passed the keys individually to the bishop of Rome, but to the Church, and especially to the martyrs. He did not say the keys are for ruling, but for opening the door to heaven.

---

[95] Hahn, n.d., "Scott Hahn on the Papacy," sec. 2, par. 19-27
[96] Tertullian, c. 205, *Scorpiace*, ch. 10
[97] Akin, 2010, *The Fathers Know Best*, Kindle location 2788

Rome's Audacious Claim

Akin's citation of this passage is a symptom of what Protestant apologist James White calls "the Peter Syndrome."[98] It is the propensity of Roman Catholic apologists to apply anything written about Peter to the pope whether or not the writer mentioned the bishop of Rome.

Tertullian had more to say about the keys, but his further comments require some context. A few years after that last quote, Tertullian was opposing the churches rather than supporting them. In his earlier writings against the gnostics, he argued convincingly for the authority of the churches the apostles had established but, sadly, he was snatched away by a false prophet named Montanus.[99] Tertullian, whose tracts indicate he was frustrated by the lack of holiness in some Christians, apparently joined the Montanists.[100] He began referring to catholic[101] Christians as "the soulish" in contrast to the spiritual Montanists.[102] Thus, in this citation, he is arguing against the interpretation of the catholic churches around him. In doing so, he tells us what that interpretation is:

> I now inquire into your opinion: from what source you usurp this right to "the Church." If, because the Lord has said to Peter, "Upon this rock I will build my Church"; "to thee have I given the keys of the heavenly kingdom"; or "Whatsoever thou shalt have bound or loosed in earth shall be bound or loosed in the heavens"; you therefore presume that the power of binding and loosing has derived to you, that is, to every Church akin to Peter, what sort of man are you, subverting and

---

[98] White, 2013, "The Great Debate III," 1:45:05-1:46:00

[99] There are those who, not knowing history, think of Montanus as a reformer and true prophet (e.g., Broadbent 1931, *Pilgrim Church*, pp. 29-30). Montanus taught that the Church had had time to become mature, so God was removing allowances that were made in the New Testament. For example, widows and widowers were no longer allowed to remarry after their spouses died (Tertullian, 208-217, "On Monogamy").

[100] While it is generally thought that Tertullian joined the Montanists, some think he formed his own cult or even stayed in the Church, while remaining a supporter of Montanus.

[101] "Catholic" means "universal," and in the first few centuries of the Church it referred to all the churches that had been founded by the apostles or by the apostles' churches.

[102] *The Ante-Nicene Fathers* series, vol. III and IV, translate Tertullian as calling other Christians "the psychics," but the word he is using means "soulish."

wholly changing the manifest intention of the Lord, [who was] conferring this personally upon Peter?[103]

Tertullian is telling the catholic churches that they do not have the right to claim the promises made to Peter. The Church taught that all churches "akin to Peter" inherited the promises given to Peter. This is what we saw in his first citation as well. The keys were passed to "the Church." Against this, Tertullian argued, "It is to spiritual men that this power will correspondently appertain, either to an apostle or else to a prophet."[104]

Of course, the prophet he was most concerned about was Montanus, but Tertullian's opinion is not what we are trying to find. We are trying to find the teaching of the whole Church in his day, and he has given it to us. The Church believed that all churches "akin" (related) to Peter received his promises.

The rest of his argument drives this home. He argues that the Lord was "conferring this personally on Peter" *against* the catholic churches. They believed Jesus's promises to Peter passed to whole churches. Tertullian, as a Montanist, argued that a promise to Peter as an individual must be passed onto individuals, not churches.

This is a critical point. Today, the Roman Catholic Church teaches that Peter's promises are passed to an individual: the bishop of Rome, whom we now call "the pope." This was the position of the Montanists rather than the position of the Church. Rome regards them as heretics.[105] They are not the group the Roman Church wants to agree with!

Though the Montanists and the Roman Catholic Church agree that the promises to Peter passed to individuals, they differ on everything else. The Montanists, or at least Tertullian representing the Montanists, taught that the keys passed to multiple individuals. Further, those individuals had to be trustworthy; they had to be "spiritual."

---

[103] Tertullian, 208-220, "On Modesty," ch. 21. I removed most of the confusing parentheses the translators added. The quote reads more simply with my one insertion in brackets.
[104] Tertullian, 208-220, "On Modesty," ch. 21
[105] Chapman, 1911, "Montanists," par. 5

Rome's Audacious Claim

> What, now, (has this to do) with the Church, and your (church), indeed, Psychic? For, in accordance with the person of Peter, it is to spiritual men that this power will correspondently appertain, either to an apostle or else to a prophet.[106]

The Roman Catholic Church teaches that the keys are passed to one person, and his only qualification is that he be bishop of Rome. His personal conduct, scandalous or not, is immaterial.[107]

As for the keys themselves, it turns out that Tertullian interprets the use of the keys of the kingdom in a way that matches both my understanding and that of Scott Hahn and the Protestant commentators.

> [Peter] himself ... made first use of the key; you see which: "Men of Israel, let what I say sink into your ears: Jesus the Nazarene, a man destined by God for you" [Acts 2:22] and so forth. [Peter] himself, therefore, was the first to unbar, in Christ's baptism, the entrance to the heavenly kingdom.[108]

Tertullian says Peter used the key first. To explain where he used it, he quotes Acts 2, which is the first proclamation of the gospel after Jesus's death and resurrection. There, Tertullian, says, the key was used to "unbar, in Christ's baptism, the entrance to the heavenly kingdom."

This matches my interpretation of the keys. He goes on:

> Peter was the first of all to be endued with the Spirit, and ... to say, "And now why are ye tempting the Lord, concerning the imposition upon the brethren of a yoke which neither we nor our fathers were able to support? But however, through the grace of Jesus we believe that we shall be saved in the same way as they" [Acts 15:7-11]. This sentence both "loosed" those parts of the law which were abandoned, and "bound" those which were reserved.[109]

---

[106] Tertullian, 208-220, "On Modesty," ch. 21, parentheses in original
[107] Mann, *The Lives of the Popes: Vol. IV*, pp. vii-viii
[108] Tertullian, 208-220, "On Modesty," ch. 21, brackets mine
[109] Tertullian, 208-220, "On Modesty," ch. 21, brackets mine

Part II | Chapter 4: Matthew 16:15-19

Here Tertullian references the Jerusalem Council described in Acts 15. Peter loosed the Gentiles from the Law of Moses there. He also bound them to four laws (Acts 15:29). This is what *Meyer's NT Commentary* taught. Tertullian agrees that "binding and loosing" have to do with the things that will keep us out of the kingdom or bring us in.[110]

Whether we choose Meyer's interpretation of Jesus's promises, mine, or both (as Tertullian does), the real issue is whether Peter's role passed only to the bishop of Rome. In no other way could he validly claim to have "full, supreme, and universal power over the whole Church." We have seen that the churches around the turn of the third century, when Tertullian was writing, believed they had the keys, which the martyrs also used to open heaven for themselves.

A few decades later, probably in the late 240s, Origen, perhaps the most renowned Christian teacher of his time, wrote about the keys again. In his commentary on the Matthew 16 passage we are addressing, he taught that every Christian who confesses that Jesus is Christ and Son of God based on a revelation from the Father would receive all the promises of Peter and be a second Peter.

> Are the keys of the kingdom given by the Lord to Peter only, and will no other of the blessed receive them? ... And if anyone says, ["Thou art the Christ, the Son of the living God"] to [Jesus], not by flesh and blood revealing it to him but through the Father in heaven, he will obtain the things that were spoken according to the letter of the Gospel to that Peter.[111]

Origen did save some honor for Peter. He goes on to say that Peter has the keys "not of one heaven, but of more."[112]

This last comment by Origen is unique, and I have never heard of anyone beside him teaching such a thing. It is clear, though, that Origen did not teach that Peter was a chief steward who passed his authority on to the bishop of Rome.

More importantly, Origen wrote a commentary on Matthew that does not even mention Rome. One would think that if the Roman

---

[110] Bible Hub, 2014-2018, "Matthew 16:19"
[111] Commentary on Matthew, Bk. XII, ch. 11, brackets mine
[112] Commentary on Matthew, Bk. XIII, ch. 31

bishop had "full, supreme, and universal power over the whole Church" in Origen's time, he would have mentioned it in a commentary on Matthew 16!

A decade later, during the 250s, Cyprian, a bishop and from Carthage like Tertullian, quotes Matthew 16 several times and uses the passage to defend the authority of the bishops of all churches,[113] but he never comments on the keys of the kingdom. This makes sense if Cyprian believed Peter used the keys to open the kingdom to the Jews, Samaritans, and Gentiles, and then they were never used again, but it is extremely odd if he believed the bishop of Rome was in possession of Peter's keys. We will cover Cyprian thoroughly in chapters 20 and 21.

With that, we will leave the keys of the kingdom behind. No matter what the Roman Catholic Church teaches about them now, and even if Protestant commentators agree with them, the churches formed by the apostles knew nothing about the relation between Matthew 16 and Isaiah 22. They knew nothing about a dynasty of individuals descended from Peter, and they knew nothing about the "full, supreme, and universal power" of the bishop of Rome.

The Ante-Nicene Fathers series, from which I am drawing the quotes in this book, is ten volumes long. The keys of the kingdom are not found until the third volume. The first two volumes have over 550 pages of writings each. The pages are large, and the print is small, and so the typical page in my edition has over 800 words. This means 880,000 words were written during the second century without a single mention of the keys of the kingdom.

This "argument from silence" is strengthened by a quotation Roman Catholic apologists love to repeat. Irenaeus—in his spectacular tome *Against Heresies*—argues for the greatness of the Roman church and says that every church needs to agree with it. He says they have "preeminent authority" based on their careful preservation of apostolic truth.[114] Yet, despite such praise, he never mentions Matthew 16, the keys of the kingdom, nor any of the other promises to Peter.

Irenaeus also wrote a book called *The Proof of the Apostolic Preaching*, which did not make it into the ten volumes of *The Ante-*

---

[113] "Cyprian to the Lapsed," Ep. XXVI; "On the Unity of the Church," par. 1; "On the Advantage of Patience," par. 9, 249-259

[114] Irenaeus, c. 185, *Against Heresies*, Bk. III, ch. 3, par. 2

Part II | Chapter 4: Matthew 16:15-19

Nicene Fathers series. My PDF copy of the book covers eighty-three pages. Irenaeus wrote it to a friend named Marcianus, and Irenaeus explained to him the purpose of the document in these words:

> We send you ... a manual of essentials, that [little] by little you may attain to much, learning in short space all the members of the body of the truth, and receiving in brief the demonstration of the things of God.[115]

Not only does this 25,000-word "manual of essentials" not mention the keys to the kingdom of heaven, it does not mention Rome. In fact, it does not even mention Peter! Rome's Audacious Claim was apparently not a part of "the body of truth" to Irenaeus; nor was it to any other Christian writer of the second century.

We must conclude that the Christians of the second century had no idea that the keys of the kingdom represented a position, much less an authority that existed in the church in their time. They knew nothing about a person, the bishop of Rome or anyone else, who possessed "full, supreme, and universal power over the whole Church."

Roman Catholic Cardinal Yves Congar, who played an influential role in Vatican II, recognizes this omission in the early fathers:

> But it does sometimes happen that some Fathers understood a passage in a way that does not agree with later Church teaching. One example: the interpretation of Peter's confession in Matthew 16:16–19. Except at Rome, this passage was not applied by the Fathers to the papal primacy.[116]

"Except at Rome" is unnecessary here. There is no evidence this passage was applied to Papal Primacy even in Rome until at least the middle of the third century. Even then, the Roman elders appealed not to Matthew 16, but to Romans 1 for a testimony of their greatness:

> The apostle would not have published such praise concerning us, when he said "that your faith is spoken of throughout the whole world" [Rom.1:8], unless already from there that vigor had borrowed the roots of faith from those times; from which

---

[115] Robinson, n.d., The Demonstration of the Apostolic Preaching, sec. 1
[116] Congar, 1998, *Tradition and Traditions*, pp. 397-399

> praise and glory it is a very great crime to have become degenerate.[117]

Rome was a great church for several hundred years, noted for generosity to less affluent churches, solid adherence to the apostolic faith, and producing and supporting brave martyrs. No less than four of its bishops would give their lives for the faith during the one decade from 249 to 258.

The Roman church, and any church, is only great as long as it adheres to the apostolic faith and boldly confesses Christ against the protestations of the world. With this, the elders who led the church in Rome in 250 agree, saying it would be a "very great crime" to fall away from such glory.

Again, Rome was great in the second and third centuries. The church there was renowned for courage, generosity, and faithfulness to the truth. Their greatness, however, had nothing to do with Peter nor because of any perceived authority in its bishop.

Dr. Klaus Schatz, church history professor at a Jesuit college, writes:

> If one had asked a Christian in the year 100, 200, or even 300 whether the bishop of Rome was the head of all Christians, or whether there was a supreme bishop over all the other bishops and having the last word in questions affecting the whole Church, he or she would certainly have said no.[118]

Catholic apologist Stephen Ray writes: "Sometimes silence is more eloquent than words. This is especially true in Church history. We hear so much about what the Fathers say and so little about what they do not say."[119] Assuming he gets a chance to read this chapter, he might not be so quick to point out the strength of an argument from silence.

Binding and Loosing

On the matter of binding and loosing, we have Tertullian's witness again. We covered both these quotes in the previous section:

---

[117] "Epistles of Cyprian," 250, Epistle 30 (Oxford 30), par. 2, brackets mine
[118] Schatz, 1996, *Papal Primacy*, p. 3
[119] Ray, 2007, *Reasons to Believe*, Kindle location 78-79

Part II | Chapter 4: Matthew 16:15-19

> Peter was the first of all to be endued with the Spirit, and ... to say, "And now why are ye tempting the Lord, concerning the imposition upon the brethren of a yoke which neither we nor our fathers were able to support? But however, through the grace of Jesus we believe that we shall be saved in the same way as they" [Acts 15:7-11]. This sentence both "loosed" those parts of the law which were abandoned, and "bound" those which were reserved.[120]

Tertullian begins by saying that Peter loosed parts of the law, at least for the Gentiles, at the Jerusalem Council in Acts 15. The four parts of the law that were "bound" to them in that chapter were not to eat meat sacrificed to idols, nor blood, nor meat from strangled animals, and not to marry unlawfully.[121] All other parts of the Law of Moses, and especially circumcision, were "loosed" for the Gentiles. Binding and loosing were the prerogative of Jewish rabbis in apostolic times.[122] Tertullian attributes this binding and loosing to Peter as an individual, rather than the whole council.

This seems to be a "win" for Roman Catholic apologists regarding the authority of Peter. Tertullian grants Peter the specific authority to bind and loose laws upon the Gentiles. That is indeed great authority! It is not significant, however, because neither Tertullian nor anyone in the first three centuries of the Church, applied Peter's authority to the bishop of Rome.

Tertullian added the following regarding binding and loosing:

> [Peter] himself was the first to unbar, in Christ's baptism, the entrance to the heavenly kingdom, in which are "loosed" the sins that were "bound" in the past.[123]

---

[120] Tertullian, 208-220, "On Modesty," ch. 21, brackets mine

[121] "Marry unlawfully," as found in the NABRE, is an unusual translation. The U.S. Conference of Catholic Bishops' online commentary explains that this prohibition is a reference to the marrying of close relations as described in Leviticus 18 (United States Conference of Catholic Bishops, 2019, "Acts, Chapter 15," note on 15:13-35). While the Greek text does not justify this, it is an ingenious solution to the problem that "sexual immorality," a more exact translation, is the only moral prescription among the four prohibitions. The others are more cultural than moral.

[122] Biblehub, 2004-2018, "Matthew 16:19," sec. "Gill's Exposition of the Entire Bible," par. 2

[123] Tertullian, 208-220, "On Modesty," ch. 21

Rome's Audacious Claim

While Scott Hahn and Protestant commentators justifiably argue that binding and loosing have to do with the authority of a steward, the Roman Catholic Church itself applies binding and loosing primarily to the forgiveness of sins. Paragraph 553 of the *Catechism of the Catholic Church* says:

> The words bind and loose mean: whomever you exclude from your communion, will be excluded from communion with God; whomever you receive anew into your communion, God will welcome back into his.[124]

They go on to say that the authority of binding and loosing was also assigned to all the apostles, though they add "united to its head," by which they mean Peter and the succession of bishops in Rome.[125]

Except for assigning the succession from Peter to Rome, I agree with this definition of binding and loosing. All churches have the right to exclude from communion and receive anew into communion. This is directly said in Matthew 18:17-18. As Tertullian tells us, the catholic churches believed all churches inherited the promises of Peter.[126]

The authority to bind and loose is the last promise made to Peter in Matthew 16:15-19, so we are done with this passage. Peter was the first to receive these promises, but later they were given to the rest of the apostles and passed to all the churches. The one exception was the use of the keys to open the doors of God's kingdom to the Jews, Samaritans, and Gentiles. That one thing was Peter's unique privilege.

We also defined the keys of the kingdom. They have to do with excluding or admitting to the communion of the church. The other apostles and the churches are given this authority in Scripture (Matt. 18:15-18; Jn. 20:22-23).

We see then that Matthew 16 does not justify Rome's Audacious Claim. Peter did not receive any authority that the other apostles and their churches did not also receive.

The other passage on which the Roman Catholic Church hangs the authority of Peter is John 21:15-17.

---

[124] *Catechism of the Catholic Church*, 1995, par. 553
[125] *Catechism of the Catholic Church*, 1995, par. 1444
[126] Tertullian, 208-220, "On Modesty," ch. 21

Chapter 5: John 21:15-17

> Jesus said to Simon Peter, "Simon, son of John, do you love me more than these?"
> He said to him, "Yes, Lord, you know that I love you."
> He said to him, "Feed my lambs." (Jn. 21:15)

This exchange between Jesus and Peter happened three times. It ended with Jesus prophesying that Peter would eventually be martyred.

This passage is the only other passage to which the *Catechism of the Catholic Church* appeals to defend their claim that Jesus made Peter "shepherd over the whole Church." It says:

> Jesus, the Good Shepherd, confirmed this mandate after his Resurrection: "Feed my sheep." The power to "bind and loose" connotes the authority to absolve sins, to pronounce doctrinal judgments, and to make disciplinary decisions in the Church.[127]

Jesus tells Peter to feed his sheep, but he does not specify who those sheep are. Peter himself comes much closer to specifying which sheep were his to shepherd.

> So I exhort the presbyters among you, as a fellow presbyter and witness to the sufferings of Christ and one who has a share in the glory to be revealed. Tend the flock of God in your midst, [overseeing] not by constraint but willingly, as God would have it, not for shameful profit but eagerly. Do not lord it over those assigned to you, but be examples to the flock. And when the chief Shepherd is revealed, you will receive the unfading crown of glory. (1 Peter 5:1-4, brackets in original)

Peter points out what should be obvious. One can only shepherd those who are near you. The word "tend" in that passage is literally "shepherd," and he tells the elders (presbyters) that they should shepherd the flock of God "in their midst."

---

[127] *Catechism of the Catholic Church*, 1995, par. 881

Rome's Audacious Claim

Notice too that Peter calls himself a "fellow presbyter" and assigns the Chief Shepherd role to Jesus, who can be "with us always" (Matt. 28:20). Peter, not being omnipresent, cannot do this.

For example, if Jesus came to me and told me to shepherd his lambs, I would be confident he meant the Christians in my church, along with any other Christians that he put in front of me or to whom he sent me. After all, I can't shepherd any of Jesus's sheep in Papua New Guinea because I don't know any of them. I would certainly not assume that he was installing me as the shepherd of all churches everywhere.

Peter was much greater than I am. The Gospels portray him as the leader of the apostles, and he plays a leading role throughout his life. Nonetheless, it is just as impossible for Peter to shepherd every Christian in the world as it would be for me. Today the pope in Rome could at least attempt to shepherd all the churches in the world using the internet. Peter, though, could not have shepherded the whole church even by letter. The apostles took the gospel into the Persian Empire, India, Ethiopia, and probably even the British Isles and southern China during Peter's lifetime. Even letters would take months to reach those locations.

John 21:15-17 does not give us enough information to draw any conclusions about the extent of Peter's shepherding. We would need some other evidence to conclude that Peter was shepherd over more than just the sheep allotted to him in Jerusalem, Antioch, Corinth, or Rome, churches in which history testifies he played a role.

Roman Catholic apologist Jimmy Akin tries to bolster John 21:15-17 with Luke 22:32. He points out that in this verse Jesus tells Peter to "strengthen your brothers" in the presence of the other apostles. Thus, he concludes, Peter has a special place among the apostles.[128]

This is no argument for Rome's Audacious Claim. We cannot deny Peter had a special role among the apostles. Strengthening his brothers, however, is not the same as having "full, supreme, and universal power" over them. "Full, supreme, and universal authority" is rather the opposite of the kind of leadership Jesus gave to any of the apostles. He told them that while the Gentiles exercise lordship and

---

[128] Akin, 2017, "What Is the Evidence for Papal Primacy?," 2:00-3:30

authority over one another, "it shall not be so among you" (Mk. 10:42-43).

If there is evidence that Peter had supreme authority over the other apostles or the whole Church, it must be found outside the Scriptures. Roman Catholic apologists try to find that evidence in early Christian history but, as we are forewarned by the Roman Catholic Church's own authorities,[129] that evidence does not exist.

It is time to look at the evidence.

---

[129] See chapter 2.

Rome's Audacious Claim

Part III

New Testament History

Rome's Audacious Claim

Chapter 6: Popes, Patriarchs, and the Episcopacy

We have a long journey in front of us, from the promises and charges to Peter in Matthew 16 and John 21, to the playing out of Peter's role in the New Testament, to the development of bishops, the rise of metropolitans and patriarchs, and finally to the most supreme office a Christian can hold: pope.

We cannot make that journey without some definitions. "Pope," "patriarch," "metropolitan," "bishop," "overseer," "presbyter," "priest," "elder," and "deacon" are all words we will encounter as we explore the development of Rome's Audacious Claim. The best way to teach you these terms is to tell you how each arose.

Let's begin this section with Peter's own words concerning the shepherding of the Church.

> So I exhort the presbyters among you, as a fellow presbyter and witness of the sufferings of Christ and one who has a share in the glory to be revealed. Tend the flock of God in your midst, [overseeing] not by constraint but willingly, as God would have it.... Do not lord it over those assigned to you, but be examples to the flock. And when the chief Shepherd is revealed, you will receive the unfading crown of glory. (1 Pet. 5:1-4)

The NABRE chooses the word "presbyters" in this passage, where most Protestant translations would use "elders." These two terms are the first we will learn. They are equivalent. Peter originally wrote in Greek. The Greek word *presbuteros* means "elder," and it is easy to see how *presbuteros* could be rendered into English as "presbyter."

"Elder" or "presbyter" was an appointed position in the apostles' churches. In Titus 1:5, Paul directs Titus to appoint presbyters in every town. In 1 Timothy 4:14, Paul says that Timothy received a spiritual gift when the "presbyterate" laid hands on him.

With this, we come to our next term: "presbytery," which the NABRE renders "presbyterate." In New Testament times, a presbytery was the group of elders who led the church in each town. Titus was to appoint presbyters, and those presbyters would together be a presbytery. Since "elder" and "presbyter" mean the same thing, most

histories use "college of elders" rather than "presbytery." I will do the same in this book. A college of elders is the presbytery mentioned in 1 Timothy 4:14.

Paul, after telling Titus to appoint presbyters, gives him the qualifications for a "bishop" (Tit. 1:7-9). The Greek word for "bishop" is *episkopos*. It means "overseer" or "supervisor." Thus, the presbyters each filled the office of "bishop," and "bishop" and "overseer" (as some Bible versions translate *episkopos*) are equivalent.

In the New Testament, or at least in the writings of Peter and Paul, presbyters (or elders) held the position of bishop. You can also see this in 1 Peter 5:1-4. Peter tells the elders that they are to "tend the flock of God" and to "oversee." The word "oversee" is the verb form of the noun *episkopos* (bishop of overseer). Peter tells elders to oversee because, like Paul, his elders were also the bishops.

Peter not only tells the elders (presbyters) to oversee the flock but also to "tend" it. The Greek word for "tend" is *poimanate*. The sentence can also be translated "shepherd the flock of God."

We have two more words now, "shepherd" and "pastor." Again, these two words mean the same thing. Both the NABRE and many Protestant translations render *poimenas* as "pastors" in Ephesians 4:11. You can see the similarity between the plural noun *poimenas* and the command *poimanate*. These "pastors" are shepherds. Even in English, "pastor" and "shepherd" are synonyms.

So now we have learned bishop, overseer, elder, presbyter, presbytery, pastor, and shepherd, but all these words refer to the same people!

No one contests this understanding of New Testament leadership, not even the Roman Catholic Church. Paul and Peter's churches were led by a college of elders. That is why Paul and Barnabas "appointed presbyters … in each church" (Acts 14:23). We see another example of this when Paul summons the elders of the church in Ephesus and reminds them that they were appointed "overseers" (Acts 20:17, 28).

It is important to point out that this form of church government did not last long. It is very likely that the role of overseer (or bishop) was separated from the role of elder (or presbyter) in the churches of Asia Minor from the time of the apostles. By the middle of the second century, all churches of the vast Roman Empire had one bishop who led the college of elders. What did not change was that the bishops and

Part III | Chapter 6: Popes, Patriarchs, and the Episcopacy

elders were the ones who pastored the churches. There was not a "pastor" role separate from the bishop and his elders. They *were* the pastors.

Eventually, both bishops and elders came to be called "priests." Elders in particular, perhaps because of language descent, are called "priests" in both Eastern and Western churches in the third century. In the eyes of Protestants (and mine) this is a very problematic deviation from both Scripture and church history (cf. Heb. 7-8). The use of "priest" to refer to presbyters only arose after Latin became the common language of Western churches in the 200s.

I have left out deacons, but we should address them now. The role of deacons will be irrelevant to this book, but the term will come up. The Greek word for "deacon" is *diakonos*, which means "servant." Paul required deacons to meet a standard not much different than bishops in the New Testament (1 Tim. 3:8-12).

1 Timothy 3:11 brings up the question of whether women can be deaconesses. *Gunaikas* can mean "wives" or "women" in that verse. Also, the apostle Paul commended a woman named Phoebe as a "minister" of the church in Cenchreae (Rom. 16:1). The Greek word there is the feminine of *diakonos*.

Whether the early churches had deaconesses or just deacons will have no influence on this book. For men or women, the job of the deacon was service, not leading the churches.

By the mid-third century, a new office arose. A bishop in larger cities came to be known as a "metropolitan." A metropolitan had the oversight not only of his own city, but of surrounding smaller towns. Those towns had their own bishops, but they were subordinate to the metropolitan. The metropolitan's own city might also have subordinate bishops.

After another century, the role of patriarch developed. If you will excuse the terminology, they were basically super metropolitans. Metropolitans were bishops who served a city and its surrounding area. Patriarchs were bishops who led whole regions.

The first patriarchs were the bishops of Rome, Alexandria, and Antioch. The Council of Nicea in 325 confirmed their vast areas of supervision, and Canon 6 of that council has become a point of hot

contention for the Roman Catholic apologists. We will look at that canon in the chapter on the fourth century.[130]

The bishop of Jerusalem, who did not have nearly the area of supervision of the others, was made an honorary patriarch, also at the Council of Nicea.[131] After Constantinople was established in 330, its bishop quickly became a patriarch because Constantinople was the "new Rome." When Persian King Yazdegerd temporarily ended persecution in Persia, the Council of Seleucia Ctesiphon organized the churches of Persia and bestowed a similar status ("Grand Metropolitan") on Mar Isaac, the bishop of Seleucia Ctesiphon.[132]

In 451, the Council of Chalcedon excommunicated Dioscorus, the patriarch of Alexandria. Many Egyptian churches stayed loyal to him, and today they call themselves the Coptic Orthodox Church. They call their patriarch "pope" as well. Other "Orthodox" branches of Christianity are affiliated with the Coptic pope, including two patriarchs, one in Ethiopia and one in Eritrea.[133]

The Orthodox Church in Russia made the bishop of Moscow a patriarch in 1448, and Constantinople approved the designation in 1589. Constantinople gave the approval because Rome split from all the Eastern patriarchs in 1054, an event known as the "Great Schism."

The Great Schism had a lot to do with Rome's Audacious Claim, but the roots of the schism arose long before the eleventh century. In 476, the Roman Empire lost the city of Rome and all of Italy to barbarian tribes. By then, the Roman emperor in Constantinople was an established fixture in the rule of the churches in the empire. Rome, however, was now outside the empire. The barbarian tribes who competed for control of Europe were "Christian," and they accepted the religious authority of the bishop of Rome, the only patriarch in Western Europe. This circumstance had much to do with Rome's

---

[130] Chapter 23
[131] Canon 7
[132] The Persian churches are known as the "Church of the East." They united with the Syrian churches after Nestorius, bishop of Constantinople, was excommunicated at the Council of Ephesus in 431.
[133] These Orthodox Churches include the Armenian Apostolic, the Eritrean Orthodox Tawahedo, the Ethiopian Orthodox Tawahedo, the Malankala Orthodox Syrian, and the Syrian Orthodox Churches.

Part III | Chapter 6: Popes, Patriarchs, and the Episcopacy

increasing claim to "full, supreme, and universal power over the whole Church."

It was during these centuries of separation that the Roman bishop became known not only as "patriarch," but also as lone claimant to the title "pope." The word "pope" means simply "papa." In the early centuries of the Church, the title was applied to all bishops, especially in the East. Since the fifth century, the churches of the Roman Empire have limited the title "papa" to the bishop of Rome.[134] As noted, the Coptic Orthodox Church, separated since the Council of Chalcedon, continues to refer to the Alexandrian patriarch as "pope."

As we progress, it will be important to remember that the pope is the pope by virtue of being the bishop of Rome. The bishop of Rome is the pope, and the pope is the bishop of Rome.

We need to add one more word that does not fit neatly into the story: "cardinal."

"Cardinal" developed from the Latin word *cardinalis*, which originally meant "every priest permanently attached to a church." Today, though, the cardinals of the Roman Catholic Church are assistants to the pope. They must be bishops, and they elect the popes. They report only to the pope and can only be deposed by him. Cardinal is the highest dignity, other than pope, to which a Roman Catholic bishop can ascend.[135]

This brings us to the final word that we must examine: "catholic."

One Holy, Catholic, and Apostolic Church

"Catholic" means "universal." The great creeds of the united Church—the Nicene and Apostles' Creeds—each express a belief in "one holy, catholic, and apostolic Church."

"Apostolic" indicates descent from the apostles. The churches founded by the apostles and by missionaries from those churches form the one apostolic Church. Together, they hold to the teachings of the apostles, both those written in the Scriptures and those passed down orally (cf. 2 Thes. 2:15).[136] "Catholic" means universal, and indicates the unity of the apostolic churches. The churches descended from the

---

[134] Schatz, 1996, *Papal Primacy*, pp. 28-29
[135] Trinity Communications, 2019, "Catholic Dictionary: Cardinal"
[136] We will devote a lot of attention to oral tradition in the chapter on Irenaeus/

apostles and united in faith are (or were) the catholic churches. Together they are "the" Catholic Church.

This is what "catholic" meant for a thousand years, even though The Councils of Ephesus (431) and Chalcedon (451) cut off entire countries and kingdoms. When the patriarchs of Constantinople and Rome excommunicated each other in 1054, what remained of the Catholic Church split in half.

It violates the definition of "catholic" to refer to one segment of a fractured body as the Catholic Church. I will refer to the segment of the former Catholic Church that is now led by the Roman bishop as the "Roman Catholic Church" throughout this book. The other segments of the Catholic Church all refer to themselves as "Orthodox" more commonly than "Catholic," sparing me any conflict in referring to them.

There can, however, still be "apostolic" churches.

Protestants and Apostolic Churches

The various Orthodox Churches, in agreement with the Roman Catholic Church, argue that a legitimate physical descent from the apostles through a lineage of bishops and elders is necessary for being apostolic. There are also Protestant denominations that claim apostolic succession as well, such as the Anglicans, Episcopalians, and Lutherans. Most other Protestant denominations do not care about nor try to claim such a succession.

However, Protestants who do not have such a lineage have support from at least one of the early church fathers, who writes:

> But if there be any (heresies) which are bold enough to plant themselves in the midst of the apostolic age ... let them unfold the roll of their bishops, running down in due succession from the beginning in such a manner that the first bishop shall be able to show for his ordainer and predecessor some one of the apostles or of apostolic men,—a man, moreover, who continued steadfast with the apostles.[137]

Tertullian wrote this shortly after the year 200, and his argument was directed against gnostic churches that rejected the God of Israel

---

[137] Tertullian, c. 200, "Prescription Against Heretics," ch. 32

Part III | Chapter 6: Popes, Patriarchs, and the Episcopacy

despite claiming to believe in Jesus. These churches could not claim to be apostolic in origin. Like the Roman Catholics and Orthodox would today, he challenges those churches on their descent. Where did they originate?

But Tertullian does not end there:

> But should they even effect the contrivance, they will not advance a step. For their very doctrine, after comparison with that of the apostles, will declare, by its own diversity and contrariety, that it had for its author neither an apostle nor an apostolic man.[138]

An "apostolic man" is a man who was a companion of the apostles. In the previous quote, Tertullian told us that these men could also establish apostolic churches, as long as they "continued steadfast with the apostles."[139]

In this quote, he points out that having a roll of bishops back to the apostles will do no good if a church's doctrine is contrary to the apostles' doctrine. Then he says there are churches who…

> … although they derive not their founder from apostles or apostolic men (as being of much later date, for they are in fact being founded daily), yet, since they agree in the same faith, they are accounted as not less apostolic because they are akin in doctrine. Then let all the heresies, when challenged to these two tests by our apostolic church, offer their proof of how they deem themselves to be apostolic.[140]

It is important to note that there are two tests that this early third-century writer requires, not one. It was not enough to show a lineage from the apostles, the church must also have apostolic doctrine.

Even more importantly, Tertullian argues that a church without a roll of bishops back to the apostles is apostolic because its doctrine agrees with the apostles. Thus, at least for Tertullian, the test of doctrine supersedes the test of succession. For twenty-first century Christians, this means our churches can be apostolic by learning and adhering to apostolic doctrine. Of course, we must also live obediently

---

[138] Tertullian, c. 200, "Prescription Against Heretics," ch. 32
[139] Tertullian, c. 200, "Prescription Against Heretics," ch. 32
[140] Tertullian, c. 200, "Prescription Against Heretics," ch. 32

Rome's Audacious Claim

to Jesus; disobedient churches receive harsh penalties from the Lord (Rev. 2-3).

The Roman Catholic Church claims "full, supreme, and universal power" for its bishop, even if he has abandoned the faith or possesses no regard for it at all. Horace Mann, in his history of the tenth-century popes, writes, "Have I not also the assurance of St. Leo I, the Great, that 'the dignity of Peter is not lost even in an unworthy successor'?"[141]

Pope Leo must have turned over in his grave when Mann used his words to defend a person like Pope John XII. Leo's sermon was about himself, and he meant that humble unworthiness which all godly men feel before the perfect love of our Lord Jesus.[142] He certainly did not intend to justify a man whose lewd behavior made respectable women afraid to go to Rome on pilgrimage and whose court was called a brothel![143]

With that assessment of the word "catholic," we have covered all the words we need to define in advance.

The following list should help you as we proceed, and I have added a list of definitions at the back of this book. Hopefully, this chapter will be enough for you to memorize the various ranks within the Roman Catholic Church and the churches of Christendom throughout history. You can also bookmark this list, which is ranked from the highest authority to lowest.

- The **pope** is the bishop of Rome and claims a primacy of authority and jurisdiction.
- **Patriarchs** are bishops who preside over regions. For example, the patriarch in Moscow is lead bishop for all of Russia (among the Russian Orthodox churches).
- A college of **cardinals** began electing the popes in 1059 by the order of Pope Nicholas II.
- A **metropolitan** is a bishop who leads a city and surrounding areas. He has bishops under him.
- A **bishop** supervises a city or town. They hold an office called an **episcopate** and govern an area called a **see**.

---

[141] Mann, 1925, *The Lives of the Popes: Vol. IV*, p. viii
[142] Leo I, 440-661, "Sermons," Sermon III
[143] Mann, 1925, *The Lives of the Popes: Vol. IV*, p. 255

Part III | Chapter 6: Popes, Patriarchs, and the Episcopacy

- A priest is a **presbyter** or **elder**. All clergy, including bishops, cardinals, and popes are considered priests by the Roman Catholic Church, and they give lip service to the scriptural teaching that all believers are priests. When a person is called a "**priest**" without further clarification, though, it generally means he is an **elder**.
- A **deacon** serves the congregation and the leaders of the congregation.

The Roman Catholic Church now has monsignors, archbishops, subdeacons, and other gradations of the offices above. You will see these here and there in this book.

With our definitions covered, let us begin our historical survey of Rome's Audacious Claim in the New Testament era. We will begin with a historical look at Peter himself.

Rome's Audacious Claim

Chapter 7: Peter the Presbyter

In his first letter, Peter tells his fellow shepherds, "Do not lord it over *those assigned to you*" (1 Pet. 5:3, italics mine). The Roman Catholic Church would argue that the whole Church is assigned to Peter.[144] The verse itself reads as though Peter, a "fellow presbyter" to the presbyters he is addressing (1 Pet. 5:1), has just one portion of the flock of God, just as the others do. We will devote this chapter to determining the extent of the portion assigned to Peter.

A presbyter, says Peter, is not a lord, but an example to the flock (1 Pet. 5:3). Hebrews 13:7 expands on this, telling us, "Remember your leaders who spoke the word of God to you. Consider the outcome of their way of life and imitate their faith." A shepherd is an example, and the flock is to know and imitate him.

The entire Church could not possibly imitate Peter. His biography was not in circulation in the first century, nor was CBS broadcasting news about "the first pope" on the radio to believers in Alexandria. The apostle Thomas went all the way to India. Those believers could not imitate Peter's faith because they did not know him. Peter could not be an example to him because he was thousands of miles away.

An elder shepherds those in his congregation. That is why the letter to the Hebrews goes on to say,

> Obey your leaders and defer to them, for they keep watch over you and will have to give an account. (13:17)

It would not be just to hold Peter accountable for believers in India or Egypt while he was living in Rome. He could not possibly "watch over" the saints in either place. According to Peter, presbyters must "tend the flock of God" in their "midst" (1 Pet. 5:2). It is impossible for a mere human to watch over or to tend the entire flock of God. Only Jesus, who promised to be with all of us always (Matt. 28:20), can personally shepherd all of us. Peter directly acknowledges this, contradicting the Roman Catholic Catechism by calling Jesus the "chief Shepherd" (1 Pet. 5:4).

The apostle Paul spent twelve verses appealing to the example he and his companions set for the Thessalonians. He says they did not

---

[144] *Catechism of the Catholic Church*, 1995, par. 882

Rome's Audacious Claim

flatter, nor seek praise, but were gentle like "a nursing mother cares for her children" (1 Thes. 2:1-12). This kind of shepherding cannot be done from a distance.

Clement of Alexandria gives an excellent example of this in a tale about the apostle John. Clement says that John took care of a number of churches in Asia Minor, much as an itinerant preacher might have in America's frontier churches. On one of his visits, he converted a young man. Since John moved from place to place, he left the young man with the overseer of the local church.

When John returned many months later, he demanded of the overseer the "deposit" he had left with him. This puzzled the bishop; he thought John meant money. Finally, John told him he was talking about the young man.

The overseer told him the tragic story. The young man had fallen in with the wrong crowd, and now he was spending his time with a band of robbers.

John did not take the news well. "It was a fine guard of a brother's soul I left!" he exclaimed. Then he called for a horse and left town to find the robbers. He was a very old man by this time, so when the gang saw him approaching, they did him no harm. They simply stopped him. John got down from the horse and demanded to see the young man, calling him by name.

It turned out the young man had become the band's leader. They took John to him, but as soon as he saw John, he fled. John ran after him, and the robbers marveled.

Eventually, the young man stopped and turned around. John told him it was not too late to repent, and the young man fell at his feet in tears. When John brought the young man back to town, he upbraided the overseer for being a pitiful watchman and told him to take better care of his charge.[145]

This is shepherding. This is what Jesus had in mind when he told Peter to shepherd his sheep. He did not tell Peter he was shepherd of all churches and all Christians; he wanted Peter to feed those who were with him: those he could tend to and those who could follow his

---

[145] Clement of Alexandria, 182-202, *Who Is the Rich Man Who Must Be Saved?*, ch. 42

example. Jesus himself would take care of his sheep in India through Thomas and those in Asia Minor through John.

Someone might be CEO over the Church in the whole world, but ruling is not shepherding. A person who owns a massive enterprise in wool and lamb chops might employ hundreds or thousands of shepherds, but he himself would not be one. He would be a CEO or president.

Peter has many firsts in the Bible. He used his keys to open the doors to the kingdom of God when he first preached the gospel in Jerusalem (Acts 2). He opened the doors of the kingdom for the Samaritans and Gentiles as well (Acts 8:4-25; 10:1-49). Being first, however, is not the same as being a shepherd. We find Peter behaving as one who is the first, but we do not find him behaving as one who is shepherd over every other shepherd. This is most apparent in his interactions with James, the Lord's brother and first bishop of the church in Jerusalem.

Peter and James

In Acts 15, we find the first council the Church held. Certain members of the Jerusalem church had come to Antioch to teach converted Gentiles that they must be circumcised in order to be saved (v. 1). Paul tells us later that he refused to submit to this "even for a moment" (Gal. 2:5). Instead, he brought the matter to the apostles and elders in Jerusalem (Acts 15:2).

Luke (the author of Acts) tells us almost nothing of the proceedings, saying only, "After much debate had taken place, Peter got up and said.... " (Acts 15:7).

Now here is testimony for Peter's authority! Everyone disputed, and then Peter stood up and gave a final argument. When he was done, "... the whole assembly fell silent" (v. 12).

For our purposes, Peter's specific words don't matter. Everyone was arguing, then Peter spoke, then everyone was silent and willing to listen to Paul and Barnabas. That is a remarkable testimony of Peter's authority.

But it is not the end of the story.

Peter spoke, and then he just stopped. No one can argue the fact that he carried enough authority in the council to stop the debate and get the local believers, who were all Jewish and mostly zealous for the

Law, to listen to Paul and Barnabas. We must notice, though, that Peter did not end the council. He gave his argument, then sat down. Yes, that speech silenced all other arguments and got those at the council to listen to the apostles to the Gentiles (cf. Rom. 11:13), but Peter issued no decree.

After Paul and Barnabas spoke, James was the one who concluded the council, and he did issue a decree:

> "It is my judgment, therefore ..." (v. 19)

This is a statement of authority: "It is my judgment" that we do such and such. Peter argued with them, telling the others that to require circumcision from the Gentiles was to tempt God. James, however, rendered judgment: "It is my judgment" that the following is what we should do.

There is no continuation of the talk after James gave his decision. He told them to write a letter with certain content, and they determined who would carry that letter. The end.

Thus, we find that it is James, not Peter, who presided at the Council of Jerusalem. While it is historically certain that James became the bishop of Jerusalem, this cannot be the reason Peter let him take the lead. The letter that James dictated was carried to Antioch, Syria, and Cilicia as well (Acts 15:23). In fact, it affected Gentile churches much more than it affected the primarily Jewish Jerusalem church, whose members were all circumcised already (Acts 21:23-26). James, not Peter, gave the final decision in a council that decided an issue affecting every Gentile church.

Thus, if there is evidence that anyone was "shepherd of the whole Church," that shepherd was James, not Peter. Fortunately, no one is claiming that James has supreme authority and passed that authority to the bishops who succeeded him in Jerusalem. That might be a harder argument to tackle!

Part III | Chapter 7: Peter the Presbyter
Hypocrisy in Antioch: Who Was Submitting to Whom?

> James and Cephas[146] and John, who were reputed to be pillars, gave me and Barnabas their right hands in partnership, that we should go to the Gentiles and they to the circumcised.... And when Cephas came to Antioch, I opposed him to his face because he clearly was wrong. For, until some people came from James, he used to eat with the Gentiles; but when they came, he began to draw back and separated himself, because he was afraid of the circumcised. And the rest of the Jews [also] acted hypocritically along with him, with the result that even Barnabas was carried away by their hypocrisy. (Gal. 2:9, 11-13; brackets in original)

In this passage we have two evidences that James exercised authority even over Peter. This almost certainly was not an official, assigned authority, but rather the sort of authority that prevails naturally in groups of men, even in churches. We don't read about an official appointment, but we see from Scripture that James became the "alpha male" in these earliest churches.

The first evidence we see is that Paul lists James first and not Peter. "James, Cephas, and John" were pillars, not, "Cephas, John, and James," the order one would expect.

The second evidence we see is Peter's fear of James. On his own, Peter did what he knew was right. Antioch was not the first place he had eaten with Gentiles. He ate with Cornelius and his household when God sent him to preach the gospel to them (Acts 11:3). When "some people" came from James, though, he was afraid, and he stopped eating with them.

This has to have infuriated Paul, who devoted his life to pursuing and proclaiming the righteousness of God apart from the Law. Peter is to be commended for listening when Paul confronted him "in front of all" (Gal. 2:14). What a tragedy it would have been to Jesus's Church had Peter bristled and proclaimed his own authority! Though Peter deserved the rebuke, this story should never be told without

---

[146] *Kephas* is the Aramaic word for "rock." It is spelled "Cephas" in many Bible translations. Peter is referred to by his Aramaic name a half dozen times in the New Testament.

mentioning Peter's humility. He chose to listen, to stay in fellowship with Paul, and to preserve the unity of God's people.

The point we want to make here, though, is that Peter gave deference to James, even in Antioch. He gave so much deference that he changed his behavior just at the presence of unnamed men from James.

The relationship between James and Peter leads us to the same conclusion we have already been drawing: Peter did not behave like he was "shepherd of the whole Church," and he was not treated as such, even in Jerusalem.

Chapter 8: Paul and Peter

The apostle Paul has much to say that applies to whether or not Peter was the "pastor of the entire Church."[147]

We have already seen that Paul listed James before Peter in his list of those "reputed" to be pillars (Gal. 2:9). Not only did he list James first, but his use of the word "reputed" suggests he did not necessarily agree with the estimation others had made. In fact, a little earlier in Galatians 2:6, he wrote:

> From those who were reputed to be important (what they once were makes no difference to me; God shows no partiality)—those of repute made me add nothing.

Paul was bold and brash, but we cannot accuse the famous apostle of being rebellious. Yet here is Paul saying that "what they once were" (and so "what Peter was") made no difference to him. God, he says, is not partial to anyone, not even to James, Peter, or John.

Paul could not have said that he did not care what Peter was if he thought Peter had "full, supreme, and universal power over the whole church." In fact, dismissing the reputation of James, Peter, and John implies that he saw a "full, supreme, and universal power" over all three. Paul assigned all his actions and opinions to the one "full, supreme, and universal" authority that Scripture does mention: Jesus Christ (Matt. 28:18).

That same authority, Jesus, is called the "chief Shepherd" by Peter himself (1 Pet. 5:4). Peter also called Jesus the shepherd and guardian of our souls (1 Pet. 2:25).[148] Jesus is the Bishop of bishops and the Shepherd of shepherds, not Peter. Jesus can be a universal Shepherd because he can be with all of us always (Matt. 28:20).

Paul also had some important things to say about Peter to the Corinthians. He complains about the divisions in the Corinthian church. Each one of them is saying, "I belong to Paul," or, "I belong to Apollos," or "I belong to Cephas," or "I belong to Christ" (1 Cor. 1:12). Cephas, as we have seen, is Peter. Paul goes on to ask them if

---

[147] *Catechism of the Catholic Church*, 1995, par. 882
[148] In 1 Peter 2:25, the NABRE reads "shepherd and guardian," but the word for "guardian" there is *episkopos*, which means "bishop" or "overseer."

Rome's Audacious Claim

Christ is divided, or if Paul was crucified for them, or if they were baptized in the name of Paul (v. 13).

We see here that there is no commendation given to those who are "of Peter" because he is "shepherd of the whole church." Of course, neither is commendation given to those who say they are "of Christ," because Paul's concern was their divisiveness. Using one's allegiance to our King to divide his kingdom is hardly commendable behavior.

There is an out here for those who want to defend Peter's authority. If the Corinthians were not even to say they were "of Christ" in contrast to their brothers and sisters, it is no wonder that they cannot do so with Peter. Nonetheless, this passage is an important foundation for the rest of what Paul says in the Corinthian letter.

He tells us it is not the work of a man that matters. The work of God matters. One may plant, one may water, but it is God who gives the growth (3:7). He then ends with this statement:

> So let no one boast about human beings, for everything belongs to you, Paul or Apollos or Cephas, or the world or life or death, or the present or the future: all belong to you, and you to Christ, and Christ to God. (3:21-23)

The question that arises from this discussion is why Peter is even mentioned. In 1 Corinthians 4:6, Paul says that he has applied the discussion to himself and Apollos. We can be confident from reading this first Corinthian letter that Apollos had been through Corinth and gained a following. He does not mention Peter in chapter four, however. He mentions Peter only among the names of Corinthian divisions.

Why Peter?

One plausible interpretation is that the Corinthians knew that Peter was "shepherd of the whole Church," but we have seen evidence against this in Acts. More likely, Judaizers in their midst, whom Paul constantly battled, claimed Peter as their authority since Peter, James, and John were apostles to the circumcision (Gal. 2:9).

Either way, Paul gives not a hint that Peter carried any legitimate authority in the Corinthian church, attributing all authority and power to God and warning them not to "boast about human beings" (1 Cor. 3:21).

Part III | Chapter 8: Paul and Peter

Later, in his second letter to the Corinthians, when Paul felt obligated to defend his ministry to them, he writes, "For I think that I am not in any way inferior to these 'superapostles'" (11:5).[149]

Who were these "superapostles"? The context does not make it clear. Paul's letter to the Galatians hints that he might be referring to James, Peter, and John. There he said they were "reputed to be important" (Gal. 2:6), and in 2 Corinthians "superapostles." We don't have to know, though. It is enough to point out that the superapostles are multiple men and that Peter is not singled out.

The absence of Peter as "chief apostle" among the superapostles is important. Again, arguments from silence are prone to be untrustworthy but, as we proceed, they will pile up. The number of situations where Peter or a "supreme" authority on earth seems relevant but is not mentioned reaches a level that cannot be ignored.

Let's look at some examples in Scripture.

Paul wrote three letters late in life to understudies: two to Timothy and one to Titus. He taught them how to raise up a church and teach them sound doctrine. In 1 Timothy 3:15, for example, he tells Timothy, "If I should be delayed, you should know how to behave in the household of God, which is the church of the living God, the pillar and foundation of truth."

To Titus, he writes, "You must say what is consistent with sound doctrine," and, "Say these things. Exhort and correct with all authority" (2:1, 15).

Despite this emphasis on sound doctrine and on how to live as a member of God's family, he mentions neither Peter nor Rome. It is not plausible that Paul knew that Peter had "full, supreme, and universal power," was "pastor of the entire Church" and sole possessor of the keys of the kingdom, yet he never mentioned this in a letter emphasizing the things consistent with sound doctrine.

Finally, we need to add in the testimony of Paul's companion, Luke, who wrote the book of Acts. At the end of Acts, we find Paul in Rome under house arrest. He taught from there for two years. Although Paul was in Rome and teaching, Luke finds it unnecessary to mention Peter or the authority of the church of Rome.

---

[149] "Superapostles" is an interesting translation. The Greek reads *lian apostolōn*, literally meaning "very great apostles."

Rome's Audacious Claim

These arguments from silence are all any historian has when something did not happen. We cannot find arguments against Peter or Roman bishops having "full, supreme, and universal power over the whole Church" because no one protests something that does not exist. Since neither Peter nor the bishops of Rome made any such claim in the early history of the Church, we will never find anyone writing against the claim.

Our arguments from silence will suffice, however, as the situations that seem to call for the mention of Peter multiply. The silence will become loud indeed, so loud that the Vatican, the U.S. Conference of Catholic Bishops, and Roman Catholic scholars have backed off the claim of an early papacy.[150]

With that, let us hurry on to the history many of my readers have not seen: the writings of the early church fathers.

---

[150] See chapter 2.

Part IV

The Apostolic Fathers

Rome's Audacious Claim

Chapter 9: Clement of Rome

In 95 or 96 AD, the church at Rome sent a letter to the church at Corinth. It is the only Christian writing outside the New Testament that is confidently dated in the first century. It is known as "First Clement" because later Christians tell us that Clement, one of the bishops at Rome, wrote it.

The letter itself says it came from the church at Rome. It does not mention Clement, but no one disputes he wrote it. The letter is well-known and cited early and repeatedly in history, and a manuscript of 1 Clement was included at the end of the New Testament of one of the more famous codex Bibles of the fourth century, *Codex Alexandrinus*.[151]

The subject of the letter was a leadership dispute that was dividing the Corinthians. In fact, at least two elders had been unseated.[152]

That sounds familiar, doesn't it? Paul, too, had written the Corinthians about division some forty years earlier (1 Cor. 1-3). First Clement reminds the Corinthians of this. It begins by commending them heartily for their deep repentance and excellent testimony since Paul's letter,[153] then moves on to long teaching against envy and pride and sharp rebuke for their return to old problems.

In the process, Clement talks about how leadership is supposed to work in the church:

> The apostles ... went forth proclaiming that the kingdom of God was at hand. Thus preaching through countries and cities, they appointed the firstfruits, having first proven them by the Spirit, to be bishops and deacons of those who would believe later. Nor was this any new thing, since indeed many ages before it was written concerning bishops and deacons ... "I will appoint their bishops in righteousness, and their deacons in faith" [Is. 40:17, LXX, loosely quoted].[154]

---

[151] Roberts & Donaldson, 1867-1873, "Introductory Note to the First Epistle of Clement to the Corinthians," in *The Ante-Nicene Fathers*, vol. I
[152] Clement of Rome, 95-96, "1 Clement", ch. 44
[153] Clement of Rome, 95-96, "1 Clement," chs. 2-3
[154] Clement of Rome, 95-96, "1 Clement," ch. 42, brackets mine

Rome's Audacious Claim

In the quote above, Clement mentions only bishops and deacons. Because deacons are servants, they are not part of the leadership of the Church. Because there are spiritual qualifications for being a servant, they are often influential men (or women, like Phoebe in Romans 16:2), but they are not "clergy."

Thus, Rome's letter mentions only bishops as leaders, not elders, and "bishops" is plural. We have already seen this as the pattern in both Peter's churches and Paul's. They had a college of elders, all called bishops. The testimony of the ancients is that Peter and Paul founded the Roman church,[155] so it should not surprise us to find collegiate leadership there just thirty years after they were martyred.

We see this again a couple chapters later.

> Our sin will not be small if we eject from the episcopate those who have fulfilled its duties without blame and in holiness. Blessed are those presbyters who ... have obtained a fruitful and perfect departure [by death], for they have no fear that anyone will deprive them of the place appointed them.[156]

Presbyters, as we learned in chapter 6, are elders. "Episcopate" comes from the Greek word for bishop or overseer, *episkopos*, and it means "office of overseer" or "office of bishop." Clement says here that elders are being ejected from the office of bishop. He uses bishop and elder as equivalent terms, just as Paul and Peter did. Again, since Paul founded the church in Corinth (Acts 18:7-8), and Peter and Paul the church in Rome, this is what we would expect. Father Richard O'Brien, once the president of the Catholic Theological Society of America, acknowledges this:

> There is no evidence that there was even a monoepiscopal [single bishop] form of ecclesiastical governance in Rome until the middle of the second century, beginning perhaps with the pontificate of Pius I (ca. 142– ca. 155). Before that time, the Roman community seems to have had a corporate or collegial form of pastoral leadership.[157]

---

[155] e.g., Irenaeus, c. 185, *Against Heresies*, Bk. III, ch. 3, par. 2
[156] Ch. 44, brackets mine
[157] McBrien, 2016, "The Papacy," Kindle location 6967-6969, brackets mine, parentheses in original

Part IV | Chapter 9: Clement of Rome

The point of this, of course, is that there was no monarchial bishop in Rome to receive Peter's "full, supreme, and universal power," an authority which, as we have seen, Peter never had anyway.

Clement as Messenger

I am surprised that more writers have not suggested what I consider to be an obvious reason that Clement would be specified as the author of a letter that has no specific person assigned as author. I attribute the problem to the translation of one word, which few seem to question.

In Revelation chapters 2 and 3, Jesus sent seven letters to churches in Asia Minor. The location of these churches is not a surprise if we accept that the apostle John wrote Revelation. After John was released from Patmos, he settled in Ephesus and oversaw the surrounding churches.[158] Each of the churches that received letters from Jesus were in Asia Minor within a hundred miles of Ephesus.

The letters were sent to the "angels" of the seven churches. To this day, almost two thousand years later, theologians puzzle over who those angels might be. A lot of commentators suggest that they might be the bishops of those churches, but they do not seem satisfied with this conclusion.[159]

One of the problems in determining who the angels of the churches might be is the lack of awareness that the Greek word for angel, *angelos*, is literally "messenger." While it is true that most New Testament messengers are heavenly ones, not all of them are. For example, John the Baptist sent two "angels" to ask if Jesus was "the One" (Luke 7:19-24), and Jesus sent two "angels" into Samaria before he went there (Luke 9:52). No versions of the Bible translate *angelos* as "angels" in those two passages. Translators use "messengers" in these two passages, but the Greek word is the same when Gabriel appears to Mary (Luke 1:26).

If we translate *angelos* in Revelation 2 and 3 as "messenger," then the interpretation is simple: Each church had a messenger responsible for sending and receiving letters.

---

[158] Clement of Alexandria, 182-202, *Who Is the Rich Man Who Must Be Saved?*, ch. 42, brackets mine
[159] Bible Hub, 2004-2018, "Revelation 1:20"

Rome's Audacious Claim

That messenger would have been a very important person in the church. The seven men chosen to distribute food to widows in Acts 6 had to be full of the Spirit and wisdom (v. 3). It would be even more important that a messenger be spiritual, wise, and of the highest reputation. The church was trusting the messengers to speak for them and to handle all their correspondence.

We have an extant work claiming that this was exactly Clement's role. *The Pastor of Hermas*[160] tells us that Clement had permission to send writings to foreign countries.

The Pastor of Hermas is a unique book, filled with visions, similes, and commands given by "the Angel of Repentance." The date of this work is hard to determine, but it was written in Rome no later than the 160s. It may have been written earlier. Irenaeus, a bishop in Gaul (modern France), referred to it as "Scripture."[161]

The Angel tells Hermas:

> You will write two books, and you will send the one to Clemens and the other to Grapte. Clemens will send his to foreign countries, for permission has been granted to him to do so. Grapte will admonish the widows and the orphans. But you will read the words in this city, along with the presbyters who preside over the church.[162]

"Clemens" is Clement. Notice first that *The Pastor of Hermas*, written in the city of Rome, gives us one more statement that presbyters presided over Rome, not a monarchial bishop.[163] Clement would have been one of those elders. His role was not monarchial bishop, but messenger.

If Clement had been the supreme authority over the whole Church, his name would be essential to the letter to the Corinthians. The doctrine of Papal Primacy invests the authority in the bishop of Rome, not the church at Rome.

Clement's position as messenger also explains the later lists that trace the lineage of Roman bishops back to Clement and his

---

[160] Also called The Shepherd of Hermas.
[161] Irenaeus, c. 185, *Against Heresies*, Bk. IV, ch. 20, par. 2
[162] Hermas, 100-160, *The Pastor of Hermas*, Vision 2nd, ch. 4
[163] A "monarchial" bishop has individual rule in the church. Once the office of bishop was separated from the role of elder, all bishops were monarchial.

Part IV | Chapter 9: Clement of Rome

predecessors. Irenaeus, for example, lists Clement as the third bishop of Rome after Linus and Anacletus. Richard McBrien, quoted earlier, explains:

> Those counted among the earliest popes may very well have been the individuals who presided over the local council of elders or presbyter-bishops, or were simply the most prominent pastoral leaders of that community, or, like Clement (ca. 91– ca. 101), acted as the official representative of the Roman church in its correspondence with other churches throughout the ancient Mediterranean world.[164]

Roman Catholic author J. Michael Miller agrees:

> Before the monarchial episcopacy took place in Rome, ecclesial matters there might have been in the hands of a group of presbyters/bishops. As Brown comments, however, "inevitably in that group an individual stood out as a natural and implicitly recognized leader for a specific purpose." Clement, for example, would have been one such leader, though not a monarchial bishop in the later sense of the term. Lists of the bishops of Rome preserved the names of outstanding individuals such as Clement in the community.[165]

These Roman Catholic scholars confirm what is apparent. Peter and Paul established collegiate leadership in Rome; Clement uses bishops in the plural and describes the presbyter as holding the office of bishop; and later lists were incorrect in describing Clement and his predecessors as monarchial bishops. Roman Catholic apologists, however, are not willing to give up on this without a fight.

Answers to Roman Catholic Apologist Arguments

The only real argument for Papal that Primacy Roman Catholic apologists make is that the church at Rome exercised authority over the church in Corinth by writing an authoritative letter to them.

If we had other evidence that the church at Rome had authority as far away as Greece in the late first century, that might be a legitimate conclusion. In the absence of any other evidence that Rome had

---

[164] McBrien, 2016, "The Papacy," Kindle locations 6970-6973; parentheses in original
[165] Miller, 1997, The Shepherd and the Rock, p. 62

Rome's Audacious Claim

authority over Corinth, however, it is more reasonable to conclude that the Roman church was acting out of love and responsibility in writing to the Corinthians. They had heard of the division in the Corinthian church, and they got involved. This is nothing more than the kind of thing one Southern Baptist congregation might do for another.

Trent Horn disagrees. He points out that the church in Corinth read 1 Clement and other letters from Rome in the Corinthian church as late as the reign of Bishop Soter, who led Rome from 166 to 175.[166] He cites Philip Schaff, the famed Protestant historian, who wrote that 1 Clement was "the first example of the exercise of a sort of papal authority." Schaff also points out that the apostle John was very likely still alive and living in Ephesus, closer to Corinth than Rome was.[167]

Schaff was offended by this idea. He writes, "The hierarchical spirit arose from the domineering spirit of the Roman church."[168] The fact that Schaff, a Protestant, saw "a sort of papal authority" in 1 Clement is a good argument. But it is not a strong argument, because it is hard to back it up from the letter itself.

I do not see a domineering spirit in 1 Clement. It is a long and beautiful intervention into a terrible situation in Corinth. Some presbyters had been removed from their positions out of pure envy, apparently with no bad conduct involved.[169] Clement's letter strongly addresses the problem, but not with a domineering spirit.

Scott Hahn, another Catholic apologist, gives the details of Schaff's perceived domineering spirit. He titles one of his points "Clement requires obedience to his epistle." As an example of this, he quotes paragraph 63:

> For ye will give us great joy and gladness, if ye render obedience unto the things written by us through the Holy Spirit, and root out the unrighteous anger of your jealousy, according to the entreaty which we have made for peace and concord in this letter.[170]

---

[166] Eusebius, *Church History*, Bk. 4, ch. 23, par. 10-11
[167] Schaff, 1901, *History of the Christian Church: Vol. 2*, p. 158, cited by Horn, 2017, *The Case for Catholicism*, Kindle location 1663-1671
[168] Schaff, 1882, History of the Christian Church: Vol. II, p. 112
[169] Clement of Rome, 95-96, "1 Clement," par. 44
[170] Hahn, 2007, *Reasons to Believe*, Kindle location 1070

Part IV | Chapter 9: Clement of Rome

Clement wrote a passionate letter to Corinth. He appeals to them to repent from envy by using stories from all over the Bible. To finish with, "you will give us great joy and gladness" if you obey is hardly "requiring obedience." In fact, Clement calls the letter an "entreaty." An entreaty does not "require" obedience; it pleads for it.

There is one section that sounds authoritative. In chapter 59, Clement writes:

> If, however, any shall disobey the words spoken by Him through us, let them know that they will involve themselves in transgression and serious danger; but we shall be innocent of this sin.

This passage does sound authoritative, but the authority comes from heaven, not from Rome. The church at Rome does not threaten discipline or excommunication if the Corinthians disobey the letter. Clement simply warns that they will be in "transgression and serious danger." He spent most of the letter proving from the Scriptures that division and envy bring about the serious danger of judgment from God. That is not a threat of authoritative judgment by Rome upon Corinth, but a conclusion from Scripture that the Corinthian church was sinning and in danger of the judgment of God.

Later, we will see that Dionysius of Alexandria had to write letters to Rome to correct Bishop Stephen's rash attempt to excommunicate every church that did not agree with him on a Roman tradition. Stephen was martyred, and his successor Xystus listened to Dionysius and dropped the matter. No one concludes that Dionysius had authority over the church in Rome. In the same way, Rome's letter to Corinth is no evidence of an authority over Corinth without other evidence.

Rome was considered a great church in its time. Its sisterly relationship with other churches was enhanced by its wealth and generosity. The same bishop, Dionysius of Corinth, who told us that Rome's letter was read in the Corinthian church decades later, also tells us, "From the beginning it has been your practice to do good to all the brethren in various ways, and to send contributions to many churches in every city."[171]

---

[171] Eusebius, *Church History*, Bk. 4, ch. 23, par. 10

Rome's Audacious Claim

Such a relation with the other churches would entirely explain why Rome would feel free to intervene in the affairs of the Corinthian church, especially when so great a problem as the expulsion of blameless elders had occurred.

We must not forget that Rome's Audacious Claim is not that the Roman church was a great church that other churches looked to in the first few centuries of the Church. If it were, we would not be able to refute the argument. We will talk about that in the chapter on Irenaeus.[172]

Rome's Audacious Claim is that the Roman bishop himself, not the Roman church as a whole, has God-given authority over every church in the world. They believe this authority is based on promises to Peter in Matthew 16, not on the holiness or worthiness of Peter's successor.[173] It is that claim that we are refuting. The intervention of a holy and respected church in the problems of a sister church does not support that claim.

Here are the important points from First Clement.

- Clement equates bishops and elders and speaks of them in the plural (chs. 42 and 44). This indicates that Rome still had the collegiate leaders typical of Peter and Paul's churches.
- Clement leans on the experience of both Peter and Paul in exhorting the Corinthians (ch. 5), confirming the statements of later writers that Rome was built on Peter and Paul, not just Peter.
- Clement writes anonymously in the letter. He does not appeal to personal authority as the bishop of Rome.
- The letter is written in an admonishing and pleading tone, called by Clement himself an "entreaty" (p. 63).

Let us move on now to a man who was undeniably a monarchial bishop and a contemporary or near-contemporary of Clement. To do so, we will need to look briefly at the origin of monarchial bishops.

---

[172] Chapter 15
[173] Catholicism.org, 2005, "Infallibility of the Pope," sec. "How is this note of infallibility exercised?," par. 7

Chapter 10: The Origin of Monarchial Bishops

The leadership pattern in Peter and Paul's churches was a college of elders, all also called bishops. Rome still had collegiate rather than monarchial leadership in the late second century. Nonetheless, there were several churches in the late part of the first century who did have monarchial leadership.

Two in specific are well known: Ignatius and Polycarp. Polycarp was appointed by apostles in Smyrna and had at least met the apostle John.[174] Ignatius was the second bishop in Antioch, the first being Evodius, whom tradition holds was appointed by Peter.[175]

Ignatius was martyred in either 107 or 116. The date is uncertain because a textual problem in "The Martyrdom of Ignatius" prevents us from knowing whether Ignatius appeared before the emperor Trajan in the emperor's ninth or nineteenth year.[176]

Ignatius is even more important because he was bishop of Antioch, the church that originally sent out Paul and Barnabas (Acts 13:1-2). Paul returned to Antioch after each of his missionary journeys (Acts 14:26-28; 15:30-35). In other words, Ignatius was one step removed from Peter and was bishop of the apostle Paul's home church. That's quite a pedigree!

Polycarp was bishop of Smyrna for a very long time. He received a letter from Ignatius in either 107 or 116. He had to have been bishop from one of those two dates until his martyrdom between 155 and 165, between thirty-nine and fifty-eight years.

If he was appointed by an apostle, as tradition holds, then that apostle must have been John, and Polycarp must have been bishop at least as early as the year 100, which is the latest that John could have died. This is believable because he told the proconsul at his martyrdom that he had been serving Jesus as King for eighty-six years![177]

---

[174] Irenaeus, *Against Heresies*, Bk. III, ch. 3, par. 4
[175] Chapman, 1909, "Evodius," par. 1
[176] "Martyrdom of Ignatius," 107 or 116, ch. 2
[177] "Martyrdom of Polycarp," c. 155-165, ch. 9

Rome's Audacious Claim

Smyrna, the church Polycarp oversaw, was one of only two churches that received no rebuke from Jesus in the book of Revelation (chs. 2-3).

In either 107 or 116, Ignatius was taken to Rome to be killed by beasts in the arena. Along the way, he wrote seven letters. One was to Polycarp, and six were to churches: Ephesus, Magnesia, Tralles, Philadelphia, Smyrna, and Rome. All of them, except Rome of course, were in Asia Minor (which is modern Western Turkey). The furthest distance between any of them was about a hundred miles.

In each of these, except Rome, Ignatius addresses a monarchial bishop—with great enthusiasm, I should add. For now, let's consider why these churches had monarchial bishops.

Magnesia and Tralles were both southeast of Ephesus and close to it. Magnesia was only about fifteen miles away, and Tralles was another twenty. Smyrna was fifty miles to the north, and Philadelphia was about one hundred miles to the northeast. The five churches to which he wrote that were not Rome were within a hundred-mile oval extending from Ephesus to Philadelphia.[178]

In the book of Revelation, we read that Jesus, through the apostle John, sent seven letters as well (chs. 2-3). The letters were to seven churches, and these were, in the order given in the Revelation: Ephesus, Smyrna, Pergamum, Thyatira, Sardis, Philadelphia, and Laodicea. Every one of these churches is in the same hundred-mile oval,[179] and three of them—Ephesus, Smyrna, and Philadelphia—are addressed by both Jesus and Ignatius.

"The Martyrdom of Ignatius" tells us that Ignatius was a disciple of the apostle John.[180] This would explain his writing to the same churches that John did, even though he was bishop of Antioch of Syria some five hundred miles away. Clement of Alexandria, a teacher in the late second century (not to be confused with Clement of Rome), tells us this about what the apostle John was doing toward the end of his life:

> When, upon the tyrant's death, [John] returned to Ephesus from the Isle of Patmos, he went away, being invited, to the

---

[178] EmersonKent.com, 2016, "Map of Asia Minor"
[179] EmersonKent.com, 2016, "Map of Asia Minor"
[180] "Martyrdom of Ignatius," 107 or 116, ch. 1

Part IV | Chapter 10: The Origin of Monarchial Bishops

contiguous territories of the nations, here to appoint bishops, there to set in order whole churches, there to ordain such as were marked out by the Spirit.[181]

"Contiguous territories" mean bordering ones. The reference to "the nations" is not a reference to far-spun countries, but simply means "territories of the Gentiles." Thus we find Clement of Alexandria agreeing with the book of Revelation as to the territory of the apostle John's oversight. He was setting churches in order and appointing bishops in the areas "contiguous" to Ephesus. Tertullian even refers to the seven churches of Revelation 2 and 3 as "John's foster churches."[182]

From these facts, I suggest that John did not establish the same form of leadership that we find Paul and Peter establishing in Scripture. They established collegiate leadership in the form of a group of elders, but John appointed one bishop who was over the elders.

In 3 John 9-10, we find that at least one of John's churches had a monarchial leader, though it was in mutiny. John writes:

> I wrote to the church, but Diotrephes, who loves to dominate, does not acknowledge us. Therefore, if I come, I will draw attention to what he is doing, spreading evil nonsense about us. And not content with that, he will not receive the brothers, hindering those who wish to do so and expelling them from the church.

Shortly thereafter, John adds, "Demetrius receives a good report from all, even from the truth itself" (v. 12).

There was a dispute over leadership in one of the churches John oversaw. Diotrephes craved his authority, his monarchial authority, so much that he was willing to oppose the apostle John himself! John, however, recommends Demetrius, seemingly as the appropriate replacement for Diotrephes.

Thus we see that the letters of Ignatius, the Third Epistle of John, and the book of Revelation are all evidence that the apostle John did not follow the pattern of church government that Paul and Peter did.

---

[181] Clement of Alexandria, 182-202, *Who Is the Rich Man Who Shall Be Saved*, ch. 42
[182] 197-220, *Against Marcion*, Bk. IV, ch. 5

Rome's Audacious Claim

I propose that the apostle John originated the monepiscopal (one bishop) form of leadership. We know from Scripture and 1 Clement that Peter and Paul established churches led by a college of elders. It is apparent that "John's foster churches" had monarchial bishops. Even Antioch, Paul's home church, had a monarchial bishop within his lifetime. That seemingly out-of-place monarchial bishop was a disciple of John.[183] If John instituted monarchial bishops, it would help explain the fact that all churches adopted monarchial leadership within a century of Paul and Peter's martyrdom.

I have been chastised for the uniqueness of this theory, but historian Philip Schaff says that many others hold it. He asks, "Was the episcopate directly or indirectly of apostolic [Johannean] origin?"[184] The footnote to this question reads:

> This is the Greek, the Roman Catholic, and the high Anglican theory. It is advocated by a very few Continental Protestants as Chevalier Bunsen, Rothe and Thiersch (an Irvingite), who trace episcopacy to John in Ephesus.[185]

I propose, then, that the church government form that includes one bishop and a group of elders is every bit as apostolic as Peter and Paul's collegiate leadership. Again, this would also explain its adoption throughout catholic Christianity in the second century.

With that established, let us see how Polycarp and Ignatius weigh in on the authority of the bishop of Rome.

---

[183] "Martyrdom of Ignatius," 107 or 116, ch. 1
[184] Schaff, 1882, History of the Christan Church, Vol. II, p. 96, brackets in original
[185] Schaff, 1882, History of the Christian Church, Vol. II, p. 96, footnote 160

Chapter 11: Ignatius of Antioch

In the letters that Ignatius wrote to the churches of Asia Minor and to Polycarp, there is an interesting pattern. Ignatius puts an emphasis on the bishop of the churches to which he writes that is unique to his letters. No other second-century writing is like it.

Here are examples from each of those letters. The letter to Polycarp was to be read aloud in Smyrna, and so Ignatius has no chapter addressed to Polycarp's flock.

- To the church at Smyrna: "See that you all follow the bishop, even as Jesus Christ does the Father, and the presbytery as you would the apostles."[186]
- To the church at Tralles: "Let all reverence the deacons as an appointment of Jesus Christ and the bishop as Jesus Christ, who is the Son of the Father, and the presbyters as the sanhedrin of God."[187]
- To the church at Magnesia: "It becomes you not to treat your bishop too familiarly on account of his youth, but to yield him all reverence, having respect to the power of God the Father, as I have known even the holy presbyters do...."[188]
- To the church at Ephesus: "It is fitting that you should run together in accordance with the will of your bishop, which you also do. For your justly renowned presbytery, worthy of God, is fitted as exactly to the bishop as the strings are to the harp."[189]
- To the church at Philadelphia: "[Your] bishop ... is in harmony with the commandments, even as the harp is with its strings. Therefore my soul declares his mind towards God a happy one, knowing it to be virtuous and perfect."[190]

---

[186] ch. 8
[187] ch. 3
[188] ch. 3
[189] ch. 4
[190] ch. 1

Rome's Audacious Claim

- To Polycarp: "Give ye heed to the bishop, that God also may give heed to you. My soul be for theirs that are submissive to the bishop, to the presbyters, and to the deacons, and may my portion be along with them in God!"[191]

These are not the only quotes that could be given from these letters. In his letters to the churches in Asia Minor, Ignatius gives effusive praise to the bishops, elders, and deacons. He exhorts absolute adherence to the bishop and to the will of the bishop, as though he were God himself.

Oddly enough, in his letter to the Romans he does not mention a bishop at all!

When I originally wrote this chapter, I addressed the various explanations, both Catholic and Protestant, for why Ignatius might not have mentioned a bishop in Rome. As I wrote, though, I found none of them adequate, all for the same reason. Not only does Ignatius not mention a bishop in Rome, he does not mention the elders either. He makes no greeting to leaders, urges no submission to leaders, and does not urge anyone to unity, all hallmarks of his other letters.

Ignatius's letter to Rome pleads with Romans not to intervene to prevent his death. Except for the introduction, where he greets the church at Rome, rather than their leaders, with much honor, he spends the whole letter pleading with them to love him by doing nothing to prevent his martyrdom.

There is no good explanation why Ignatius does not take the time to greet the leaders in Rome or urge submission to their leadership, which explains why there are so many theories.

It is possible that Ignatius did not know who the elders were, but that is not a very satisfying conclusion. He mentions the names of the leaders in most of his letters to the other churches, but he does not do so in all of them. He praises the clergy in the letter to the Philadelphians, but he does not mention them by name. Instead, he simply urges unity with the unnamed "bishop, elders, and the deacons."[192] He does not do this in the Roman letter.

---

[191] ch. 6
[192] Ignatius, 107 or 116, "Epistle to the Philadelphians," introduction

Part IV | Chapter 11: Ignatius of Antioch

Roman Catholic apologists like to argue that Ignatius did not urge submission to the bishop of Rome because everyone already knew that they should submit to the bishop of Rome. He was the "full, supreme, and universal power" over the Church, and everyone knew it.

If you'll excuse the pun, this is no more than a "Hail Mary" in an effort to cover a glaring problem. How could Ignatius possibly ignore mention of "the pope," if there was one in the early part of the second century? Saying that everyone already knew to submit to him is hardly an answer. Surely the Christians of Ephesus, Smyrna, Tralles, Philadelphia, and Magnesus knew that they should submit to the bishop and fight for unity, yet Ignatius pleads for them to do so anyway.

I can only postulate that Ignatius had but one thing on his mind when he wrote to Rome: his martyrdom.

Ignatius's relationship with the apostle John and his status as bishop of Antioch (Paul's home church) probably made him influential in the churches of Asia Minor. He had also stopped in Smyrna and been visited by leaders from these churches. While Ignatius explicitly says he has no authority among those churches,[193] his letters convey a shepherd's care. Even his letter to the great Polycarp, who would have been at least twenty years younger, is full of exhortation and guidance.

Rome, however, could not have been part of the flock assigned to Ignatius (1 Pet. 5:3). Ignatius, then, was not thinking of advice to Rome, which was not under his care. He was focused on ensuring that his martyrdom was not hindered.

In any case, it is not my task in this book to explain why Ignatius writes to Rome so differently than he writes to other churches. It is my task to show that Ignatius knows of no supreme authority in Rome, nor that its bishop had inherited primacy from Peter. Therefore, we will address the arguments Catholic apologists use to try to create a reference to Rome's supremacy in the letters of Ignatius.

Answers to Roman Catholic Arguments

In the introduction to the Epistle to the Romans, Ignatius says that the church in Rome "presides in the region of the Romans" and that it "presides over love" or "presides in love." Somehow Roman Catholic

---

[193] Ignatius, 107 or 116, "Epistle to the Ephesians," ch. 8

apologists have managed to interpret this as meaning that Ignatius knew that Rome had authority over all the churches in the world.

If we had seen evidence already that Peter was supreme over all the other apostles, and if we had seen evidence that Rome had received the keys of the kingdom from Peter, then perhaps we could make a gigantic interpretive leap and argue that "the region of the Romans" was the entire empire and that the church at Rome presided over all other churches in the empire. Of course, that would still leave out the churches in Syria, Persia, and India, which we know already existed. Everything we have seen and will see makes it clear that Rome was not presiding even over the Roman Empire.

The answer to their argument is simple. "The region of the Romans" was either just Rome and its surroundings, or perhaps all or a large section of Italy. Italy contained Romans. The church in Corinth was Greek, not Roman. The church in Alexandria was Egyptian, not Roman.

Even two hundred years later, the church in Rome did not have jurisdiction across the empire. The Council of Nicea described a jurisdiction for the bishop of Alexandria, "based on ancient custom," that included Egypt, Libya, and Pentapolis. The council goes on to say that "the like is customary for the bishop of Rome also."[194]

The issue at hand was a rebellious bishop named Meletius who was appointing new bishops from among those who agreed with him. The mentioned jurisdiction was the right of the bishop of Alexandria to approve or reject the appointments of all bishops in Egypt, Libya, and Pentapolis.[195]

The council's "the like is customary for the bishop of Rome also" can only mean that Rome's bishop had right of approval for Italian and other Western bishops. We will see in the chapter on Cyprian that this was so in the 250s all the way into Spain and down into North Africa.

I cite the canon here to show that even in 325 Rome's rule was limited to certain areas. To "preside in the region of the Romans" is to preside, more or less, over Italy rather than in the region of the Greeks or the Syrians or the Egyptians. J. B. Lightfoot renders the phrase "hath the presidency in the country of the region of the Romans."[196]

---

[194] Pavao, 2009-2019, "Canons of the Council of Nicea," Canon 6
[195] Socrates Scholasticus, 439, *Ecclesiastical History*, Bk. 1, ch. 9
[196] Kirby, 2001-2019, "Ignatius to the Romans," ch. 0

Part IV | Chapter 11: Ignatius of Antioch

Ignatius also says that the church in Rome "presides over love." Scott Hahn makes a big deal of this and takes it to an extreme. He quotes Frances Glimm, the Catholic translator of *Apostolic Fathers*,[197] as saying:

> Whether St. Ignatius has in mind a pre-eminence of authority or charity, the context seems to imply that he means a universal not merely a local pre-eminence.[198]

I am not sure where Glimm got his context. The context in *The Ante-Nicene Fathers* series is:

> ... the Church which is beloved and enlightened by the will of Him that willeth all things which are according to the love of Jesus Christ our God, which also presides in the place of the region of the Romans, worthy of God, worthy of honour, worthy of the highest happiness, worthy of praise, worthy of obtaining her every desire, worthy of being deemed holy, and which presides over love, is named from Christ, and from the Father....[199]

To be honest, I am not sure what "presides over love" might mean, but the context shows it has nothing to do with the extent of Rome's leadership. Ignatius has already stated the extent of their presiding when he said they preside in the "place of the region of the Romans." He does not change his mind a few words later.

As Orthodox apologist Andrew Damick points out, Ignatius tells the Romans that with his upcoming death, the church in Syria now has only God for its Shepherd. Surely, he would have said more if he believed that the Roman bishop had jurisdiction over the whole Church. He could have asked Rome to send a temporary bishop to preside in Antioch until a replacement could be appointed.[200] In fact, if the Roman bishop was "pastor of the entire Church," it would have been insulting to say that Antioch was left with only God as their Shepherd.

---

[197] Glimm, 1947, *The Apostolic Fathers*
[198] Ray, 2009, *Upon This Rock*, footnote 46, Kindle location 4777
[199] Ignatius, 107 or 116, "Epistle to the Romans," introduction
[200] Damick, 2015, "One Quote from St. Ignatius," par. 12-14

Rome's Audacious Claim

There is nothing else in Ignatius's letter to Rome that hints at supremacy for the bishop of Rome, so we will leave Ignatius's letters with a simple nod to the fact that Ignatius seems unaware of a "chief shepherd over the whole church" living there.

These are the conclusions we can draw from Ignatius, his seven letters, and "The Martyrdom of Ignatius."

- Ignatius oddly leaves out any reference to the leadership of the church at Rome, despite the strong emphasis on the clergy in his other letters to churches.
- Monepiscopal church government seems to have arisen in Asia Minor under the leadership of the apostle John. It had not reached Rome yet.[201]
- After Ignatius's death, God would be the Shepherd of the church in Syria, not the bishop of Rome.

With that, let us move on to the other early monarchial bishop who wrote a letter that is still in our possession.

---

[201] O'Brien, 2008, *The Church*, p. 44

Part IV | Chapter 12: Polycarp of Smyrna

Chapter 12: Polycarp of Smyrna

We know that Polycarp was a monarchial bishop because Ignatius addresses him as "bishop of the church of the Smyrneans" in his letter.[202] Oddly enough, Ignatius does not mention Polycarp's name when he refers to the bishop in his letter to them.[203]

Polycarp's letter to Philippi was written after Ignatius's letter, which we know because he mentions Ignatius's martyrdom in it. You could never tell from Polycarp's letter, though, that he was a monarchial bishop. He greets the Philippians with, "Polycarp and the presbyters with him, to the church of God sojourning at Philippi."[204]

Later, in chapters 5 and 6, he addresses the duties of deacons and elders, never mentioning a bishop.

On the surface, it seems unusual that the bishop of Smyrna would not call himself a bishop in his greeting to the Philippians and that he mentions only elders in his discussion of the duties of appointed men. There is actually nothing strange about it, however. The church in Philippi was founded by Paul (Acts 16). It is no surprise that it was led by a college of elders.

We must conclude that Polycarp politely does not mention a bishop, nor even state his own position as bishop, because Philippi had no such office. Thus, his letter is one more evidence that Paul's churches—in this case, Philippi—had collegiate leadership into the second century.

Roman Catholic apologists do not appeal to Polycarp in support of Rome's Audacious Claim, so we will not address his letter further. We will now look briefly at other works which probably date to the time of Clement of Rome, Ignatius, and Polycarp.

---

[202] Ignatius, 107 or 116, "Epistle to Polycarp," introduction
[203] Ignatius, 107 or 116, "Epistle to the Smyrneans," ch. 8
[204] Polycarp, 110-140, "Epistle of Polycarp to the Philippians," introduction

Chapter 13: The Didache and Other Early Works

There are several other works from the late first or early second centuries. These include the anonymous "Epistle to Diognetus" and *The Didache* and the "Epistle of Barnabas." Barnabas's epistle is often called "Pseudo-Barnabas" because few believe Paul's companion Barnabas wrote it.[205]

The Ante-Nicene Fathers series attributes the Epistle to Diognetus to someone named Mathetes. *Mathetes*, however, is just the Greek word for "disciple." No one knows who wrote the letter. It is a very early work that expresses early Christian ideas, such as the idea that God has never wanted sacrifices.[206] It neither quotes nor references any scriptures, neither from the Old nor the New Testament.

The Epistle of Barnabas is a very interesting work, with some insight into types in the Old Testament, but it is entirely irrelevant to Rome's Audacious Claim.

The *Didache* is also called *The Teaching of the Twelve Apostles*. It is a very early church manual, though the exact date it was written cannot be determined. It is the only one of the three that has any relevance to this book, and that relevance is minor. In chapter 15, it gives instructions for bishops and deacons, adding one more testimony that early church government was collegiate rather than monepiscopal.

There is no footing to gain or lose in these works, so let us move on to the much more important "apologists."

---

[205] e.g., Tixeront, 1920, *Handbook of Patrology*; in Kirby, 2001-2019, "Handbook of Patrology," sec. 4

[206] Anonymous, 50-120, "Epistle of Mathetes to Diognetus," ch. 3; cf. Jer. 7:22

Part V

The Apologists

Rome's Audacious Claim

Chapter 14: The Apologists

"The apologists" are a set of Christians who wrote from the mid-second century into the early third century. These authors argued in defense of the faith of the apostles against various heresies and against Roman paganism. They also wrote to emperors to argue against the persecution of Christians.[207]

We will deal primarily with Irenaeus and Tertullian because they are the only ones who say anything about Rome, but that very fact leads us to say something in general about the apologists.

The apologists include Quadratus (120-130), Aristides (117-138), Justin (150-160), Tatian (c. 165), Melito of Sardis (165-175), Apollinarius (160-180), Athenagoras (175-180), Theophilus of Antioch (180-185), Irenaeus (175-185), Clement of Alexandria (182-202), Tertullian (197-220), and Minucius Felix (160-230).[208] Of these, only two say anything at all about the church in Rome. Those two speak of Rome in glowing terms, but neither ties Peter specifically or Matthew 16 to the bishop of Rome. The rest are silent, despite the fact that three of them, Justin, Hippolytus, and Minucius Felix, lived in or near Rome.

No one mentions the idea because no one had ever heard that there was a vicar of Christ on earth. Jesus the Messiah, the one who will eventually conquer all kingdoms, represents himself on earth through one body made up of many parts (1 Cor. 12:12), not through one bishop of Rome. As the apostle Paul says, "If they were all one part, where would the body be?" (1 Cor. 12:19). He follows by saying, "Now you are Christ's body, and individually parts of it" (1 Cor. 12:27). It is all of us together who are the vicar of Christ, not the bishop of Rome or any other bishop.

Once we have noted the absence of reference to the bishop of Rome by almost all the apologists, we can address the ones who do mention Rome and why.

I want to remind you again, through all that follows, that the position of the Roman Catholic Church in the twenty-first century is

---

[207] e.g., Justin, c. 155, *First Apology*; Tertullian, 197-220, *Apology*
[208] Encyclopedia Britannica, inc., 2019, "Apologist," par. 2. These dates are from Kirby, 2019, *Early Christian Writings*, and are not necessarily used in the rest of this book or its bibliography.

that the Roman bishop, whom we call the pope, has "power over all, both pastors and faithful," that he is "Vicar of Christ and pastor of the whole Church," and because of this "has full, supreme and universal power over the Church," which he is "always free to exercise."[209] Today the Catholic Church argues, both in the documents of Vatican II and in their *Catechism*, that all this authority comes from Jesus through Peter and is based on Jesus's words to Peter in Matthew 16:15-19 and John 21:15-17.[210]

The position of the twenty-first century Roman Catholic Church is not that the church at Rome was the best and most visible representation of apostolic truth in the late second century, dwelt in the capitol city of the empire, and thus carried immense truth-based authority 1,800 years ago. If that were their position, we would all have to concede their argument and admit the solid teaching and glorious testimony of the Roman church in the second century. There would be no reason to write this book.

But that is not their claim. Their claim is that Peter passed his "full, supreme, and universal power" to the succession of bishops in Rome. It is this succession from Peter which allows him, they say, to wield "full, supreme, and universal power" over all "pastors and faithful."[211]

This is extremely important. If the pope's authority is based on what the Roman Catholic Church claims it is, then the pope can be immoral and still wield universal authority because of his office.[212] He can proclaim as dogma something as unknown to Scripture as the bodily assumption of Mary into heaven. Pope Pius XII did this in 1950,[213] and if he possesses authority from Peter to do so, we must add it to our beliefs.

If, however, the authority of Rome in the second century was because of its generosity, because it was the place of many martyrdoms, because Peter and Paul taught there, because it was the

---

[209] Pope Paul VI, 1964, "Dogmatic Constitution on the Church," par. 22
[210] Pope Paul VI, 1964, "Dogmatic Constitution of the Church," par. 22, notes 156 & 157
[211] Pope Paul VI, 1964, "Dogmatic Constitution of the Church," par. 22
[212] Catholicism.org, (2005), "The Infallibility of the Pope," sec. "How is this Note of Infallibility exercised," par. 7
[213] FranciscanMedia.org, n.d., "Solemnity of the Assumption of Mary," par. 1

Part V | Chapter 14: The Apologists

capital of the empire, and because the Roman church was holding steadfastly to the doctrine of the apostles without change, then the Roman bishop's authority can be judged on the basis of his faithful adherence to truth. As the Scriptures suggest, we could "consider the outcome of [his] way of life" (Heb. 13:7) and reject offhand "coarse, immoral" men like Pope John XII (955-964),[214] along with all other bishops of Rome who did not adhere to the faith of the apostles.

Irenaeus and Tertullian give the church in Rome the highest praise. Neither, though, says anything about the authority of Rome's bishop himself, nor of Matthew 16 or John 21. They do not talk about any transfer of authority or keys from Peter to Rome's bishop. Instead, they give several reasons for Rome's greatness. By far the most important of those is the Roman church's adherence to apostolic truth.

With that, let us begin with Irenaeus, whose praise for the faithfulness and preeminence of Rome in the late second century is the most effusive.

---

[214] Kirsch, 1910, "Pope John XII," par. 2

Rome's Audacious Claim

Chapter 15: Irenaeus

Irenaeus is second only to Cyprian in being quoted by Roman Catholic apologists. This is because of one quote in his five-volume book, *Against Heresies*:

> We put to confusion all those who ... assemble in unauthorized meetings ... by indicating that tradition derived from the apostles, of the very great, the very ancient, and universally known Church founded and organized at Rome by the two most glorious apostles, Peter and Paul ... which comes down to our time by means of the successions of the bishops. For it is a matter of necessity that every Church should agree with this Church, on account of its preeminent authority....[215]

I called the second chapter of this book "First-Round Knockout" because of the support of the Vatican, the U.S. Conference of Catholic Bishops, and Roman Catholic scholars. This quote by Irenaeus, however, sounds like a late-second-century knockout for the Roman Catholic apologists!

Many Protestant apologists have contested this translation of Irenaeus's Greek. The American editor of *The Ante-Nicene Fathers* series, for example, says a worse translation than "preeminent authority" would be hard to find.[216] We are not going to contest the translation. If we understand Irenaeus's argument, then we must agree that the church in Rome had "preeminent authority" *during that time period.*

Protestant apologists appeal to the puzzling words that follow: "... that is, the faithful everywhere, inasmuch as the apostolical tradition has been preserved continuously by those ... who exist everywhere."[217] They argue that this statement means that the apostolic tradition—meaning tradition from the apostles and not later—is preserved everywhere, and Christians coming into Rome are helping to preserve it there.

---

[215] Irenaeus, c. 185, *Against Heresies*, Bk. III, ch. 3, par. 2
[216] *The Ante-Nicene Fathers*, 1867-1873, Vol. I, p. 597, footnote 3313
[217] Irenaeus, c. 185, *Against Heresies*, Bk. III, ch. 3, par. 2

Rome's Audacious Claim

That could well be what Irenaeus meant, but the context of *Against Heresies* gives a clearer picture of Irenaeus's thoughts than wrangling over words. Let us go through the things Irenaeus said, and you will find his statements as easy to understand as if you had heard them from your next-door neighbor.

Introduction to *Against Heresies*

The "preeminent authority" quote is found in Book III of *Against Heresies*, but we cannot begin there because Irenaeus lays the foundation for Book III in Book I. I also should add a little introduction so you understand the purpose of the book.

By the time Irenaeus wrote *Against Heresies*, he was a very influential bishop. In his younger years, he had been part of the church in Smyrna and had sat under Polycarp's teaching.[218] Later, he emigrated to Gaul, and eventually became bishop in what is now Lyons, France.

The book itself was written against the bizarre gnostic sects that were spreading in the empire. He goes into exceptional and accurate[219] detail about various gnostic heresies, but the most important parts of the book are his explanations of the reliable sources of truth. He makes it clear, too, that all the churches think as he does.[220] It is in that section that we must begin.

Apostolic Tradition

> The Church, though dispersed throughout the whole world, even to the ends of the earth, has received from the apostles and their disciples this faith....[221]

Irenaeus introduces us here to a key element of early Christian belief: apostolic tradition.

"Apostolic tradition" is a term that refers to traditions that can reasonably be assumed to have come from the apostles. While Jesus

---

[218] Irenaeus, c. 185, *Against Heresies*, Bk. III, ch. 3, par. 4
[219] Based on my own reading of *Against Heresies* and gnostic documents such as those found at The Gnostic Society Library's "Nag Hammadi Library," http://www.gnosis.org/naghamm/nhl.html.
[220] Irenaeus, c. 185, *Against Heresies*, Bk. I, ch. 10, par. 2
[221] Irenaeus, c. 185, *Against Heresies*, Bk. I, ch. 10, par. 1

Part V | Chapter 15: Irenaeus

rejects "the traditions of men" (Mark 7:6-8), the traditions of the apostles formed the foundation of early Christianity. The apostle Paul told the Thessalonian church, "Stand firm and hold fast to the traditions that you were taught, either by an oral statement or by a letter of ours" (2 Thes. 2:15). He rebuked the proud Corinthians, saying, "If anyone thinks that he is a prophet or a spiritual person, he should recognize that what I am writing to you is a commandment of the Lord" (1 Cor. 14:37). He praised them because they "hold fast to the traditions, just as I handed them on" (1 Cor. 11:2). There is a difference between the traditions of men and the traditions of the apostles, who were guided by the Holy Spirit into "all truth" (Jn. 16:13).

It is Irenaeus who first fully introduces the concept of apostolic tradition, though Tertullian builds on it spectacularly, as we shall see in the next chapter. Nonetheless, the idea of apostolic tradition can also be found in the writers preceding Irenaeus. The church in Rome, for example, wrote to Corinth, saying:

> The apostles have preached the Gospel to us from the Lord Jesus Christ; Jesus Christ [has done so] from God. Christ therefore was sent forth by God, and the apostles by Christ. Both these appointments, then, were made in an orderly way, according to the will of God. Having therefore received their orders, and being fully assured by the resurrection of our Lord Jesus Christ, and established in the word of God, with full assurance of the Holy Ghost, they went forth proclaiming that the kingdom of God was at hand. And thus preaching through countries and cities, they appointed the firstfruits, having first proved them by the Spirit, to be bishops and deacons of those who should afterwards believe.[222]

Apostolic tradition is the foundation for this quote. The apostles taught what they received from God through Jesus. They were the authorities. Ignatius, bishop of Antioch in the late first and early second centuries, wrote, "Study ... to be established in the doctrines of

---

[222] Clement of Rome, c. 81-96, "1 Clement," ch. 42

the Lord and the apostles so that in everything, whatever you do, you may prosper."[223]

Anything the apostles taught, whether orally or written down in Scripture, was the foundation and authority of the church. This concept dates to the very beginning, when the first converts rushed to the temple every day to listen to them (Acts 2:42, 46). Later, Jude would warn his readers "to contend for the faith that was once for all handed down to the holy ones" (1:3). It was the apostles who handed that faith down.

Irenaeus gives this description of the faith that the apostles delivered to the churches:

> [She believes] in one God, the Father Almighty, Maker of heaven, and earth, and the sea, and all things that are in them; and in one Christ Jesus, the Son of God, who became incarnate for our salvation; and in the Holy Spirit, who proclaimed through the prophets the dispensations of God, and the advents, and the birth from a virgin, and the passion, and the resurrection from the dead, and the ascension into heaven in the flesh of the beloved Christ Jesus, our Lord, and His manifestation from heaven in the glory of the Father "to gather all things in one" [Eph. 1:10] and to raise up anew all flesh of the whole human race, in order that to Christ Jesus, our Lord, and God, and Saviour, and King, according to the will of the invisible Father, "every knee should bow, of things in heaven, and things in earth, and things under the earth, and that every tongue should confess" to Him, and that He should execute just judgment towards all; that He may send "spiritual wickednesses" [Php. 2:10-11] and the angels who transgressed and became apostates, together with the ungodly, and unrighteous, and wicked, and profane among men, into everlasting fire; but may, in the exercise of His grace, confer immortality on the righteous, and holy, and those who have kept His commandments, and have persevered in His love,

---

[223] Ignatius, 107 or 116, "Epistle to the Magnesians," ch. 13

Part V | Chapter 15: Irenaeus

some from the beginning ... and others from ... their repentance, and may surround them with everlasting glory.[224]

This statement of faith is the earliest we have in writing. I hope that you will read it carefully; however, the passage most pertinent to this book is the next one.

> The Church, having received this preaching and this faith, although scattered throughout the whole world, yet, as if occupying but one house, carefully preserves it. She also believes these points just as if she had but one soul, and one and the same heart, and she proclaims them, and teaches them, and hands them down, with perfect harmony, as if she possessed only one mouth.... Nor will any one of the rulers in the Churches, however highly gifted he may be in point of eloquence, teach doctrines different from these ... nor, on the other hand, will he who is deficient in power of expression inflict injury on the tradition. For the faith being ever one and the same, neither does one who is able at great length to discourse regarding it, make any addition to it, nor does one, who can say but little diminish it.[225]

Irenaeus hammers home the point that the tradition of the apostles is not to be tampered with. The summation of the faith that Irenaeus gives here is not all of the apostolic tradition. Apostolic tradition is anything that can reasonably be traced to the apostles.

Tertullian, whom we will cover in the next chapter, gives a list of practices received among the churches so far before his time that he concludes they certainly came from the apostles. These are held up as apostolic tradition as well.[226]

The same reasoning cannot apply to the twenty-first century. In the year 200, if all the churches, and especially the churches founded by apostles, had some common practice, such as "in all the ordinary actions of daily life, trac[ing] upon the forehead the sign [of the

---

[224] Irenaeus, c. 185, *Against Heresies*, Bk. I, ch. 10, par. 1; parentheses mine, brackets in original
[225] Irenaeus, c. 185, *Against Heresies*, Bk. I, ch. 10, par. 2
[226] Tertullian, 204, *De Corona*, ch. 3

cross]," then Christians could reasonably assume that such a tradition was apostolic.[227]

Whether you or I agree, Irenaeus and Tertullian certainly thought this way. If a tradition came from the apostles, it was to be followed. It was not to be changed, no matter how eloquent or brilliant or even "anointed" a Christian might be and no matter what position he held.

We will see as this book proceeds that this idea reigned in the churches into at least the fourth century.

With that in mind, let us get back to those all-important chapters that begin the third book of *Against Heresies*.

Apostolic Succession

Apostolic succession is a central doctrine of the Roman Catholic and Orthodox Churches today. That doctrine was first espoused by Irenaeus, and it is important that we find his definition of the idea. Fortunately, he explains it well, and his words reveal his conception of apostolic succession with little need for comment.

He had, as we have seen, explained his conception of apostolic tradition in the first book. As he begins to describe apostolic succession, he reaffirms apostolic *tradition* in the strongest of terms:

> We have learned from none others the plan of our salvation, than from those through whom the Gospel has come down to us, which they did at one time proclaim in public, and, at a later period, by the will of God, handed down to us in the Scriptures, to be the ground and pillar of our faith. For it is unlawful to assert that they preached before they possessed perfect knowledge, as some do even venture to say, boasting themselves as improvers of the apostles. For, after our Lord rose from the dead, [the apostles] were invested with power from on high when the Holy Spirit came down ... were filled from all [His gifts], and had perfect knowledge.[228]

As pointed out above, the apostles are everything. God gave the gospel and the whole faith to Jesus, Jesus gave it to the apostles, and the apostles gave it to the bishops and elders of the churches, whose

---

[227] Tertullian, 204, "De Corona," chs. 3-4; brackets mine
[228] Irenaeus, c. 185, *Against Heresies*, Bk. III, ch. 1, par. 1

job it was to preserve it unchanged. Then Irenaeus warns of the dangers of ignoring apostolic tradition:

> If anyone does not agree to these truths, he despises the companions of the Lord; nay more, he despises Christ Himself the Lord; yea, he despises the Father also, and stands self-condemned, resisting and opposing his own salvation.[229]

It frustrated Irenaeus that the gnostic heretics did not get this concept. He complains:

> When ... they are confuted from the Scriptures, they turn round and accuse these same Scriptures, as if they were not correct, nor of authority ... that they are ambiguous, and that the truth cannot be extracted from them by those who are ignorant of tradition.... that the truth was not delivered by means of written documents, but *viva voce* [orally]. Therefore, [they say,] Paul declared, "But we speak wisdom among those that are perfect, but not the wisdom of this world" [1 Cor. 2:6].[230]

Yes, the gnostics used Scripture as well. Irenaeus had a marvelous illustration of their misuse of Scripture, which is well worth reading here:

> Their [Scripture interpretation] is just as if one, when a beautiful image of a king has been constructed by some skillful artist out of precious jewels, should then take this likeness of the man all to pieces, should rearrange the gems, and so fit them together as to make them into the form of a dog or of a fox, and even that but poorly executed; and should then maintain and declare that this was the beautiful image of the king which the skillful artist constructed.[231]

We ourselves must beware that we do not do the same thing with Scripture. Let me emphasize, though, that the heretics that Irenaeus was refuting argued that the God of Israel was a false god who was not

---

[229] Irenaeus, c. 185, *Against Heresies*, Bk. III, ch. 1, par. 1
[230] Irenaeus, c. 185, *Against Heresies*, Bk. III, ch. 2, par. 1; brackets mine
[231] Irenaeus, c. 185, *Against Heresies*, Bk. 1, ch. 8, par. 1; brackets mine

the Father of our Lord Jesus. They were not an alternative branch of Christianity, as some argue today.[232]

Irenaeus had another weapon to present to the gnostics: apostolic tradition.

> When we refer them to that tradition which originates from the apostles, [and] which is preserved by means of the succession of presbyters in the Churches, they object to tradition, saying that they themselves are wiser not merely than the presbyters, but even than the apostles, because they have discovered the unadulterated truth.... It comes to this, therefore, that these men do now consent neither to Scripture nor to tradition.[233]

It is here that Irenaeus bolsters his argument from tradition by introducing a new argument, for apostolic succession. From here on, his words are crucial to this book, and I do not skip words from quote to quote. The citations are separated only by my commentary.

Note that apostolic tradition is preserved not only by bishops, but by the whole presbytery. This is a good thing! In the chapter on Cyprian's epistles, we will discuss letters he exchanged with the Roman presbytery while they were without a bishop because of persecution. If the presbyters were not preserving apostolic traditions along with the bishops, Rome would have lost its succession between early 250, when Fabian was martyred, and 251 when Cornelius replaced him.

Since Irenaeus's concern is the teaching of the apostles and the truth of the Christian faith, it does not matter whether a monarchial bishop or a college of elders preserves them. What matters is that the faith is preserved. Irenaeus's concern is truth, not any one person's authority over another.

He goes on:

> If the apostles had known hidden mysteries, which they were in the habit of imparting to "the perfect" apart and privily from the rest, they would have delivered them especially to those to whom they were also committing the Churches themselves. For they were desirous that these men should be very perfect

---

[232] Bock, 2006, *The Missing Gospels*, pp. xxii-xxiii
[233] Irenaeus, c. 185, *Against Heresies*, Bk. III, ch. 2, par. 2; brackets in original

and blameless in all things, whom also they were leaving behind as their successors, delivering up their own place of government to these men; which men, if they discharged their functions honestly, would be a great boon [to the Church], but if they should fall away, the direst calamity.[234]

The gnostics claimed that their teachers ("the perfect") had received secret teachings from Jesus. Jesus kept the more famous apostles in the dark, they claimed. Thus, the gnostics produced such works as "The Gospel of Judas" and "The Gospel of Mary Magdalene." They argued that Jesus's real message was passed on through these less famous disciples. Of course, the things taught in these Gospels, as the commentators on *The Ante-Nicene Fathers* series point out, are so strange that, "Nothing more absurd than these has probably ever been imagined by rational beings."[235]

> Since, however, it would be very tedious, in such a volume as this, to reckon up the successions of all the Churches, we do put to confusion all those who, in whatever manner, whether by an evil self-pleasing, by vainglory, or by blindness and perverse opinion, assemble in unauthorized meetings; [we do this, I say,] by indicating that tradition derived from the apostles, of the very great, the very ancient, and universally known Church founded and organized at Rome by the two most glorious apostles, Peter and Paul.[236]

If he had known about any such claim, this would have been an excellent time for Irenaeus to bring up Jesus's promises to Peter in Matthew 16. But he does not. Irenaeus is not thinking about the authority of a bishop. He is thinking about the traditions of the apostles and the testimony Rome and all other churches bore to it.

Irenaeus wanted to list the succession of many churches. He did not do this because it would be "very tedious." He chose the best alternative. He gave the succession of a church that was "universally known." This church, Rome, probably would not have gone off course

---

[234] Irenaeus, c. 185, *Against Heresies*, Bk. III, ch. 3, par. 1; brackets in original
[235] *The Ante-Nicene Fathers*, 1867-1873, ANF, vol. I, sec. "Introductory Note to Irenaeus Against Heresies"
[236] Irenaeus, c. 185, *Against Heresies*, Bk. III, ch. 3, par. 2; brackets in original

Rome's Audacious Claim

because it was great, ancient, and founded by the two greatest apostles. It did not stray because it was universally known. All the other churches would have noticed.

Irenaeus explains:

> ... as also [by pointing out] the faith preached to men, which comes down to our time by means of the successions of the bishops. For it is a matter of necessity that every Church should agree with this Church, on account of its preeminent authority, that is, the faithful everywhere, inasmuch as the apostolical tradition has been preserved continuously by those [faithful men] who exist everywhere.[237]

As pointed out earlier, it is impossible to take a firm stand on what the last half of this quote means. We have seen, though, what it probably means. The church in Rome was "universally known." If they had gone astray, "the faithful everywhere" who have "preserved continually" the apostolic faith, would have noticed and corrected or rejected them. Rome had not strayed, so Irenaeus adds the confirmation of the "faithful everywhere" to Rome's ancient origin and apostolic founding as evidence that Rome can be trusted.

The "preeminent authority" of Rome is based on all this. Their tradition was more trustworthy than any other church because both Peter and Paul established their tradition and because it was constantly being compared to the traditions of "the faithful everywhere." Every church needed to agree with this church, not because the bishop of Rome had authority from Peter, but because their origin and succession proved they were teaching the same faith taught by Jesus.

Irenaeus was not arguing against Ephesus or Corinth or Alexandria; they already agreed with Rome. He is saying the gnostics need to agree with Rome if they want to be churches. It is unlikely he expected the gnostics to agree with him on this. More likely, he wanted fellow Christians to trust Rome over and against the gnostic churches in order not to be deceived by them. He also hoped that by training them through his book, they would be prepared to convert individual gnostics they encountered back to the apostolic faith.

---

[237] Irenaeus, c. 185, *Against Heresies*, Bk. III, ch. 3, par. 2; brackets in original

Part V | Chapter 15: Irenaeus

This next section is long, giving the list of bishops from Linus, the first, to Eleutherius, the twelfth, who then led the church in Rome.

> The blessed apostles, then, having founded and built up the Church, committed into the hands of Linus the office of the episcopate. Of this Linus, Paul makes mention in the Epistles to Timothy [2 Tim. 4:21]. To him succeeded Anacletus; and after him, in the third place from the apostles, Clement was allotted the bishopric. This man, as he had seen the blessed apostles, and had been conversant with them, might be said to have the preaching of the apostles still echoing [in his ears], and their traditions before his eyes. Nor was he alone [in this], for there were many still remaining who had received instructions from the apostles. In the time of this Clement, no small dissension having occurred among the brethren at Corinth, the Church in Rome dispatched a most powerful letter to the Corinthians, exhorting them to peace, renewing their faith, and declaring the tradition which it had lately received from the apostles, proclaiming the one God, omnipotent, the Maker of heaven and earth, the Creator of man, who brought on the deluge, and called Abraham, who led the people from the land of Egypt, spake with Moses, set forth the law, sent the prophets, and who has prepared fire for the devil and his angels. From this document, whosoever chooses to do so, may learn that He, the Father of our Lord Jesus Christ, was preached by the Churches, and may also understand the apostolical tradition of the Church, since this Epistle is of older date than these men who are now propagating falsehood, and who conjure into existence another god beyond the Creator and the Maker of all existing things. To this Clement there succeeded Evaristus. Alexander followed Evaristus; then, sixth from the apostles, Sixtus was appointed; after him, Telephorus [*sic*], who was gloriously martyred; then Hyginus; after him, Pius; then after him, Anicetus. Sorer having succeeded Anicetus, Eleutherius does

> now, in the twelfth place from the apostles, hold the
> inheritance of the episcopate.[238]

Although Irenaeus lists all these as bishops, it is certain that, at least through Clement, they were not monarchial bishops. Irenaeus did not know this. The evidence is strong that Clement at least, though one of a college of elder-bishops, had the job of "messenger." If others were messengers before and after him, this would have provided a roll of names for Rome (and other churches that were originally collegiate) to present as a succession of bishops.[239]

For Irenaeus's purposes, it does not matter if there were a succession of bishops or a lineage of multiple elder-bishops. Earlier he said the apostolic tradition was preserved in a succession of presbyters. Obviously, a college of elders can preserve truth as well as, and probably better than, an individual bishop.

Before we return to the text, we must note Irenaeus's reference to Clement. He did not see Clement's letter as Rome exercising authority over Corinth. Instead, "from this letter" anyone may "understand the apostolical tradition of the Church."

> In this order, and by this succession, the ecclesiastical tradition from the apostles, and the preaching of the truth, have come down to us. And this is most abundant proof that there is one and the same vivifying faith, which has been preserved in the Church from the apostles until now, and handed down in truth.[240]

As pointed out, the traditions of the apostles are on his mind, not the authority of the Roman church. Irenaeus is doing one thing without losing focus. He is proving that there is "one and the same vivifying faith, which has been preserved in the Church from the apostles until now."

Once done with Rome's succession, Irenaeus proceeds to appeal to several of the churches whose succession was too tedious to list.

---

[238] Irenaeus, c. 185, *Against Heresies*, Bk. III, ch. 3, par. 3; brackets in original, scripture reference mine
[239] Clement's role and the later lists of bishops were covered in chapter 9.
[240] Irenaeus, c. 185, *Against Heresies*, Bk. III, ch. 3, par. 3; the eighth from the apostles was Telesphorus, not Telephorus.

Part V | Chapter 15: Irenaeus

But Polycarp also was not only instructed by apostles, and conversed with many who had seen Christ, but was also, by apostles in Asia, appointed bishop of the Church in Smyrna, whom I also saw in my early youth, for he tarried [on earth] a very long time, and, when a very old man, gloriously and most nobly suffering martyrdom, departed this life, having always taught the things which he had learned from the apostles, and which the Church has handed down, and which alone are true. To these things all the Asiatic Churches testify, as do also those men who have succeeded Polycarp down to the present time,—a man who was of much greater weight, and a more steadfast witness of truth, than Valentinus, and Marcion, and the rest of the heretics. He it was who, coming to Rome in the time of Anicetus caused many to turn away from the aforesaid heretics to the Church of God, proclaiming that he had received this one and sole truth from the apostles—that, namely, which is handed down by the Church. There are also those who heard from him that John, the disciple of the Lord, going to bathe at Ephesus, and perceiving Cerinthus within, rushed out of the bath-house without bathing, exclaiming, "Let us fly, lest even the bath-house fall down, because Cerinthus, the enemy of the truth, is within." And Polycarp himself replied to Marcion, who met him on one occasion, and said, "Dost thou know me?" "I do know thee, the first-born of Satan." Such was the horror which the apostles and their disciples had against holding even verbal communication with any corrupters of the truth; as Paul also says, "A man that is an heretic, after the first and second admonition, reject; knowing that he that is such is subverted, and sinneth, being condemned of himself" [Tit. 3:10]. There is also a very powerful Epistle of Polycarp written to the Philippians, from which those who choose to do so, and are anxious about their salvation, can learn the character of his faith, and the preaching of the truth. Then, again, the Church in Ephesus, founded by Paul, and having John remaining among them permanently until the

times of Trajan, is a true witness of the tradition of the apostles.[241]

If there were questions about the point Irenaeus was making, he erased them when he wrote the paragraph above. Polycarp was "a more steadfast witness of the truth" than the gnostics. The apostle John would not even talk to "corrupters of the truth." We can learn "the character of his faith and the preaching of the truth" in Polycarp's epistle to the Philippians. The church in Ephesus is a "true witness to the tradition of the apostles."

I had a discussion about this passage once with some friends who were considering joining a church with apostolic succession. As I explained to them the meaning of the passage, one of them yelled, "Truth, truth, truth! Is that all you care about, the truth?"

As a matter of fact, yes, at least in regard to these kinds of issues. More importantly, Irenaeus only cared about the truth. The words "true" and "truth" are mentioned five times in this passage.

We will end this chapter by letting Irenaeus sum up what he has been saying. Again, this next quote directly follows the previous one.

> Since therefore we have such proofs, it is not necessary to seek the truth among others which it is easy to obtain from the Church; since the apostles, like a rich man ... in a bank, lodged in her hands most copiously all things pertaining to the truth: so that every man, whosoever will, can draw from her the water of life. For she is the entrance to life; all others are thieves and robbers. On this account are we bound to avoid them, but to make choice of the thing pertaining to the Church with the utmost diligence, and to lay hold of the tradition of the truth. For how stands the case? Suppose there arise a dispute relative to some important question among us, should we not have recourse to the most ancient Churches with which the apostles held constant intercourse, and learn from them what is certain and clear in regard to the present question? For how should it be if the apostles themselves had not left us writings? Would it not be necessary ... to follow the course of

---

[241] Irenaeus, c. 185, *Against Heresies*, Bk. III, ch. 3, par. 4; brackets mine

the tradition which they handed down to those to whom they did commit the Churches?[242]

Irenaeus ends this section by making his purpose clear. Do not look for truth among the heresies ("from others"). The apostles have deposited the truth in the Church like a rich man depositing treasures in the bank. We have to avoid the heresies and instead choose the things that are in the Church "with all diligence." If there is a dispute inside our church, then appeal to "the most ancient churches."

Irenaeus then makes the interesting point that if we did not have the Scriptures, we would have to "follow the course of the tradition which [the apostles] handed down to those whom they did commit the Churches." This is interesting because he follows it with a description of what barbarian churches, among which he was working, believe even without the Scriptures.

> To which course many nations of those barbarians who believe in Christ do assent, having salvation written in their hearts by the Spirit, without paper or ink, and, carefully preserving the ancient tradition, believing in one God, the Creator of heaven and earth, and all things therein, by means of Christ Jesus, the Son of God; who, because of His surpassing love towards His creation, condescended to be born of the virgin, He Himself uniting man through Himself to God, and having suffered under Pontius Pilate, and rising again, and having been received up in splendor, shall come in glory, the Savior of those who are saved, and the Judge of those who are judged, and sending into eternal fire those who transform the truth, and despise His Father and His advent. Those who, in the absence of written documents, have believed this faith, are barbarians, so far as regards our language; but as regards doctrine, manner, and tenor of life, they are, because of faith, very wise indeed; and they do please God, ordering their conversation in all righteousness, chastity, and wisdom. If any one were to preach to these men the inventions of the heretics, speaking to them in their own

---

[242] Irenaeus, c. 185, *Against Heresies*, Bk. III, ch. 4, par. 1. I removed two unnecessary insertions, which I replaced with ellipses.

language, they would at once stop their ears, and flee as far off as possible, not enduring even to listen to the blasphemous address.[243]

Authority over churches is not in sight in *Against Heresies*. The "preeminent authority" of the church in Rome was like expert testimony in a court of law. In an injury lawsuit, a doctor might be called in to verify an injury. The more educated or respected the doctor, the more authority he has on the witness stand. Rome was the preeminent authority on apostolic teaching; therefore, it was his first witness against heresies. The apostolic tradition "has been preserved continuously by those [faithful men] who exist everywhere."[244] There was no reason to direct the argument of apostolic succession against faithful men and churches who already preserved apostolic tradition through their own succession of bishops and elders. Irenaeus directed his argument against heretics who denied apostolic tradition and to those Christians who might be deceived by them.

From Irenaeus we will now step forward just over a decade to another opposer of heretics: the acerbic lawyer from Carthage, Tertullian.

---

[243] Irenaeus, c. 185, *Against Heresies*, Bk. III, ch. 4, par. 2
[244] Irenaeus, c. 185, *Against Heresies*, Bk. III, ch. 3, par. 2; brackets in original

Part V | Chapter 16: Tertullian

Chapter 16: Tertullian

> Come now, you who would indulge ... curiosity. If you would apply it to the business of your salvation, run to the apostolic churches, in which the very thrones of the apostles still preside in their places, in which their authentic writings are read ... Achaia is very near you, you find Corinth. Since you are not far from Macedonia, you have Philippi; you have the Thessalonians. Since you are able to cross to Asia, you get Ephesus. Since, moreover, you are close to Italy, you have Rome, from which there comes even into our own hands the very authority (of apostles themselves).[245]

Tertullian believed truth could be found in all the apostolic churches, and he was confident that all the churches had preserved it. He added one line that is very pertinent to our subject: "Rome, from which there comes even into our own hands the very authority (of apostles themselves)."

But the authority of the apostles was not only in Rome. He had just written, "in which the very thrones of the apostles still preside in their places" about Corinth, Philippi, Thessalonica, and Ephesus. Tertullian was writing from Carthage, right across the Mediterranean Sea from Italy. He is simply saying that because Rome is the closest apostolic church, the truth makes its way to Carthage from Rome.

He states this more clearly in *Against Marcion*:

> That which comes down from the apostles ... has been kept as a sacred deposit in the churches of the apostles. Let us see what milk the Corinthians drank from Paul, to what rule of faith the Galatians were brought for correction; what the Philippians, the Thessalonians, the Ephesians read; what utterance the Romans also give, so very near, to whom Peter and Paul bequeathed the Gospel, sealed with their own blood. We also have St. John's foster churches. In the same manner is recognized the excellent source of the other churches.[246]

---

[245] Tertullian, 197-208, *Prescription Against Heretics*, ch. 36; parentheses in original
[246] Tertullian, 207, *Against Marcion*, Bk. IV, ch. 5

Rome's Audacious Claim

Considering our subject matter, I need to point out that Tertullian did not write "St." That was added by the translators. It is not in the Latin text.[247] The addition of a special class of saints had not yet happened in Tertullian's time.

This clarifies and establishes what Tertullian meant in the previous quote. Rome is "so very near." Oddly, the translators of *The Ante-Nicene Fathers* insert brackets indicating that Rome was "so very near [to the apostles]." This is nonsensical. How can Rome be any closer in time to the apostles than any other of the churches listed by Tertullian? Carthage really was "so very near" to Rome, a short jaunt across the Mediterranean from the boot of Italy. Just as in the previous passage, Tertullian is saying Rome is the nearest apostolic church.

The website Tertullian.org gives three additional translations of *Against Marcion*. I cannot read the French version, but there is a second English translation and a German one, which I can read. Both understand the passage as indicating geographical proximity.[248]

Tertullian then praises Rome, much as Irenaeus did.

> How happy is its church, on which apostles poured forth all their doctrine along with their blood! where Peter endures a passion like his Lord's! where Paul wins his crown in a death like John's! where the Apostle John was first plunged, unhurt, into boiling oil, and thence remitted to his island-exile! See what she has learned, what taught, what fellowship has had with even (our) churches in Africa.[249]

Tertullian adds the apostle John's name to Rome's legacy. Of course, he is not arguing for the "full, supreme, and universal power" of Rome or its bishop; he is making the same point as Irenaeus: the churches have preserved the teaching of the apostles, and Rome is the greatest of those churches. This is not to establish the authority of Rome, but to argue that the unity of the apostolic churches, all holding the truth together, is a powerful argument that they received the faith unchanged from the apostles. Tertullian writes:

---

[247] Evans, 1972, *Tertullian: Adversus Marcionem*, IV:5
[248] Tertullian Project, n.d., *Adversus Marcionem*
[249] Tertullian, 197-208, *Prescription Against Heretics*, ch. 36

Part V | Chapter 16: Tertullian

> Is it likely that so many churches, and they so great, should have gone astray into one and the same faith? No casualty distributed among men produces one and the same result. Error of doctrine in the churches must necessarily have produced various issues. When, however, that which is deposited among many is found to be one and the same, it not the result of error, but of tradition.[250]

This is a powerful argument, not only for truth, but against Rome's Audacious Claim. If these churches, whose goal was to preserve the life and teachings of whichever apostles founded them, all had the same doctrine and practice more than a century after the last apostle died, then it is the truth they all hold. It makes no sense that they would all individually go astray into the same error, unless ...

... unless Rome's Audacious Claim were true in Tertullian's time. If the bishop of Rome had "full, supreme, and universal power over the whole Church," then he could have gone into error and spread that error to all other churches.

If Tertullian knows of a supreme authority that could decree doctrine to all other churches, then he could not have made the argument he makes. His argument would disintegrate. "Yes," the heretics could answer, "so many churches could easily have gone astray into one and the same error because all the doctrines of the churches are decreed, supervised, and maintained by one bishop in Rome."

Tertullian assigns authority to the tradition of the apostles. Thus, he points his readers to apostolic churches that preserved their traditions. He praises Rome especially, as Irenaeus does, but not because of their bishop, nor because of promises to or descent from Peter. Tertullian is not a testimony to Rome's Audacious Claim, but he is the first Christian we know, outside of Matthew 16, to mention the keys of the kingdom!

---

[250] Tertullian, 197-208, *Prescription Against Heretics*, ch. 28

Rome's Audacious Claim

The Keys of the Kingdom

We cannot leave Tertullian without looking at the first time that the "keys of the kingdom" came up in church history. Oddly enough, Tertullian only mentioned them after he left the catholic churches.[251]

The Montanist movement was the first major split in the catholic churches of the second century. It began around the middle of the second century or a little later. A young Christian by the name of Montanus in one of the churches of Phrygia was in the habit of prophesying in "a sort of frenzy and ecstasy."[252] Phrygia was an area in Asia Minor west of Ephesus that included Colossae and Antioch of Pisidia, and thus was the area of Paul's first missionary journey (cf. Acts 13:14; 14:24).

Eusebius, in his *Church History*, tells us that Montanus's prophecies, and the prophecies of others with him, were challenged, rebuked, and then rejected by the churches of Phrygia and of all Asia.[253] Despite being put out of the Phrygian churches, the Montanist heresy spread. In fact, it spread all the way to Carthage and was adopted by Tertullian.

What we know about these prophecies we know mostly from Tertullian. The Montanists referred to the Holy Spirit as "the Paraclete" (Latin *Paracletos*) from the Greek word *parakletos*, which is applied to the Holy Spirit in John 14:16 and in three other places in the New Testament.

Tertullian did something similar with the Greek word *psychikos*, which means "the soulish." He Latinized it to *psychicos* and referred to the Christians who rejected Montanus as the *psychicis*. This is often rendered as "the psychics," but it means "the soulish."

The Montanists believed that the Church had had time to mature, and therefore the Paraclete had added stricter laws, such as banning remarriage for widows and widowers.[254] Tertullian, whose many tracts indicate he was frustrated by worldliness he saw in some Christians, heartily embraced the stricter rules of Montanism. The first

---

[251] As a reminder, "catholic churches" in the early centuries of the Church was a reference to all the churches founded by the apostles. Well into the third century they were united and known as "catholic" or "universal." See chapter 6.
[252] Eusebius, 323, *Church History*, Bk. V, ch. 16, par. 3
[253] Tertullian, 207, *Against Marcion*, Bk. V, ch. 16, par. 10
[254] Tertullian, 208-217, "On Monogamy," ch. 2

Part V | Chapter 16: Tertullian

explanation of the keys of the kingdom arose from Tertullian's objections to the fact that the catholic churches were willing to forgive sins like adultery after a certain time of penance.

He writes, "'But,' you say, 'the Church has the power of forgiving sins.'"[255] Tertullian, as a Montanist, then begins to examine the right of the catholic churches to call themselves "the Church."

> I now inquire into your opinion, [to see] from what source you usurp this right to "the Church." If, because the Lord has said to Peter, "Upon this rock will I build My Church," "to thee have I given the keys of the heavenly kingdom;" or, "Whatsoever thou shalt have bound or loosed in earth, shall be bound or loosed in the heavens," you therefore presume that the power of binding and loosing has derived to you, that is, to every church akin to Peter, what sort of man are you, subverting and wholly changing the manifest intention of the Lord: conferring this personally upon Peter?[256]

I have left "thou" and "thee" in the translation because Tertullian will go on to use it in his argument. Many people think that "thou" and "thee" are holy language used to address God, but this is not true. "Thou" is simply the singular form of "ye," and "thee" the singular form of "you." Until the nineteenth century, "ye" meant the same thing we now convey by "y'all" or "you guys." "Thou," on the other hand, was just one person. Tertullian will go on to argue that Jesus made a promise to Peter as an individual, not to any church, which would be a group.

We learn from Tertullian that the catholic churches claimed the right to be "the Church" and to forgive sins because of Jesus's promises to Peter in Matthew 16:17-18. According to Tertullian, the catholic churches believed the promises made to Peter apply to "every church akin [related] to Peter."

The Montanists, who were put out of the Church by the decision of several Phrygian churches, objected to this interpretation. Tertullian offers an alternative, saying that "thee" and "thou" in those two verses indicate that Jesus was talking specifically to Peter as an individual.

---

[255] Tertullian, 208-220, "On Modesty," ch. 21
[256] Tertullian, 208-220, "On Modesty," ch. 21; brackets in original

Rome's Audacious Claim

The catholic churches, then, must be wrong in applying those promises to whole churches.

> What now [has this to do] with the Church, and yours indeed, Psychic? For, in accordance with the person of Peter, it is to spiritual men that this power will correspondingly appertain, either to an apostle or else to a prophet.[257]

Tertullian then argues that the Montanist prophets are the spiritual men to whom the keys appertain.

> "The Church," it is true, will forgive sins, but it will be the church of the Spirit, by means of a spiritual man, not the Church which consists of a number of bishops.[258]

I bring up the Montanist argument just to complete Tertullian's thought. For our purposes, the part of the argument that matters is that for the first time in Church history, someone explains the meaning of the keys from the standpoint of the apostolic churches. They were given to every church related to Peter.

The fact that he opposed the doctrine of the churches makes his explanation all the more reliable. It would be foolish of Tertullian to argue against a doctrine which the catholic churches did not actually hold. He was addressing the apostolic churches on behalf of the Montanists. If this doctrine were not the true belief of the catholic churches, his audience would know it. Tertullian would be wasting his ink.

Scorpiace

For some reason, Roman Catholic apologist Jimmy Akin lists one more quote from Tertullian. It, too, provides a different interpretation of the keys than the Roman Catholic Church does. In "Antidote to the Scorpion's Sting" (*Scorpiace* in *The Ante-Nicene Fathers*), Tertullian writes:

> For though you think that heaven is still shut up, remember that the Lord left the keys of it to Peter here, and through him

---

[257] Tertullian, 208-220, "On Modesty," ch. 21
[258] Tertullian, 208-220, "On Modesty," ch. 21

Part V | Chapter 16: Tertullian

> to the Church, which keys everyone will carry with him if he has been questioned and made a confession [of faith].[259]

In this passage, "everyone" will carry Peter's keys with him if he has stood up to persecution. Tertullian is referring to a specific doctrine that you very likely do not know about.

The early churches believed that Christians who died remained in the "good side" of Hades, "Abraham's bosom," where Lazarus the beggar was carried in Jesus' story in Luke 16:19-31. Only martyrs went straight to heaven, per Revelation 6:9-11. It is to this that Tertullian refers. Martyrs received Peter's keys to the kingdom of heaven.

Thus, it is confusing that Akin quotes this passage. It contradicts Roman Catholic teaching. Rather than the keys going to the bishops of Rome, they went to "everyone" who made a good confession before interrogators. The only explanation is "Peter Syndrome," the affliction that causes Roman Catholic apologists to assume without investigation that all references to Peter are evidence for Rome's Audacious Claim.

Roman Catholic apologists do have one more argument, this one reasonable, from Tertullian's writings.

The Montanists Appeal to the Bishop of Rome

I admit I knew nothing about a Montanist appeal to Rome until I found it in *Upon This Rock*.[260] In fact, if Tertullian had not become a Montanist, no one might ever have known that, after their rejection by Phrygia, the Montanists appealed to the bishop of Rome.

> For after the Bishop of Rome had acknowledged the prophetic gifts of Montanus, Prisca, and Maximilla, and, in consequence of the acknowledgment, had bestowed his peace on the churches of Asia and Phrygia, [Praxeas], by persistently urging false accusations against the prophets themselves and their churches, and insisting on the authority of the bishop's predecessors in the see, compelled him to recall the pacific

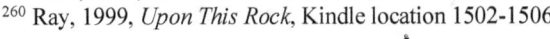

---

[259] Akin, 2010, *The Fathers Know Best*, Kindle location 2788
[260] Ray, 1999, *Upon This Rock*, Kindle location 1502-1506

letter which he had issued, as well as to desist from his purpose of acknowledging the said gifts.[261]

I was a little surprised that no one mentioned this event except Tertullian. Eusebius devotes four chapters of Book V of his *Church History*[262] to the "Phrygian heresy" of Montanus, but he never mentions an appeal to Rome.

In his *Church History*, Eusebius quotes an anonymous letter in regard to the Montanists, which says, "Those of the Phrygians that were deceived were few in number."[263] A few, however, must have been enough for the Montanist heresy to spread everywhere. Eusebius writes:

> The followers of Montanus, Alcibiades, and Theodotus in Phrygia were now first giving wide circulation to their assumption in regard to prophecy—for the many other miracles that, through the gift of God, were still wrought in the different churches caused their prophesying to be readily credited by many,—and as dissension arose concerning them, the brethren in Gaul set forth their own prudent and most orthodox judgment in the matter, and published also several epistles from the witnesses that had been put to death among them. These they sent, while they were still in prison, to the brethren throughout Asia and Phrygia, and also to Eleutherius, who was then bishop of Rome, negotiating for the peace of the churches.[264]

These letters, we learn in the next chapter, were sent by the hand of Irenaeus. A. Cleveland Coxe, he American editor of *The Ante-Nicene Fathers* series has a different take on what happened when Irenaeus arrived: "[Irenaeus] had the mortification of finding the Montanist heresy patronized by Eleutherius the bishop of Rome."[265]

Coxe is not impartial. He attacks Papal Primacy throughout his notes. Nonetheless, Tertullian does say that the bishop of Rome had

---

[261] Tertullian, 208-220, *Against Praxeas*, ch. 1
[262] chapters 16-19
[263] Eusebius, 323, *Church History*, Bk. V, ch. 16, par. 9
[264] Eusebius, 323, *Church History*, Bk. V, ch. 3, par. 4
[265] Coxe, 1886, "Introductory Note to Irenaeus Against Heresies," par. 1

Part V | Chapter 16: Tertullian

acknowledged the prophetic gifts of the Montanist leaders.[266] This could not have been a good thing. Thus, it is accurate to conclude that Gaul's "prudent and most orthodox judgment" helped deliver Eleutherius from embracing a heresy!

This interpretation is disputed. Apparently, some scholars think that Gaul's letter supported Montanus and urged Eleutherius to approve it. A Western Seminary blog, for example, says, "Eusebius writes that some Christians in Gaul wrote a letter to Rome asking for a reception of the New Prophecy for the sake of peace in the church."[267]

This is impossible. The content of the letter from Gaul is unknown to us, but it was known to Eusebius the historian. He called their letter "prudent and most orthodox."[268] Eusebius wrote more than a century after the Montanist uprising, and he condemned it. He would not have called it "prudent and most orthodox" if it had supported the Montanists.

The Montanists could not have successfully appealed to Rome, anyway. The Phrygians would not have submitted to Rome's judgment. The next bishop of Rome, Victor, tried to enforce Roman tradition upon the churches of Asia—the same churches that had rejected Montanus—and he was soundly repudiated. If Victor had no authority in Asia Minor, neither did his predecessor.

In fact, it was Irenaeus who intervened with Victor, as he had done with Eleutherius.

Let us take a look now at the Quartodeciman Controversy.

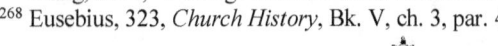

---

[266] Tertullian, 208-220, *Against Praxeas*, ch. 1
[267] Liang, 2014, "5 Things to Know about Montanism," sec. 5
[268] Eusebius, 323, *Church History*, Bk. V, ch. 3, par. 4

Rome's Audacious Claim

Part V | Chapter 17: Victor

Chapter 17: Victor

I love telling stories, and it would be easy—and pleasant—to make a long story of this one. Since that would not suit the purpose of this book, I will simply address the facts. Roman Catholic apologists draw one conclusion from the facts, and I (and Roman Catholic scholars) draw another, but little explanation is needed to see why each side draws the conclusion it does.

During the second century, all churches celebrated Passover. They still do, but we now call it "Easter" in English.[269] They did this by fasting certain days in advance—what we now call Lent—and then ending the fast on Passover with the Lord's Supper.[270] In those days, the Eucharist[271] was a meal (1 Cor. 11:21), not a cracker and a shot glass of juice. It was sufficient to break a fast.[272]

All churches celebrated Passover, but not all churches celebrated it on the same day. The churches in Asia Minor, relying on a tradition passed to them by the apostle John, celebrated Passover on the same day as the Jews: Nisan 14 on the Jewish calendar. The rest of the churches in the empire celebrated Passover on the Sunday following Nisan 14. Some churches fasted just two days before Passover, and others fasted as many as forty days. Because the churches of Asia Minor ended their fast on the Jewish calendar's Passover, it sometimes ended before other churches had even begun theirs.[273]

This caused enough controversy that Polycarp, the highly respected bishop of Smyrna, and Anicetus, the bishop of Rome, discussed the issue in Rome around the year 150. Neither would give up a tradition that came to them from an apostle, so they parted equitably.

The controversy, now known as the Quartodeciman Controversy, from the Latin word for "fourteen," was not resolved at that time. Eusebius tells us that "synods and assemblies were held on this

---

[269] Harper, 2001-2019, "Easter"; note that *Pascha* is the Greek word for "Passover"
[270] Eusebius, 323, *Church History*, Bk. V, ch. 23, par. 1; see also note 1687
[271] "Eucharist," from the Greek word for "thanksgiving," means the same thing as the Protestant "communion." "Eucharist" refers to the prayers of thanksgiving given at the meal, and "communion" refers to the fellowship of Jesus's body and blood in 1 Corinthians 10:16.
[272] Anonymous, 50-120, "The Teaching of the Twelve Apostles" or *Didache*, ch. 10
[273] Eusebius, 323, *Church History*, Bk. V, ch. 23, par. 1, note 1687

account," and that they all agreed that Passover should be celebrated on the Lord's Day (Sunday). He specifically mentions five synods and a letter from Bacchylus, bishop of Corinth, then says there were "a great many" other letters. Eusebius tells us that all the synods and letters came to the same conclusion: Passover should be celebrated on the Sunday after Nisan 14.[274]

One of the synods was held in Rome, and they sent a letter "bearing the name of Victor," the bishop of Rome from 189 to 199 (plus or minus a year). That letter apparently made demands of the churches in Asia Minor, because Polycrates, bishop of Ephesus, worded his reply strongly, but defensively:

> We observe the exact day; neither adding, nor taking away. For in Asia also great lights have fallen asleep, which shall rise again on the day of the Lord's coming, when he shall come with glory from heaven, and shall seek out all the saints. Among these are Philip, one of the twelve apostles, who fell asleep in Hierapolis, and his two aged virgin daughters and another daughter that lived in the Holy Spirit and now rests at Ephesus. Moreover, John, who was both a martyr[275] and a teacher, who reclined upon the bosom of the Lord and, being a priest, wore the sacerdotal plate.[276] He fell asleep at Ephesus; also, Polycarp in Smyrna, who was a bishop and martyr; and Thraseas, bishop and martyr from Eumenia, who fell asleep in Smyrna. Why need I mention the bishop and martyr Sagaris who fell asleep in Laodicea or the blessed Papirius or Melito, the eunuch, who lived altogether in the Holy Spirit and who lies in Sardis, awaiting the episcopate from heaven when he shall rise from the dead?

---

[274] Eusebius, *Church History*, Bk. V, ch. 23, par. 2-3

[275] Those who were captured and tortured were called "martyrs" whether they died or not. The Greek word *martus* means "witness" and is translated as such twenty-nine times in the King James Version of the New Testament. The word slowly became confined to those who had witnessed through their severe suffering or death. Tradition holds, of course, that the apostle John was boiled in oil and miraculously survived before being sent to the isle of Patmos (Tertullian, 197-220, *Prescription Against Heretics*, ch. 36; Rev. 1:9).

[276] No one is sure what Polycrates meant by sacerdotal plate. It is irrelevant to our book. Note 862 on Eusebius, 323, *Church History*, Bk. III, ch. 31, par. 3, addresses possible solutions.

Part V | Chapter 17: Victor

All these observed the fourteenth day of the Passover according to the Gospel, deviating in no respect, but following the rule of faith.[277] And I also, Polycrates, the least of you all, do according to the tradition of my relatives, some of whom I have closely followed. For seven of my relatives were bishops; and I am the eighth. And my relatives always observed the day when the people [the Jews] put away the leaven.

I, therefore, brethren, who have lived sixty-five years in the Lord, and have met with the brethren throughout the world, and have gone through every Holy Scripture, am not frightened by terrifying words. For those greater than I have said, "We ought to obey God rather than man." I could mention the bishops who were present, whom I summoned at your desire, whose names, should I write them, would constitute a great multitude. And they, beholding my littleness, gave their consent to the letter, knowing that I did not bear my gray hairs in vain, but had always governed my life by the Lord Jesus.[278]

Victor then sent out letters informing everyone that the churches in Asia Minor, along with any who agreed with them, were "wholly excommunicate." Those letters, however, were not well-received. Eusebius tells us, "Words of theirs are extant, sharply rebuking Victor."[279]

Eusebius preserved a letter from Irenaeus that reminds Victor that the churches had lived in harmony and peace since the time of the apostles, despite the difference over Passover. He mentions the peaceful attitude of Victor's predecessors and then brings up the

---

[277] The rule of faith was taught to converts at baptism, and each church had one. Irenaeus's rule of faith is given in chapter 15. After the first general Council in Nicea in 325, a rule of faith, which we now call a "creed," was determined for all the churches to hold to. In fact, Nicea's creed—as added to by the Council of Constantinople in 381 and confirmed by the Council of Chalcedon in 451—and the Apostles Creed, which are very similar, are still the official creeds of the Roman Catholic and Eastern Orthodox Churches to this day. Many Protestant churches also affirm these creeds.
[278] Eusebius, 323, *Church History*, Bk. V, ch. 24, par. 2-8
[279] Eusebius, 323, *Church History*, Bk. V, ch, 24, par. 10

discussion between Anicetus and Polycarp, bishop of Smyrna, mentioned earlier. Not only did they agree to remain in peace with one another, but Anicetus made an open display of their fellowship by letting Polycarp administer the Eucharist in the church in Rome.[280]

Eusebius's last comment on the episode is that Irenaeus then cleaned up the situation by letters "not only with Victor, but also with most of the rulers of the churches." He even comments that Irenaeus was appropriately named. His name means "peace" in Greek, and he was the peacemaker in this situation.[281]

Victor tried to exercise authority, or at least control, over the churches in Asia. Whether it was because he found it inappropriate that one small section of the unified church should hold a practice unique to themselves, or whether he was the first bishop of Rome to claim authority over all other churches, we will never know. What we do know is that he was rebuked and opposed by almost everyone and finally gave in to Irenaeus.

We should notice that bishops all over the empire had held synods concluding that Passover should be celebrated on the Lord's Day following Nisan 14. Thus, everyone was on Victor's side in the controversy except the Asia Minor churches; yet they still rebuked him for trying to enforce his will on those churches.

There could be no more solid evidence that the bishop in Rome did not have "full, supreme, and universal power over the whole Church, a power which he can always exercise unhindered."[282] In fact, the churches could not have hindered Victor's supposed power more!

We would not know about this incident if it were not mentioned in *The Church History of Eusebius*; therefore, our first report of it is 133 years after the fact. Eusebius describes this incident without reference to a succession from Peter in the Roman church and without any surprise that the bishops of the churches universally or almost universally rejected the attempted excommunication by Victor. This not only lets us know that Victor was not seen as the "supreme, full, and universal authority" in his own time, but it also lets us know that he was not regarded as supreme authority 133 years later. If Eusebius was familiar with the idea that the bishop of Rome was always free to

---

[280] Eusebius, 323, *Church History*, Bk. V, ch. 24, par. 11-17
[281] Eusebius, 323, *Church History*, Bk. V, ch. 24, par. 18
[282] *Catechism of the Catholic Church*, 1995, par. 882

Part V | Chapter 17: Victor

exercise his supreme power unhindered, he would have described the Quartodeciman Controversy as a mutiny rather than a dispute.

We have now examined all the arguments that Catholic apologists use from the second century (including Tertullian, whose writing career extended into the third century). We have found that the bishop of Rome did not have "full, supreme, and universal power" then. We will now search the third century for clues to the origin of Rome's Audacious Claim.

Rome's Audacious Claim

Part VI

The Third Century

Rome's Audacious Claim

Chapter 18: Hippolytus

We must address Hippolytus because he split the church in Rome from 217 to 235. Catholic Answers tells the fascinating story.

Hippolytus was frustrated throughout the reign of Zephyrinus, whom he felt was not properly dealing with the heresy of modalism.[283] He went over the edge when Callistus was chosen as Zephyrinus's replacement rather than himself. He found other Italian bishops to elect him as the bishop of Rome and to duly appoint him. This was the first split of a major church known to history. Hippolytus remained a separate bishop, what the Roman Catholic Church calls an "antipope," for nineteen years.[284] In the meantime, three other men continued the legitimate succession of Roman bishops.

The resolution of this split is a beautiful work of God. Pontian, who held the legitimate succession in 235, and Hippolytus were both arrested and sent to the mines during a persecution instigated by Emperor Maximinus Thrax. In the mines together, Pontian and Hippolytus reconciled, and Hippolytus repented of his schism.[285]

Hippolytus wrote *The Refutation of All Heresies*, a book very similar to Irenaeus's *Against Heresies*, yet Hippolytus never appealed to the argument of apostolic succession. It is possible he did not want to add importance to Callistus's episcopacy against his own. He excoriated Callistus's character in his writings, in defense of his splitting of the church in Rome.[286] An argument about the importance of succession from Peter, or from both Peter and Paul, might undermine his own position.

---

[283] Modalism is the belief that the Father, Son, and Holy Spirit are all one Person, rather than three. The one God simply plays the role (or the "mode") of Father, Son, and Holy Spirit, much as one actor might play three roles in a film. Today "modalism" is often called "Jesus Only," and modern adherents like the United Pentecostal Church like to say God was "the Father in creation, the Son in redemption, and the Holy Spirit in the Church."

[284] The article on Hippolytus at Catholic Answers gives the time of Hippolytus's bishopric as nineteen years. As a lover of mathematics, I want to point out that 217 through 235 can be either eighteen or nineteen years. If he were, for example, bishop from July 217 to July 235, that would just be eighteen years. If, however, he were bishop from January 217 through December of 235, then it would be nineteen years.

[285] Weidenkopf, 2014, "The Antipope Who Became a Saint," par. 6

[286] Hippolytus, 222-235, *Refutation of All Heresies*, Bk. IX, ch. 2

Rome's Audacious Claim

I found one passage that, while not important, is at least of interest. He wrote:

> By this Spirit, Peter spoke that blessed word, "Thou art the Christ, the Son of the living God." By this Spirit the rock of the Church was established. This is the Spirit, the Comforter, that is sent because of thee, that he may show thee to be the Son of God.[287]

It is safe to assume that Hippolytus, like everyone around him, regarded Peter as the rock on which Jesus built the Church, but this passage shows that he also regarded Peter's confession as the rock of the Church. That said, Hippolytus must go down as irrelevant to Rome's Audacious Claim.

Origen, however, is very relevant, and he is the next author we will cover.

---

[287] Hippolytus, 218-235, *Discourse on the Holy Theophany*, par. 9

Chapter 19: Origen

Origen is one of my favorite Church fathers. He was a deep and "out of the box" thinker. He was one of the most revered teachers of his time, but later Christians condemned some of his more innovative ideas. As we have learned, innovation was not the job of a church leader—preservation was.

All that is irrelevant to this book. What is relevant is that the most educated Christian of the early third century was apparently blissfully unaware of any claim by the bishop of Rome to supreme authority over all Christians and churches. He wrote a long book on the basic principles of Christianity, in which he refers but once to Rome, and that only because he was quoting 2 Timothy 1:17 on a different subject.[288] Apparently the authority of Rome was neither a basic principle of the faith nor even known about in Caesarea in the first half of the third century.

More pertinent is Origen's commentary on the book of Matthew. We don't have all of it, but we do have his commentary on Matthew 16 and Jesus's promises to Peter.

Origen goes verse by verse through the Gospel of Matthew. In Matthew 16:14, the apostles tell Jesus that people think he might be John the Baptist, Elijah, Jeremiah, or one of the prophets, and Origen explains the reasons that the Jews might have suggested each of those.[289] From this we can conclude that Origen was not glossing over the top of Matthew 16. He was covering every verse thoroughly, giving us context, history, and possible interpretations.

In verse 15, Jesus asks the apostles who they think he is. In verse 16, Peter answers him, and here we come to the chapters in Origen's commentary that are relevant to this book.

First, Origen tells us that "perhaps" we can be blessed like Peter if we confess that Jesus is the Christ, the Son of the living God, and we confess it by revelation from the Father.[290] If we do this, he says,

> We become a Peter ... for a rock is every disciple of Christ of whom those drank who drank of the spiritual Rock which

---

[288] Origen, 217-230, *De Principiis*, Bk. III, ch. 1, par. 20
[289] Origen, 246-248, *Commentary on Matthew*, Bk. XII, ch. 9
[290] Origen, 246-248, *Commentary on Matthew*, Bk. XII, ch. 10

> followed them, and upon every such rock is built every word of the Church, and the polity in accordance with it. For in each of the perfect, who have the combination of words and deeds and thoughts which fill up the blessedness, is the Church built by God.[291]

Origen interprets Matthew 16 the way I do in chapter 4. Peter was the first living stone, but any of us who confess Jesus as the Christ, the Son of the living God, become living stones as well, built together into a spiritual house (1 Pet. 2:5). That the bishop of Rome, or any other bishop, is shepherd of the whole Church does not creep into Origen's thoughts. Although his commentary delves deeply enough into Matthew to explore interpretations that earn only a "perhaps," Rome's Audacious Claim does not get even that.

We must also note Origen's reference to "the perfect." He defines them further down as those "who have the combination of works and deeds and thoughts which fill up the blessedness."[292] He means Christians who are fully mature in Christ.

Origen then argues against the idea that the promises apply to Peter alone!

> If you suppose that upon the one Peter only the whole Church is built by God, what would you say about John the son of thunder or each one of the apostles? Shall we otherwise dare to say that against Peter in particular the gates of Hades shall not prevail, but that they shall prevail against the other apostles and the perfect? Does not the saying previously made, "The gates of Hades shall not prevail against it," hold in regard to all and in the case of each of them?[293]

Origen doesn't stop. He claims all the promises to Peter not only for the other apostles, but for "the perfect." He continues:

> And also the saying, "Upon this rock will I build my Church"? Are the keys of the Kingdom of Heaven given by the Lord to Peter only, and will no other of the blessed receive them? But if this promise, "I will give thee the keys of the Kingdom of

---

[291] Origen, 246-248, *Commentary on Matthew*, Bk. XII, ch. 10
[292] Origen, 246-248, *Commentary on Matthew*, Bk. XII, ch. 10
[293] Origen, 246-248, *Commentary on Matthew*, Bk. XII, ch. 11

Part VI | Chapter 19: Origen

> Heaven," be common to the others, how shall not all the things previously spoken of, and the things which are subjoined as having been addressed to Peter, be common to them?[294]

Origen rounds up all the promises to Peter and assigns them to both the other apostles and "the blessed"!

I am not saying this is the correct way to interpret Matthew 16:15-19. I am saying, though, that Origen rejects the idea that those promises were for Peter alone. If they were not for Peter alone, then they were certainly not for the bishop of Rome alone!

Origen has a lot of detractors, but even his detractors agree that he was probably the greatest Christian scholar of his day.

In *History of Christian Thought*, Jonathan Hill writes:

> Origen is, together with Augustine and Luther, one of the most important figures in this book. Almost single-handedly, the 'Iron Man', as he was known, dragged Christianity into intellectual respectability. One of the greatest minds of his age, he debated with pagan philosophers as their superior. And as the first truly professional theologian, he also created the first true Christian philosophy, much of which would remain in place throughout Christendom for centuries. Yet this very originality was regarded by many as heresy. The systematic destruction of most of his writings after his death—by churchmen unworthy to inherit them—robbed the Church of one of its greatest treasures.[295]

You and I are free to join many others in condemning Origen for certain liberties he took with his theology. No one, however, can deny that if there was anyone in the eastern half of the empire who knew that the bishop of Rome had "full, supreme, and universal power" over every Christian, it was Origen. Nor can it be denied that he would have mentioned it in his commentary on Matthew 16. Obviously, Origen had never heard of Rome's Audacious Claim.

---

[294] Origen, 246-248, *Commentary on Matthew*, Bk. XII, ch. 11
[295] Hill, 2003, *History of Christian Thought*, Kindle location 710-715

Rome's Audacious Claim

We could continue Origen's commentary, but we would find only the same. A little further down, he writes, "For all bear the surname of 'Rock' who are the imitators of Christ."[296] Rome never gets a mention.

Catholic Apologists and Origen's Commentary on Matthew

Despite Origen's clear teaching against the modern Roman Catholic Church's interpretation of Matthew 16, their apologists cite him anyway!

Stephen Ray

Stephen Ray, in *Upon This Rock*, praises him repeatedly, calling him "the most accomplished biblical scholar of the early Church."[297] He not only agrees that Origen, above all others, would have known about a claim to supreme authority over all churches, he emphasizes it:

> Origen was probably the brightest scholar and most powerful intellect of all the Fathers living at the end of the second century. With unlimited access to historical and ecclesiastical documents, both in the library of Alexandria, which was second to none, and also the libraries of the Empire and the documents and traditions of the local Churches, Origen was in an unparalleled position to speak on the events of the first century, especially since he himself was born within eighty-five years of the death of the Apostle John.[298]

Why would a Catholic apologist like Stephen Ray praise the intellect and knowledge of a man who rejects the Roman Catholic Church's interpretation of Matthew 16? It can only be "Peter Syndrome." It is, apparently, an intellectual epidemic among Roman Catholic apologists. It is my prayer that this book will help them differentiate between a reference to the bishop of Rome and a reference to Peter.

Ray cites Origen—always secondhand and usually from Jurgens's *Faith of the Early Fathers*[299]—to show that Peter was crucified upside down in Rome, that the Church was built on Peter, and that the Church

---

[296] Origen, 246-248, *Commentary on Matthew*, Bk. XII, ch. 11
[297] Ray, 1999, *Upon This Rock*, Kindle location 5308-5309, footnote 57
[298] Ray, 1999, *Upon This Rock*, Kindle location 4215-4219, footnote 40
[299] 1970, Liturgical Press

Part VI | Chapter 19: Origen

should only hold to beliefs that have been held in the Church since the time of the apostles.[300] All of these things are true, but none of them are relevant to the claim that the bishop of Rome has "full, supreme, and universal power over the whole Church."

Ray is not deterred! He actually quotes Origen on Matthew 16.[301] He has to explain Origen's interpretation, of course, since it opposes his argument. He argues that Origen is only focusing on the allegorical and spiritual interpretation in his commentary. He concludes, "We can understand Origen to be simply 'spiritualizing the text.'"[302]

Ray is clearly confused by Origen's commentary on Matthew 16. He writes:

> We have already established that Origen accepted the *literal* and *historical* intent of this passage by the fact that he clearly states that Peter is the rock upon which the Church is built. So why does Origen seem to contradict this later in life?[303]

Origen did write his commentary on Matthew late in his life. It is, however, very literal about Matthew 16:15-19. Just as Peter was the rock, so everyone who confesses what he confessed by revelation of the Father is a rock as well. That is not figurative. Hahn's confusion is because he confused Origen's statement that Peter is the rock with an argument for the authority of Rome.

There are a lot of logical steps between "Peter is the rock on which Jesus will build his Church" and "The bishop of Rome has full, supreme, and universal power over the whole Church." Origen does not supply any of those steps. Instead, his argument is that if any of us do what Peter did, we all get to reap the benefits Peter reaped. Nothing figurative there.

Jimmy Akin

Jimmy Akin also quotes Origen's commentary on Matthew. Akin quotes his commentary on Matthew 18 in *The Fathers Knows Best*,[304]

---

[300] Ray, 1999, *Upon This Rock*, Kindle location 566, 1524, 1529 respectively
[301] Ray, 1999, *Upon This Rock*, Kindle location 1534-1546
[302] Ray, 1999, *Upon This Rock*, Kindle location 5363-5383
[303] Ray, 1999, *Upon This Rock*, Kindle location 5363-5383; emphasis in original
[304] Akin, 2010, *The Fathers Know Best*, Kindle location 2795-2800

passing over the commentary on Matthew 16:14-19 for obvious reasons.

Origen's commentary on Matthew 18:15-18 is intriguing, to say the least. Akin quotes him because he says that Peter has "some element superior" and that the things said to Peter have "a great difference and preeminence" over the things promised to individual Christians in Matthew 18:15-18.[305]

Matthew 18:15-18 says that if a brother offends you, you should talk to him. If he doesn't listen to you, get another person or two to talk to him with you. If he still doesn't listen, bring him before the church. If he won't even listen to the church, then he is to be treated like a Gentile and a tax collector. At that point Jesus promises "you" the power of binding and loosing with authority from heaven, just like he promised Peter in Matthew 16. Almost everyone understands this promise to apply to all churches.

Origen does not. He repeatedly refers to the person who offended as "the thrice admonished" and the people who follow these steps as "those who thrice admonished." He clearly thinks "you" in Matthew 18:18 refers to the offended individual, even though the "you" is plural in the Greek.

Jimmy Akin, however, either did not notice or did not know about Origen's use of "those who thrice admonished." This results from using a lot of secondhand sources. When you use secondary sources, you cannot see the context of the quotes you are using. Like Scott Hahn, Akin gets many of his quotes come from Jurgens' *Faith of the Early Fathers*. In this case, he does not list the quote from Origen's *Commentary on Matthew*[306] in his "Translations Used" section,[307] so I do not know his source. It is likely that Akin had no idea that Origen was comparing Peter to "those who were thrice admonished." In that case, it would be his unreferenced source that misquotes Origen by inserting misleading brackets. Akin's citation reads:

> [I]f we were to attend carefully to the Gospels, we should also find, in relation to those things that seem to be common to Peter ... a great difference and a preeminence in the things

---

[305] Origen, 246-248, *Commentary on Matthew*, Bk. XIII, ch. 31
[306] Akins, 2010, *The Fathers Know Best*, Kindle location 2795
[307] Akins, 2010, *The Fathers Know Best*, Kindle location 6360-6417

Part VI | Chapter 19: Origen

[Jesus] said to Peter, compared with the second class [of apostles].[308]

Once we reinsert the words that Akin leaves out and replace the misleading brackets, the quote reads:

> If we were to attend carefully to the Gospels, we should also find, in relation to those things which seem to be common to Peter and those who have thrice admonished the brethren, a great difference and preeminence in the things said to Peter compared with the second class.[309]

The "second class," then, are, "those who have thrice admonished the brethren," not the other apostles.

What Origen sees as the difference between Peter and "those who have thrice admonished" is strange to all of us, Protestant and Roman Catholic alike. Peter, Origen says, has the keys to many heavens, while "those who thrice admonished" have the key to only one heaven.[310]

Origen nowhere suggests that Peter is superior to or has more authority than the other apostles, except in Jimmy Akin's misquote. Again, to be fair, Akin may not have known he was misquoting; but if he did not, then his source (or his source's source) did. This is why it is not just important, but necessary, to at least check trusted original translations of the fathers. I have done that for every quote in this book.

In general, one mistake does not disqualify a whole work, but this is not a mistake. "Those who have thrice admonished the brethren" was removed from the quote, and "[the apostles]" was inserted. That is sabotage, not error.

Origen exalted the promise made to Peter over the promise made to any Christian who "thrice admonishes." That makes sense of Origen's words, but Origen is likely the only Christian in history who has argued that Peter has the key to multiple heavens.

Origen's bizarre idea is irrelevant, though. What is relevant is that the "brightest scholar and most powerful intellect of all the Fathers

---

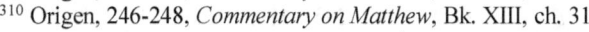

[308] Akins, 2010, *The Fathers Know Best*, Kindle location 2795; brackets in original
[309] Origen, 246-248, *Commentary on Matthew*, Bk. XIII, ch. 31
[310] Origen, 246-248, *Commentary on Matthew*, Bk. XIII, ch. 31

Rome's Audacious Claim

living at the end of the second century"[311] addressed Matthew 16 and applied the promises made to Peter to every Christian who confessed Peter's confession by the revelation of the Father.

With that, we must turn to the early Church father most quoted—and most misrepresented—by the Roman Catholic apologists: Cyprian of Carthage.

---

[311] Ray, 1999, *Upon This Rock*, Kindle location 4215-4219, footnote 40

Chapter 20: Cyprian

Cyprian's epistles are numbered one way in The Ante-Nicene Fathers *and in a different order in* The Oxford Series. *I am using the numbering system from* The Ante-Nicene Fathers *series, and I will give the Oxford numbering in the footnotes.*

Perhaps the most important early Christian witness to the authority of Peter and the bishop of Rome is Cyprian, who was bishop of Carthage in North Africa (modern Tunisia) from 249 to 258. He referenced Matthew 16 and the authority of Peter more than any other writer from the era before the Council of Nicea in 325, perhaps more often than all of them combined!

Rome Was the Nearest Apostolic Church to Carthage
Before we get started, I need to give you one bit of background information regarding Cyprian. This applies as well to the writings of Irenaeus, who was bishop west of Rome in the territory of Gaul, and Tertullian, who was from Carthage like Cyprian.

Rome was the only church founded by the apostles to the west of Greece. Cyprian was bishop in Carthage, which lay at the shortest point between Italy and Africa across the Mediterranean. The distance between Carthage and Rome, as an aircraft flies, is 367 miles. The distance to Alexandria, the capital of Egypt, is just short of 1,200 miles. Rome was by far the closest apostolic church to Carthage.

In the early centuries, churches not founded by apostles appealed to churches that were founded by apostles. As Irenaeus puts it:

> Suppose there arise a dispute relative to some important question among us, should we not have recourse to the most ancient churches with which the apostles held constant intercourse and learn from them what is clear and certain in regard to the present question?[312]

---

[312] Irenaeus, c. 185, *Against Heresies*, Bk. III, ch. 4, par. 1

Rome's Audacious Claim

The point to remember here is that Rome was Carthage's closest apostolic church. Cyprian's relationship with the Roman clergy is unique because of this. The bishops of Eastern churches, who were closer to Antioch, Alexandria, Ephesus, Philippi, and other apostolic churches, would not have had the same relationship with Rome.

I do not remind you of Carthage's relationship to Rome to bolster my argument from Cyprian. Rome's Audacious Claim would fall without it. Knowing the relationship helps us understand the volume and tone of the correspondence between Rome and Carthage.

Cyprian was bishop of Carthage from 249 to 258, around seventy years after Irenaeus wrote *Against Heresies*. He became bishop one year before Origen's death in 250 and less than five years after Origen completed his commentary on Matthew. If the pope did not have "full, supreme, and universal power" in Origen's day, he did not have it in Cyprian's.

There was a lot of interaction between Cyprian and the Roman clergy. He exchanged twenty-one letters with the elders and bishops of Rome. Those letters show a fatherly care for Cornelius, under whom Novatian split the church of Rome. Cyprian shows the same fatherly care in his letters to Lucius, who replaced the martyred Cornelius and soon faced martyrdom himself. Stephen followed, and Cyprian's conflict with him provides the fodder for many of Cyprian's eighty-two epistles. More importantly, Stephen's episcopate prompted much discussion about Peter and the promises made to him in Matthew 16.

Cyprian, Peter, and Matthew 16

Roman Catholic apologists love Cyprian because he quoted Matthew 16 regularly. He had plenty of cause to do so.

Novatian split the church in Rome early in Cyprian's episcopate, and then he sent "apostles" to churches all over the empire, including Carthage, to spread his ideas.[313] If this were not problem enough, two of the most intense Roman persecutions occurred during Cyprian's episcopate as well. Many Christians lapsed during the persecutions, and those who did not only requested readmission to the church, but demanded it!

---

[313] Cyprian, 252, Epistle 51 (Oxford 56), par. 24

Part VI | Chapter 20: Cyprian

Cyprian used Matthew 16 and the promises to Peter to argue that both the agents of Novatian and those who had lapsed were battling against more than just bishops. They were confronting the foundation, authority, and unity of the Church. The bishops represented the authority of Peter, upon whom the Church was founded. The circumstances of his tenure provided plenty of reasons to defend the bishops of all churches. Cyprian defended the bishops of Rome against the faction of Novatian; he defended himself, the bishop of Rome, and surrounding bishops from the demands of those who had lapsed during persecution; and he defended himself and the bishops of the Roman Empire against Stephen's threats of excommunication. Throughout these letters, he defined and defended the authority of the one united episcopate held by all bishops. He based that authority on the promises made to Peter.

It is not surprising, then, that Roman Catholic apologists latch on to Cyprian's references to Peter. In one letter, he complains that the lapsed have brought letters from heretics to "the throne of Peter" and "the chief church from where priestly unity takes its source"![314] What a gold mine for Rome's Audacious Claim! Stricken with "Peter Syndrome," though, they fail to notice that Cyprian applies the promises made to Peter to all the bishops of the churches, including himself!

The clearest example of this is in Epistle 26:

> Our Lord ... describing the honor of a bishop and the order of his Church, speaks in the Gospel, and says to Peter: "I say to you that you are Peter, and upon this rock will I build my Church; and the gates of hell shall not prevail against it. And I will give to you the keys of the kingdom of heaven: and whatsoever you shall bind on earth shall be bound in heaven: and whatsoever you shall loose on earth shall be loosed in heaven." From there, through the changes of times and successions, the ordering of bishops and the plan of the Church flow onwards; so that the Church is founded upon the bishops, and every act of the Church is controlled by these same rulers. Since this, then, is founded on the divine law, I marvel that some, with daring temerity, have chosen to write

---

[314] Cyprian, 252, Epistle 54 (Oxford 59), par. 14

Rome's Audacious Claim

to me as if they wrote in the name of the Church; when the Church is established in the bishop and the clergy, and all who stand [fast in the faith].[315]

To Cyprian, the Church is founded upon the bishops, not one specific bishop. Every act of the Church is controlled by "these same rulers," not by one individual ruler. Cyprian had no thought that the bishop of Rome had "full, supreme, and universal power" over the whole Church. Instead, the bishops lead the Church, and they are the foundation of its unity. This is the theology of Cyprian, and as we go, we shall see it is consistent throughout his letters and treatises and guides all that he says.

Roman Catholic theologian Richard McBrien writes:

> In a very real sense, however, every bishop is a successor of Peter. Cyprian of Carthage (d. 258) held this, and so, too, did Hilary of Poitiers (d. 367), for whom all bishops are "successors of Peter and Paul."[316]

In Epistle 26, Cyprian applies the authority of all bishops specifically to himself. The "daring temerity" he mentions comes from some of the lapsed. They had received a certificate granting them peace with the church from one of the imprisoned saints, and they demanded Cyprian receive them back into fellowship.[317] Their authority was the certificate they had received, but Cyprian tells them that the real authorities in the church were the bishop—Cyprian himself—and the clergy.

Although Cyprian attributes Matthew 16:16-19 to all bishops, he did say that Rome was the chief source of priestly unity.[318] This is no surprise to us. We have seen in the writings of Irenaeus and Tertullian that Rome was the most important church of its time. This was because of its fame, its giving, its adherence to apostolic truth, and its foundation in the two greatest apostles, Paul and Peter. In addition, as we all know, it was once said that "all roads lead to Rome." The interaction of Rome with the churches throughout the empire would

---

[315] Cyprian, 250, Epistle 26 (Oxford 33), par. 1
[316] McBrien, 2016, "The Papacy," Kindle location 6909-6910; parentheses in original
[317] Cyprian, 250, Epistle 22 (Oxford 27), par. 1
[318] Cyprian, 252, Epistle 54 (Oxford 59), par. 14

also have caused Cyprian to see it as the chief source of unity. As Irenaeus put it some seventy years earlier:

> For it is a matter of necessity that every Church should agree with [the church in Rome], on account of its pre-eminent authority, that is, the faithful everywhere, inasmuch as the apostolical tradition has been preserved continuously by those [faithful men] who exist everywhere.[319]

Rome had more interaction with other churches than any other because of its giving, the martyrdoms that occurred there, and because it was the capital of the empire. This interaction not only assured the preservation of the apostolic tradition in Rome, but it made Rome a center of unity as well. Thus, Cyprian calls it "the chief church from which unity takes its source."[320]

As for Cyprian's reference to Peter's throne, there is no denying that Cyprian and others of his time regarded the bishop of Rome as being specifically descended from Peter. Only seventy years had passed since Irenaeus gave their source as Peter and Paul, but as the role of bishop had gained prominence, so had the importance of the first bishop's ordainer. Cyprian appealed to Peter and to Matthew 16 as the authority for all bishops. Rome, though, had Peter as a founding apostle. The seeds for Rome's Audacious Claim were already planted, bedded, and fertilized in Cyprian's time. It is no surprise that Stephen took advantage of his descent from Peter.

Cyprian himself did not grant the bishops of Rome the authority of Peter. He saw the authority of Peter in the "one episcopate" consisting of all the bishops of all the churches. This is probably best seen in his ferocious battles with Stephen over Stephen's authority. These grew so heated that Cyprian called a council of eighty-seven bishops to oppose him.

The Seventh Council of Carthage

To borrow the wording of Cyprian's overly acerbic contemporary, Firmilian of Caesarea, I am "justly indignant" at Roman Catholic

---

[319] Irenaeus, c. 185, *Against Heresies*, Bk. III, ch. 3, par. 2; brackets in original
[320] Cyprian, 252, Epistle 54 (Oxford 59), par. 14

apologists who quote Cyprian in support of Papal Primacy, when they know he led a council to deny it.[321]

It is wrong, whether because of poor scholarship or purposeful deceit, to quote Cyprian's references to Matthew 16 without pointing out that he applied the promises of Peter to all bishops. It is wrong to let ignorant readers make the assumption that because Peter is mentioned, the bishop of Rome must be the target of Cyprian's statements. Those wrongs, however, cannot be compared to the wrong of quoting Cyprian to support Papal Primacy when he actually called and led a council that expressly denied it!

> Cyprian said: ... For neither does any of us set himself up as a bishop of bishops, nor by tyrannical terror does any compel his colleague to the necessity of obedience, since every bishop according to the allowance of his liberty and power, has his own proper right of judgment and can no more be judged by another than he himself can judge another.[322]

There is no doubting Cyprian's intention. He was rejecting the excommunications issued by Stephen, the bishop of Rome in 256.

Cyprian's reign as bishop of Carthage was marked by persecution, the first major division in Church history, and strife. It was so bad that at one point he was sure the Antichrist was at hand.[323] During his nine-year tenure, no fewer than five bishops of Rome were martyred: Fabius in 250, Cornelius in 254, Lucius in 256, Stephen in 257, and Sixtus II in 258, about a month before Cyprian himself was martyred.[324] At the beginning of Cyprian's tenure, the bishop's chair in Rome was empty, and the persecution was so strong that the elders could not fill it. Cyprian and the Roman elders exchanged several epistles during that time.[325]

A break in the persecution finally came, and in 251 the Roman church installed Cornelius as bishop. One elder, Novatian by name,

---

[321] Firmilian, 256, "Epistles of Cyrian," Epistle 74 (Oxford 75), par. 17
[322] "The Seventh Council of Carthage," 256, introduction
[323] Cyprian, 257, Epistle 67 (Oxford 67), par. 7
[324] Wikipedia, 2019, "List of Popes." The Wikipedia dates are based on the *Annuario Pontificio*, an annual published by the Roman Curia; Cyprian's date of martyrdom is from Frend, 2018, "St. Cyprian, Christian Theologian and Bishop [Died 258]," par. 1.
[325] Epistles 2, 3, 14, 22, 28-30 (Oxford 8, 9, 20, 27, 30, 35-36)

took offense at being passed over. He issued charges against Cornelius and found three Italian bishops to install him as bishop against Cornelius.

Novatian's schism stuck. He sent emissaries everywhere in defense of his bishopric. They reached Carthage, prompting Cyprian to look into the charges against Cornelius. After doing so, Cyprian and most other bishops took their stand for Cornelius and against Novatian. Novatian, however, gathered enough support that his schism lasted with strength through the fourth century, making it the first lasting split among the apostolic churches.[326]

Cyprian was indignant on behalf of the true bishops of Rome, first Cornelius, then Lucius, then Stephen. Novatian had split the Church, and Cyprian went after him and any who associated with him with boundless energy, even calling on Stephen to excommunicate a bishop in Spain who was openly supporting Novatian.[327] Despite such strong support for the true line of Roman bishops, Cyprian found himself in a heated conflict with Stephen.

Some Novatians were returning to the catholic churches. Some of those had come to Christ through the Novatians and been baptized by them.[328] It seemed obvious to Cyprian that these needed to be baptized again by the one Church, whose unity was based on Peter. Novatian had violated that unity, and Cyprian was convinced there could be no valid baptism outside the Church.

Stephen, even though he held the episcopal seat that Novatian had snubbed, accepted the Novatian schism's baptisms as valid! Apparently, previous bishops had accepted the baptisms of the heretic Marcion in the second century.[329] This seems bizarre to me, because Marcion rejected the God of Israel and considered him to be a false god.[330]

---

[326] They are mentioned in Canon 8 of the Council of Nicea in 325. They played a role in ending the Arian Controversy in 383 (Pavao, 2014, *Decoding Nicea*, pp. 130-134). The Catholic Encyclopedia tells us they still had a church in Alexandria as late as the year 600 (Chapman, 1911, "Novatian and Novatianism," last paragraph).
[327] Cyprian, 254, Epistle 66 (Oxford 68).
[328] The Novatians believed nothing different than the catholic/apostolic churches, except they refused to grant readmittance to those who had committed major sins such as adultery, murder, or lapsing under persecution.
[329] Cyprian, 256, Epistle 72 (Oxford 73), par. 4
[330] Irenaeus, c. 185, *Against Heresies*, Bk. I, ch. 27, par. 2

Rome's Audacious Claim

Cyprian had no regard for Stephen's tradition. He wanted tradition that was traceable to the apostles.[331] As pointed out in the chapter on Irenaeus, apostolic tradition is the only tradition that was acceptable to the churches. Firmilian, the bishop of Caesarea at the time, gives a little clearer explanation of this argument than Cyprian does:

> As respects what Stephen has said, as though the apostles forbade those who come from heresy to be baptized, and delivered this also to be observed by their successors, you have replied most abundantly, that no one is so foolish as to believe that the apostles delivered this, when it is even well known that these heresies themselves … arose subsequently [i.e., after the apostles]; when even Marcion the disciple of Cerdo is found to have introduced his sacrilegious tradition against God long after the apostles, and after long lapse of time from them.[332]

Firmilian argues that Stephen's tradition, accepting the baptism of heretics, could not possibly be apostolic because all the heretics came after the time of the apostles. This argument is wrong. It is probable that Peter encountered gnostics in Rome before his death. The early churches charged Simon the Magician (Acts 8:9-24) with beginning the gnostic movement, and Irenaeus puts him in Rome during the reign of Claudius Caesar, around a decade before Peter's martyrdom there.[333]

Though his argument is inaccurate, this quote shows Firmilian, bishop of Caesarea, regarded apostolic tradition as authoritative, just as Irenaeus and Tertullian did.

Here is Cyprian's version of the argument against tradition that is not apostolic.

> "Let nothing be innovated," says [Stephen], "except what has been handed down." From where is that tradition? Does it descend from the authority of the Lord and of the Gospel, or does it come from the commands and the epistles of the apostles? God witnesses and admonishes that those things which are written must be done, saying to Joshua the son of

---

[331] Cyprian, 254-257, Epistle 73 (Oxford 74), par. 2
[332] Firmilian, 256, Epistle 74 (Oxford 75), par. 5; brackets mine
[333] Irenaeus, c. 185, *Against Heresies*, Bk. I, ch. 23, par. 1-2

Part VI | Chapter 20: Cyprian

> Nun: "The book of this law shall not depart out of your mouth; but you shalt meditate in it day and night, that you may observe to do according to all that is written therein" [Josh. 1:8].[334]

Cyprian argues that a tradition must come from the Lord in the Gospels or from commands in the letters of the apostles. This would be a powerful passage for a Protestant to quote in defense of *sola scriptura*, or the teaching that the Scriptures should be the sole authority in the churches, but it would not fairly represent Cyprian.

Cyprian, like all other bishops and teachers of his age, believed that tradition is only valid if there is good reason to believe it descended from the apostles. Scripture, however, was not the only way to show a tradition was from the apostles. One also could show that all the churches held it. They believed, accurately at the time, that the churches could only come to the same doctrine because of dissemination from all the apostles. Error, as Tertullian taught us, necessarily results in variety as it spreads, not in unity.[335]

That argument is only true as long as there is not a central authority that can decree doctrine to the churches. Once ecumenical councils began decreeing dogma to all the churches in the fourth century, the united belief of the churches was no longer a testimony to apostolic origin. An ecumenical council could spread a new belief, and thus possible error, to all the churches.

In Cyprian's time, though, a tradition common to all the churches was still likely to be apostolic. It had been just 150 years since the death of the last apostle. Cyprian appeals to that united tradition of the churches in a letter to a Spanish church (or churches):

> For which reason you must diligently observe and keep the practice delivered from divine tradition and apostolic observance, which is also maintained among us, and almost throughout all the provinces; that for the proper celebration of ordinations all the neighboring bishops of the same province should assemble with that people for which a prelate is

---

[334] Cyprian, 254-257, Epistle 73 (Oxford 74), par. 2; brackets mine
[335] Tertullian, 197-208, *Prescription Against Heretics*, ch. 28

ordained. And the bishop should be chosen in the presence of the people, who have most fully known the life of each one.[336]

This tradition is not in the Scriptures, yet Cyprian calls it "divine" tradition. We cannot use Cyprian to justify *sola scriptura*. Pulling quotes out of context to make an author seem to believe what he does not believe is called "quote mining." Catholic apologists do this all the time, especially with Cyprian. We should not.

Despite the arguments Firmilian and Cyprian presented regarding the rebaptism of heretics, Stephen tried to excommunicate Cyprian over this matter. Not only that, but he wrote letters to churches in the East threatening them with excommunication if they rebaptized any heretics.[337]

Cyprian's response was not a letter—but a council. Eighty-seven bishops came together to reject Stephen's decision, and Cyprian began the council by announcing, "… neither does any one of us set himself up as a bishop of bishops." He even added, "nor by tyrannical terror does any compel his colleague to the necessity of obedience."[338] The "tyrannical terror" was, of course, a reference to Stephen's attempt to excommunicate other churches.

Catholic apologists love to quote Cyprian's various references to a succession from Peter as though Cyprian was referring to the bishop of Rome. They give no context, but simply quote him, then claim Cyprian supported Papal Primacy. Several are honest enough to mention that Firmilian and Cyprian disagreed with Stephen on the baptism of heretics, but even those then claim that neither bishop denied Stephen's right to compel the obedience of other bishops.[339]

This is false. We have just looked at Cyprian's denial of Stephen's authority. Firmilian, the bishop of Caesarea, did not have much regard for it either:

> But let these things which were done by Stephen be passed by for the present, lest, while we remember his audacity and

---

[336] Cyprian, 257, Epistle 67 (Oxford 67), par. 5
[337] Eusebius, 323, *Church History*, Bk. VII, ch. 5, par. 4
[338] "Seventh Council of Carthage," 256, introduction
[339] e.g., Butler, Dahlgren & Hess, 1996, *Jesus, Peter, and the Keys*, p. 223; Ray, 2009, *Upon this Rock*, Kindle location 87-88

pride, we bring a more lasting sadness on ourselves from the things that he has wickedly done. (Epistle 74:3)

Surely by calling Stephen's action wicked, Firmilian is denying his right to take it! He goes further:

> But the greatness of the error and the depth of the blindness of one who says that remission of sins can be granted in the synagogues of heretics, and does not abide on the foundation of the one Church which was once based by Christ upon the rock, may be perceived from this, that Christ said to Peter alone, "Whatsoever thou shalt bind on earth shall be bound in heaven, and whatsoever thou shalt loose on earth shall be loosed in heaven" [Matt. 16:19]. And again, in the Gospel, when Christ breathed on the apostles alone, saying, "Receive ye the Holy Spirit; whoever's sins ye remit, they are remitted to them, and whoever's sins ye retain, they are retained" [Jn. 20:22-23]. Therefore, the power of remitting sins was given to the apostles, and to the churches that they who were sent by Christ established, and to the bishops who succeeded to them by vicarious ordination.[340]

In a surprising twist, Firmilian uses the promises of Matthew 16 *against* Stephen! Like Cyprian, he understands all the bishops of the churches to wield Peter's authority; therefore, when Stephen acts against those bishops, he has left the foundation of the one Church.

Firmilian and Cyprian both emphatically denied the authority of Stephen to enforce his views on other churches. The claim that they did not shows that the writers are not familiar enough with their topic to write a book on it—or that they were dishonest. This is just the tip of the iceberg, however. Cyprian references Jesus's promises to Peter a lot, and the Roman Catholic apologists make a habit of misrepresenting him.

Misuse of Cyprian's Writings by Catholic Apologists

As I stated earlier, it is one thing to pull quotes out of context to bolster an argument. It is wrong, and even dishonest, but the sad fact is that authors do it all the time on all sorts of subjects. It is one step

---

[340] Firmilian, 256, Epistle 74 (Oxford 75), par. 16; brackets mine

Rome's Audacious Claim

worse, however, to cite Cyprian in defense of Papal Primacy while completely ignoring the Council of Carthage, where Cyprian led eighty-seven bishops in rejecting the right of Stephen of Rome to compel the obedience of other bishops. As bad as this is, Catholic apologists not only do it, but do it often!

- In *The Fathers Know Best*, Jimmy Akin mentions or cites Cyprian fifty-one times. He actually quotes the Seventh Council of Carthage in defense of baptismal regeneration twice, but he ignores the council's statement that no bishop can rule over another.[341]
- In his *Catholic Church Fathers*, Dave Armstrong cites or mentions Cyprian eighteen times, but he never mentions the Seventh Council of Carthage.
- In *The Case for Catholicism*, Trent Horn mentions or cites Cyprian forty-seven times, without mention of the Seventh Council of Carthage.
- In *Upon This Rock*, a 350-page book specifically defending Papal Primacy, Stephen Ray mentions or cites Cyprian seventy-five times, but he never mentions the Seventh Council of Carthage.

Upon This Rock leads us to the next problem with Catholic apologists and the way they deal with Cyprian. In it, Ray writes:

> There is good reason to believe that the controversy influenced Cyprian's full submission to Roman primacy. By 257, when Stephen was martyred, Cyprian appears to have accepted the Roman bishop's position on baptism.[342]

This is not true. *A History of the Councils of the Church* gives the true story.

> The persecution which soon afterwards broke out against the Christians under the Emperor Valerian, in 257, probably appeased the controversy. Pope Stephen died as a martyr during this persecution, in the month of August 257. His successor Xystus received from Dionysius the Great [bishop

---

[341] Akin, 2010, *The Fathers Know Best*, Kindle location 3875 and 4296-4303
[342] Ray, 2009, *Upon This Rock*, Kindle location 5391

Part VI | Chapter 20: Cyprian

of Alexandria], who had already acted as mediator in this controversy on the baptism of heretics, three letters in which the author earnestly endeavoured to effect a reconciliation; the Roman priest Philemon also received one from Dionysius. These attempts were crowned with success; for Pontius, Cyprian's deacon and biographer, calls Pope Xystus *bonus et pacificus sacerdos* [good and peaceful priest].[343]

Cyprian never agreed with Stephen on the rebaptism of heretics. Stephen was martyred with his opinion, and Cyprian was martyred with his. Hefele tells us that the letters of Dionysius resulted in peace between Stephen's successor and the church in Carthage.

We find confirmation of Hefele's version of the story in Eusebius's *Church History*. Eusebius quotes Dionysius letter to Xystus, then says, "So much in regard to the above-mentioned controversy."[344]

Trent Horn makes another unique, unjustified, and inexplicable assertion in his book *Why We're Catholic*. He tells us, "Some Church Fathers, such as St. Cyprian of Carthage, criticized the pope's decisions; but even Cyprian believed the pope could not lead the Church astray."[345]

Quite to the contrary, Cyprian attacked Stephen's position with such vehemence that he wondered whether Stephen would be acquitted on the day of judgment. He sent a copy of a letter from Stephen to Pompey, bishop of an unknown church, and says the following about it:

> We must consider, for the sake of the faith and the religion of the sacerdotal office which we discharge, whether the account can be satisfactory in the day of judgment for a priest of God who maintains, approves, and acquiesces in the baptism of blasphemers ... Does he give glory to God who communicates in the baptism of Marcion? ... Does he give glory to God, who, a friend of heretics and an enemy to Christians, thinks that the

---

[343] Hefele, 1871, *A History of the Councils of the Church*, p. 130; brackets mine
[344] Eusebius, 323, *Church History*, Bk. VI, ch. 5, par. 6
[345] Horn, 2017, *Why We're Catholic*, Kindle location 1326-1327

priests of God, who support the truth of God and the unity of the Church, are to be excommunicated?[346]

Cyprian questioned whether it would go well on the day of judgment for Stephen. It follows that if Stephen were able to convince all bishops to agree with him, then Cyprian would question the final judgment of all bishops. Surely that would qualify as leading the Church astray!

The final example of the way Catholic apologists mistreat Cyprian is also from Trent Horn. He quotes Cyprian as saying, "The throne of Peter ... from whom no error can flow." He gives "Epistle 54:14" as a reference.[347]

Epistle 54 is quoted above. It contains the paragraph in which Cyprian calls Rome the chief source of priestly unity and grants that their bishop's chair is the throne of Peter. If Cyprian also said that no error can flow from Rome, it would not establish that he believed in Papal Primacy, but it would sure be a major commendation for Rome!

But he did not. Trent Horn, or his unknown source, manufactured this reading.

The context of the letter is that Cyprian is appalled that people who lapsed during persecution would dare approach such a church as Rome to demand peace. He marvels that they "set sail ... to bear letters from schismatic and profane persons to the throne of Peter and to the chief church from which priestly unity takes its source." He wonders why they could be so brazen as not to consider "that these were the Romans, whose faith was praised in the preaching of the apostle, *to whom faithlessness could have no access.*"[348]

This reading makes much more sense. "Schismatic and profane persons" should definitely consider that "faithlessness could have no access" to the great church of Rome. Cyprian was saying that these lapsed and unrepentant Christians, who are thus "faithless," could not corrupt such a faithful church as Rome.

On the other hand, it makes little or no sense to say that these persons should have considered that no error could flow out of Rome.

---

[346] Cyprian, 256, Epistle 73 (Oxford 74), par. 8
[347] Horn, 2017, *Why We're Catholic*, Kindle location 1328
[348] Cyprian, 252, Epistle 54 (Oxford 59), par. 14; emphasis mine

The issue here is not what flows out of Rome, but error trying to flow into Rome. Cyprian is exclaiming, "They should have known better!"

Nonetheless, I looked for translations that might support Horn's rendering. I knew many of the Roman Catholic apologists get their quotes from *Faith of the Early Fathers*.[349] William Jurgens does cite the passage, but his quote is similar to *The Ante-Nicene Fathers* translation: "... among whom it is not possible for perfidy to have entrance."[350]

I also found a translation that used the Oxford numbering of Cyprian's letters. The phrase in question is in paragraph 18 of Epistle 59 there, but it is rendered almost exactly the same as *The Ante-Nicene Fathers* version: "... to whom faithlessness can have no access."[351]

I am not going to assume that Trent Horn invented "from whom no error could flow." He may have run across a pro-Roman-Catholic translation somewhere, but the translation he used is in error. Thus, we find one more way to misrepresent Cyprian: mistranslation.

These examples should suffice to show that Catholic apologists are routinely either uneducated or dishonest in regard to their handling of Cyprian. In the next chapter, we will find that handling his writings honestly reveals deep care for the flock of Christ and a depth of thought that is both enriching and inspiring.

Initial Conclusions and Summary

In discussing the relationship between Cyprian and Rome, and even more so between Cyprian and Stephen, the basic truths about Cyprian's opinions about Rome are:

- The Church is built on Peter, the Rock.
- All the bishops of the catholic churches together inherit the promises given to Peter. The Church is built upon them, and the unity of the Church is established in their oneness.
- Cyprian regards Rome as the source of the priestly unity of the bishops. He continues Irenaeus's and Tertullian's high regard for Rome.

---

[349] Jurgens, 1970, Liturgical Press
[350] Jurgens, 1970, Faith of the Early Fathers: Volume I, p. 232
[351] Archive.org, n.d., "Full Text of 'The Epistles of Cyprian,'" Epistle 59, par. 18

Rome's Audacious Claim

- Neither the church at Rome, the Roman bishop, nor any other bishop has authority over other bishops, nor can any bishop compel other bishops to obedience.

The Seventh Council of Carthage settles the matter of Cyprian's opinion of Rome's authority all by itself. It is important to establish, however, that all of Cyprian's references to Peter, to Matthew 16, and to the church in Rome fit comfortably into the outline of his opinions I have just given. It is important to look at every one of Cyprian's epistles that mentions Rome, Peter, or Matthew 16, as well as each of the twenty-one epistles that were exchanged between Cyprian and the church in Rome.

The next chapter is necessary to nail down Cyprian's opinion beyond contradiction. Looking at all those letters is a long process, however. Those who do not need convincing may want to skip to chapter 22.

Chapter 21: Cyprian's Epistles and Treatises

In this chapter we will examine all of Cyprian's letters that mention Rome, Peter, or Matthew 16. We will also cover the twenty-one letters exchanged between Cyprian and the church in Rome. The Oxford numbering of the epistles is in parentheses.

Epistle 2(8): The Roman Clergy to the Carthaginian Clergy, 250

The clergy—the elders and servants (deacons)—in Rome wrote this letter to the clergy in Carthage because they had heard "the blessed father Cyprian" had hidden himself in order to avoid Carthage losing their bishop to martyrdom like Rome did. They do not object to this, saying Cyprian "acted rightly," but they are concerned about both Rome and Carthage being without their leading shepherd. Fabian, the bishop of Rome, had been recently martyred.

The letter is full of exhortation to be good shepherds in the stead of the bishops, and the Roman clergy apply the exhortations to themselves as well as the Carthaginians. It is an important letter, because they quote and expound on John 21:15-17.

> To Simon, too, He speaks thus: "Do you love me?" He answered, "I do love you." He says to him, "Feed my sheep." We know that this saying arose out of the very circumstance of his withdrawal, and the rest of the disciples did likewise. We are unwilling, therefore, beloved brethren, that you should be found hirelings, but we desire you to be good shepherds, since you are aware that no slight danger threatens you if you do not exhort our brethren to stand steadfast in the faith. (par. 1-2)

The important point in this passage is that the Roman clergy apply the exhortations to shepherd the sheep to the Carthaginian clergy. They do not think this passage was uniquely for Peter. It was not only for "the rest of the disciples," but, in this letter, for the Carthaginian clergy as well.

Epistle 3(9): Cyprian to the Elders and Deacons in Rome, 250

In this letter, Cyprian acknowledges receiving a letter from "Crementius the subdeacon," saying that Bishop Fabian had been martyred. Cyprian refers to him as "an excellent man" and "my colleague." It is a short letter and contains nothing pertinent to Rome's Audacious Claim.

Epistle 14(20): Cyprian to the Elders and Deacons in Rome, 250

This is Cyprian's response to Rome's letter to his clergy (Epistle 2). Cyprian explains to the elders and deacons at Rome that his withdrawal did not mean he had forsaken his duties as shepherd. Though he had withdrawn at the demand of the people, he made sure that "neither counsel to the clergy, nor exhortation to the confessors, nor rebuke, when it was necessary, to the exiles, nor my appeals and persuasions to the whole brotherhood, that they should entreat the mercy of God were lacking" (par. 2).

In this epistle, we also learn about the huge problem both Cyprian and the Roman clergy were facing. Those who had lapsed during persecution were petitioning "the martyrs with importunate and excessive entreaties" (par. 2).

This is unusual wording because typically a martyr is someone who was put to death for the faith. Someone who is still alive is a "confessor."[352] Apparently Cyprian distinguished between those condemned to die and those who were beaten or tortured and then released. Those condemned to die must have been, in his eyes, already martyrs.

It got so bad that "some of the lapsed ... broke forth with a daring demand, as though they would endeavor by a violent effort to extort the peace promised them by the martyrs and confessors" (par. 3).

Cyprian tells the clergy of Rome that he has been writing many letters telling the martyrs and confessors not to give in to these people. He gives more details in later letters, but he adds a conclusion to this letter that is important to our subject.

> I had read your letter which you lately wrote hither to my clergy by Crementius the subdeacon, to the effect that assistance should be given to those who might, after their

---

[352] Department of Christian Education, n.d., "Martyrs and Confessors"

Part VI | Chapter 21: Cyprian's Epistles and Treatises

lapse, be seized with sickness, and might penitently desire communion; I judged it well to stand by your judgment, lest our proceedings, which ought to be united and to agree in all things, should in any respect be different. (par. 3)

Here we see that the clergy in Rome, who were without a bishop, wrote instructions to the elders and deacons in Carthage. Cyprian agreed to their instructions, but not because Rome had any special authority over Cyprian. We have already seen that Cyprian believed no bishop was subject to another. Instead, Cyprian "judged it well" and wanted to preserve unity. Later, Stephen's decision on the rebaptism of heretics would not be judged as well!

Epistle 22(27): Cyprian to the Elders and Deacons in Rome, 250

This letter explains the problem of the lapsed more fully. This is important because it gives a context to Cyprian's correspondence with Bishop Cornelius later.

A confessor named Lucian had handed out certificates in the name of a couple martyrs to many of the lapsed. The certificates granted them peace with the church. This meant that they could return to full communion. Cyprian speaks highly of Lucian's faith, but makes it clear to the Roman clergy that Lucian was lacking in the Lord's wisdom. We saw the result in Epistle 14: some of these lapsed were demanding readmittance with threats of violence (par. 2-3)!

Cyprian says that he has been writing letters trying to get this terrible situation under control. He also thanks the Roman clergy for a letter they sent saying the same things, which Cyprian says "much assisted me in my labor here" (par. 4).

Epistle 26(33): Cyprian to the Lapsed, 250

This letter was written to the lapsed to resolve the problems described in Epistle 22 (Oxford 27). In it, Cyprian applies Matthew 16:18-19 to himself (par. 1). We covered the passage in the last chapter. We need not address it here.

Epistle 28(35): Cyprian to the Elders and Deacons in Rome, 250

In this letter Cyprian gives a report to the Roman clergy, who still do not have a bishop installed. The reason he gives for the report is not that he is under Rome's supervision, but that "our common love" and

the importance of the situation "demand ... that I should keep back from your knowledge nothing of those matters which are transacted among us" (par. 1). It is a very short letter, but Cyprian says he attached letters from the lapsed saying that Paulus, through Lucian, had already given them peace and a letter from Cyprian in response. The attached letter from Cyprian was probably Epistle 26.

Epistle 29(36): The Elders and Deacons of Rome to Cyprian, 250

The elders and deacons of Rome addressed this letter to "Father Cyprian." They expressed their broken hearts over the situation with the lapsed, then said Cyprian moderated their pain by the way he was dealing with the issue (par. 1). Finally, they thanked him for the warnings and let him know they were up-to-date on what was happening (par. 4).

One of their concluding statements is pertinent to this book: "It becomes us all to watch for the body of the whole Church, whose members are scattered through every various province" (par. 4). Though John 21:15-17 is not mentioned, as it is in Epistle 2, it is clear the Roman clergy, in the year 250, believed that the shepherding assigned to Peter was the duty of all the shepherds of the Church.

Epistle 30 (30): The Roman Elders and Deacons to Cyprian, 250

This letter, too, is addressed to "Father Cyprian." There is a passage in this letter addressing Cyprian as "brother Cyprian" rather than "father."

> Those are worthy of double praise, who, knowing that they owe their conscience to God alone as the judge, yet desire that their doings should be approved also by their brethren themselves. It is no wonder, brother Cyprian, that you should do this, who, with your usual modesty and inborn industry, have wished that we should be found not so much judges of, as sharers in, your counsels, so that we might find praise with you in your doings while we approve them; and might be able to be fellow-heirs with you in your good counsels, because we entirely accord with them. (par. 1)

Part VI | Chapter 21: Cyprian's Epistles and Treatises

Here the Roman elders and deacons call Cyprian "brother" rather than "father," though they began the letter calling him "father." "Father" was apparently not a required title for bishops at that time.

The Roman clergy then tell Cyprian that he is worthy of double praise because he has sought approval from them, even though only God is his judge. This is important. Remember that Irenaeus attributed "preeminent authority" to the church in Rome, not to the bishop of Rome. This authority was based on adherence to the truth of the apostolic teaching. It was much like a citing the famed bishop of Durham, N. T. Wright, as an "authority" on the New Testament. Rome had "preeminent authority" to declare what was true.

Here we see that the Roman clergy agrees. Only God is Cyprian's judge, not the church in Rome.

In paragraph 2, we find one of the more interesting passages in the letters of Cyprian. It is important specifically because it came from the Roman clergy:

> For what is there either in peace so suitable, or in a war of persecution so necessary, as to maintain the due severity of the divine rigor? Which he who resists, will of necessity wander in the unsteady course of affairs, and will be tossed hither and thither by the various and uncertain storms of things; and the helm of counsel being, as it were, wrenched from his hands, he will drive the ship of the Church's safety among the rocks.

There is more to this passage, but we need to take note of what they said. The Roman clergy said that it is a good thing to hold the helm of leadership ("counsel") steady in time of peace, but absolutely necessary in persecution. Otherwise, they said, if a leader does not follow through on his duties in such a time, "he will drive the ship of the Church's safety among the rocks."

The Roman clergy were not simply hanging on, believing that they were safe because the gates of Hades could not prevail against the Church (Matt. 16:18).[353] Instead, they declared that it is the duty of

---

[353] The claim that the Roman Catholic Church can never fall away is made repeatedly by Roman Catholic apologists. One example is on the apologetic site Catholic.com (Catholic Answers, 2018, "Papal Infallibility," sec. "Based on Christ's Mandate," par. 1).

Rome's Audacious Claim

both Cyprian and themselves to hold tight to the helm in times of trouble so that the Church would not suffer shipwreck.

A couple sentences later, they continue with an important statement concerning Rome's special position among the churches of the empire. This passage will be very important later when we discuss the centuries when the bishop of Rome did have supreme authority in the West and the occasional acknowledgment of it in the Eastern Roman Empire.

> Nor is it now but lately that this counsel has been considered by us, nor have these sudden appliances against the wicked but recently occurred to us; but this is read of among us as the ancient severity, the ancient faith, the ancient discipline, since the apostle would not have published such praise concerning us, when he said "that your faith is spoken of throughout the whole world" [Rom.1:8] unless already from there that vigor had borrowed the roots of faith from those times; from which praise and glory it is a very great crime to have become degenerate. (par. 2, brackets mine)

The elders and deacons of Rome told Cyprian that they did not start thinking about their responsibility until recently. They knew that the apostle Paul, in Romans 1:8, had told them "your faith is spoken of throughout the whole world." They were not resting on their laurels or claiming they could not fall, but they were laying hold of the vigor of their ancestry. Then they made a very pertinent concession: If they were to lose that praise and glory, it would be a "very great crime."

The Roman Catholic Church today believes that no matter how corrupt a pope or their church might have been or might become, the pope's succession from Peter and his inheritance of his authority remain unchanged.[354] The Roman clergy of the third century, however, thought it was a very great crime to fall from the praise and glory that marked the Roman church in those early centuries. It seems safe to conclude from this that they would not agree that their authority would remain unchanged if they were to become corrupt.

---

[354] e.g., Catholic Answers, 2018, "Papal Infallibility," sec. "Based on Christ's Mandate," par. 1

Part VI | Chapter 21: Cyprian's Epistles and Treatises

In disagreement with the opinions of their more modern descendants, the Roman clergy of the year 250 have more to say about this "very great crime."

> For it is less disgrace never to have attained to the heraldry of praise, than to have fallen from the height of praise; it is a smaller crime not to have been honored with a good testimony, than to have lost the honor of good testimonies; it is less discredit to have lain without the announcement of virtues, ignoble without praise, than, disinherited of the faith, to have lost our proper praises. For those things which are proclaimed to the glory of anyone, unless they are maintained by anxious and careful pains, swell up into the odium of the greatest crime. (par. 2)

It is apparent the elders in Rome in 250 rejected the idea that a church with the "odium" of the greatest crime—and even more so a church that is "disinherited of the faith"—could have authority over other churches. They therefore promise to give "anxious and careful pains" to maintain their holiness and virtue.

It would be a joy to expound on the rest of this Roman epistle. It is full of brotherly cooperation and deep respect for Cyprian, and it also discusses the treatment of the lapsed with attention both to mercy and the "medicine" of repentance. The heart of true shepherds shines through in this brilliant letter.

Unfortunately, I must continue on with my purpose: to expound upon, expose, and refute Rome's Audacious Claim. I will, however, pause to press home a truth to Protestants—and, more precisely, my evangelical brethren—from these praiseworthy third-century Roman elders. It is irrelevant to this book, but deeply relevant to every one of our lives. They wrote, "The whole mystery of faith is understood to be contained in the confession of the name of Christ" (par. 3).

This is no small thing, but is an acknowledgment of what was said repeatedly by Origen and others: Peter was the rock because he was the first to confess Jesus as the Christ. Thus, as modern Rome acknowledges,[355] his confession is also the rock on which Jesus builds his Church. It is a glaring lack in many Protestant churches that we are

---

[355] *Catechism of the Catholic Church*, par. 424

not following Jesus's plan to build the Church on the confession that Jesus is the Christ. Instead, we are trying to build on the confession that Jesus died for our sins.

As important as the atonement is, Jesus did not say he would build the church on the confession that he died for our sins. He said he would build it on the confession that he is the Christ, the Son of the living God (Matt. 16:16-18). In our rush to refute anything attached to the papacy, we have neglected this passage to our peril.

Let me drive this point home with a shocking fact. The only record we have of the apostles' preaching to the lost is the book of Acts. Although the atonement is discussed in almost every letter of the New Testament, the apostles never told a lost person that Jesus died for their sins. They told them that Jesus forgives sins, but they never said Jesus provided that mercy on the cross. The atonement was central to their letters to Christians, but in proclamations to the lost in the Acts of the Apostles, there is nary a word. Instead, you will find them emphasizing the resurrection to establish that Jesus is Lord, Christ, Son of God, and judge of the living and the dead.[356]

If you will excuse that important digression, we will now return to Cyprian's epistles.

Epistle 39(43): Cyprian to the People of Carthage, 251

In this letter, Cyprian is reporting to his people, still from his hiding place, that certain elders were trying to rise up against him again. From the beginning of his episcopate, there was opposition to his leadership, because, though not a young man, he was a relatively new Christian. Now, while he was away, certain of the elders, "the faction of Felicissimus," were clamoring against him, trying to have him removed from authority. Their goal was to restore the lapsed to the communion of the church without the time of penance Cyprian was requiring.

In Cyprian's eyes, Felicissimus and his faction were breaking the unity of the church, and thus they had placed themselves outside its protection. He complains, "They are now offering peace who do not have peace themselves; they are promising to bring back and recall the

---

[356] You can verify this by reading the book of Acts; or see Pavao, 2013, *The Apostles Gospel*.

lapsed into the church, who themselves have departed from the church" (par. 5).

Then he writes, "There is one God, Christ is one, and there is one Church and one chair founded upon the rock by the Word of the Lord" (par. 5).

Here "founded upon the rock" is a certain reference to Peter. Cyprian often called Peter the rock because Cyprian appeals so often to Matthew 16:18. Rev. Ernest Wallis, the translator of Cyprian's letters in *The Ante-Nicene Fathers* series, must agree; he would have capitalized "rock" if he thought it referred to Jesus.

This passage is important because it is Cyprian's authority that is being challenged. The "chair" that is being threatened is his own, yet he refers to it as the "one chair" founded upon the rock of Peter. He can do this because, in his ecclesiology, all bishops sit upon the one chair, himself every bit as much as the bishop of Rome.

Epistle 40(44): Cyprian to Cornelius, Bishop of Rome, 251

This is the first letter to Cornelius, the new bishop of Rome, whom he addresses as "his brother." Cyprian told him that he had heard of the "wickedness of an unlawful ordination" of Novatian, and he gives Cornelius a full explanation of his support.

> I and several of my colleagues ... were awaiting the arrival of our colleagues Caldonius and Fortunatus, whom we had lately sent to you as ambassadors, and to our fellow-bishops, who were present at your ordination, in order that, when they came and reported the truth of the matter, the wickedness of the adverse party might be quelled through them by greater authority and manifest proof. But there came, in addition, Pompeius and Stephanus, our colleagues, who themselves also ... put forward manifest proofs ... so that it was not even necessary that those who had come, as sent by Novatian, should be heard any further. And when in our solemn assembly they burst in with unwarranted abuse and turbulent clamor, demanding that the accusations, which they said that they brought and would prove, should be publicly investigated by us and by the people, we said that it was not consistent with our gravity to suffer the honor of our colleague, who had already been chosen and ordained and approved by the

laudable sentence of many, to be called into question any further by the abusive voice of rivals. (par. 1)

The following comment by Cyprian reveals the attitude of the Church in its days of unity in regard to the appointment of bishops.

> Nor shall we cease to command them to lay aside their pernicious dissensions and disputes, to be aware that it is an impiety to forsake their Mother [the Church], and to acknowledge and understand that when a bishop is once made and approved by the testimony and judgment of his colleagues and the people, another can by no means be appointed. (par. 2, brackets mine)

Epistle 41(45): Cyprian to Cornelius, 251

This letter is the official notice to Cornelius that Cyprian and the church in Carthage accepted his ordination. Cyprian says he has sent letters to the bishops of surrounding churches asking them to send similar letters to Cornelius. He assures Cornelius that those bishops already support him and that he has notified them of his support for Cornelius against Novatian (par. 1-2).

He writes that Novatian's party has "rejected the bosom and embrace of its root and mother" (par. 1). "Mother" is always a reference to the Church. The idea is that God is our Father and the Church is our mother. Galatians 4:26 tells us that the heavenly Jerusalem is the mother of us all. As the bride of Christ, heavenly Jerusalem is rightly associated with the Church (Rev. 21:2). This phrase, "root and mother," will matter more when we get to Epistle 44.

In paragraph 3, Cyprian writes:

> For this, my brother, we especially labor for, and we ought to labor for: to be careful to maintain as much as we can the unity delivered by the Lord and through his apostles to us his successors.

Note that Cyprian chooses the words "us his successors," not "you his successor."

In paragraph 4, Cyprian tells Cornelius that "he will do better" if Cornelius has Cyprian's recent letters read in the church along with the letters of Caldonius and Fortunatus. Now, these are not just any letters.

Part VI | Chapter 21: Cyprian's Epistles and Treatises

It would be possible to argue that Cyprian felt free to give instruction like this to Cornelius because these letters supported his ordination. As we will see, though, Cyprian feels free to give strong instruction in his letters to all three Roman bishops to whom he wrote.

Epistle 42(47): Cyprian to Cornelius, 251

This third letter to Cornelius is short. Cyprian felt compelled to write to the confessors (those imprisoned for the faith) in Rome who had been deceived by Novatian, exhorting them to return to the church. He sent the letters to Cornelius because he was writing to people in Rome. A subdeacon carried them to Cornelius, and Cyprian says that subdeacon will deliver them if Cornelius approves.

Cyprian requested approval for these letters from Cornelius because they were sent to members of Cornelius's church in Rome.

Epistle 43(46): Cyprian to Maximus and Nicostratus and Other Confessors, 251

This is the letter Cyprian asked Cornelius if he could send. We get a feel for what matters to Cyprian in this plea:

> For as our unanimity and concord ought by no means to be divided, and because we cannot forsake the Church and go outside her to come to you [confessors], we beg and entreat you with what exhortations we can, rather to return to the Church your Mother, and to our brotherhood. (par. 1)

Cyprian's great care is unity. Though he had such a fierce disagreement with Stephen over the baptism of heretics and used such strong words in the conflict, he never wanted to cut off or excommunicate Stephen. It is joining with Novatian, who split the Church of Jesus Christ, that cut men off from God and his Church. Cyprian did not try to expel such, because they had already expelled themselves. Earlier in the letter he writes:

> The intolerable grief of a smitten, almost prostrate, spirit seizes me, when I find that you there, contrary to ecclesiastical order, contrary to evangelical law, and contrary to the unity of the catholic institution, had consented that another bishop should be made. That is what is neither right nor allowable to be done; that another church should be set up; that Christ's

members should be torn asunder; that the one mind and body of the Lord's flock should be lacerated by a divided jealousy.

There is no missing Cyprian's immense care about the unity of the Church.

Epistle 44(48): Cyprian to Cornelius, 251

In this epistle, Cyprian explains to Cornelius that for a short time after his ordination, Carthage addressed letters to the elders and deacons in Rome rather than to Cornelius because Carthage was still looking into the contested ordination. He then assures Cornelius that everyone around Carthage has fully acknowledged and defends his ordination.

In this letter, Cyprian writes that everyone that Carthage sends to Rome is exhorted to acknowledge "the root and matrix [lit. womb] of the catholic Church" (par. 3, brackets mine). Roman Catholic apologists, of course, interpret this phrase to mean the pope.[357] We have seen, however, that Cyprian believes the bishops are the root of Catholic unity, not just one bishop.

Further, this wording is not new to us. Cyprian referred to Novatian's rejection of his "root and mother" in Epistle 41 (par. 1). If "root and mother" is a reference to the whole Church, "root and womb" is not different.

Epistle 45(49): Cornelius to Cyprian, 251

Here we find out that Cyprian's letter to the confessors in Rome worked (Epistle 43)! Not only did the confessors return to the church, but Maximus, one of those specifically addressed, had been restored to his position as elder.

There is an interesting contrast in this letter with Epistle 41. In Epistle 41, Cyprian tells Cornelius, "You will do better, brother, if you will also bid copies of the letters I sent to you ... to be read for the common satisfaction ... declaring your ordination" (par. 4). In this letter, Cornelius tells Cyprian, "I think, brother, that you ought to send these letters also to the other churches, that all may know that the craft ... of this schismatic and heretic are from day to day being reduced to

---

[357] Horn, 2017, *Why We're Catholic*, Kindle location 1790; Ray, 2009, *Upon This Rock*, Kindle location 5403

nothing" (par. 3). This seems like an appeal from Cornelius. Cyprian, though he had only been bishop for two years, writes to Cornelius like a father would, or at least like a big brother. He has no qualms about giving direction to the bishop of Rome.

Epistle 46(51): Cyprian to Cornelius, 251
Though I have not been mentioning it, Cyprian and Cornelius refer to one another as "brother" throughout these epistles. In this one, Cyprian rejoices that the confessors returned.

Epistle 47(1): Cornelius to Cyprian, 251
Here Cornelius warns Cyprian that Nicostratus, one of the confessors addressed in Epistle 43, has left the church. Cornelius says he embezzled funds from both his Roman patroness and from the church.

This epistle also refers to Novatus, a cohort of Novatian who is sometimes confused with him. Cyprian always refers to Novatian as "Novatian" and not "Novatus." Cyprian wrote in Latin. Greek-speaking authors like Eusebius call him "Novatus."[358]

Epistle 48(52): Cyprian to Cornelius, 251
In this letter, Cyprian acknowledges the crimes of Novatus described to him by Cornelius and expands on them. He was a problem in Carthage as well as in Rome. Novatian and Novatus are mentioned together in the first sentence. They are two men, not one.

Cyprian writes in this letter that "Rome from her greatness plainly ought to take precedence of Carthage" (par. 2). Though Roman Catholic apologists love to latch onto phrases like this, we have seen that Rome's second- and third-century greatness has nothing to do with Jesus's promise to Peter, but with their solid faith and testimony. Their foundation in Peter and Paul is part of their greatness, but that is because of their continuation of the apostles' faith, love, and holiness. Their greatness was not based on a promise to Peter that applied no matter how they or their bishop behaved.

---

[358] Eusebius, 323, *Church History*, Bk. 6, ch. 48

Rome's Audacious Claim

As the Roman elders said themselves, they would lose their greatness if they did not continue in it, and such a loss would be "the greatest crime."[359]

Epistle 51(55): Cyprian to Antonianus, 252

This is an important epistle, both because it again reveals the heart of Cyprian for the unity of the Church, and because Cyprian describes the seat of the Roman bishop as being the seat of Peter. He writes:

> Moreover, Cornelius was made bishop by the judgment of God and of His Christ, by the testimony of almost all the clergy, by the suffrage [vote or affirmation] of the people who were then present, and by the assembly of ancient priests and good men, when no one had been made so before him; when the place of Fabian, that is, when the place of Peter and the degree of the sacerdotal throne was vacant. (par. 8, brackets mine)

Cyprian refers to the chair of Peter only twice (here and in Epistle 54, par. 14). The wording here is "place of Peter," but he follows it by mentioning the priestly throne. ("Sacerdotal" means "priestly," and "throne" and "chair" both represent a bishop's authority.) In both cases, he is referring to the office of bishop in Rome. The "place of Peter" was empty because there was no bishop until there was a break in the persecution.

Cyprian contrasts Cornelius's ordination, which was to the empty "chair of Peter," to Novatian's ordination, which was schismatic because the office of bishop was already filled in Rome. This is the primary issue that concerned Cyprian.

In this book, however, we have a different concern. We must determine whether the bishop of Rome had "full, supreme, and universal power over the whole Church" in Cyprian's time. If Cornelius, the bishop of Rome, filled the "chair of Peter," does that mean he received all the promises of Peter?

Roman Catholic apologists answer this with "yes." They assume that any reference to the authority of Peter is a reference to the

---

[359] "Epistles of Cyprian," 250, Epistle 30 (Oxford 30), par. 2

Part VI | Chapter 21: Cyprian's Epistles and Treatises

authority of the pope. As mentioned earlier, James White refers to this as the "Peter Syndrome."[360]

We will consider this reference to Peter logically. Cyprian agrees Cornelius sat on the throne of Peter, but Cyprian was also sure that no bishop could rule over another.[361]

Cyprian, along with all the bishops of the mid-third century, believed that the bishop of Rome's succession was from Peter. They did not believe that Peter's successor in Rome inherited "full, supreme, and universal power over the whole Church." Cyprian's letters, along with the Seventh Council of Carthage, are perhaps the surest evidence they did not.

The episcopate is "one and undivided," each bishop having "part ... of the whole,"[362] All the bishops hold the "one chair" (Epistle 39, par. 5), but each apostolic church was founded by a specific apostle. The bishop of Alexandria, in Cyprian's eyes, was sitting in the "chair of Mark" because Mark founded the church in Alexandria.[363] The bishops in India, or at least one of them, were sitting on the chair of Thomas because he founded churches there.[364] Ironically, the bishop of Antioch also sat on the chair of Peter, because Eusebius tells us it was Peter who appointed Evaristus as the first bishop there.[365]

Cyprian confirms his opinion at the end of this letter. "There is one Church, divided by Christ throughout the whole world into many members, and also one episcopate diffused through a harmonious multitude of many bishops" (par. 24).

Cyprian did not forget or renounce his belief in one episcopate when he calls Rome the chair of Peter. In doing so, though, he and those who followed seem to forget Paul was co-founder of the church in Rome.

Irenaeus based the unity of the Church on one truth, given by the apostles and faithfully preserved by the bishops and elders of all the churches. This made Paul important in the founding of Rome. Cyprian and his contemporaries shift this idea, ascribing unity to the bishops

---

[360] 2013, "The Great Debate III," 1:45:05-1:46:00
[361] "Seventh Council of Carthage," 256, introduction
[362] Cyprian, 251, "On the Unity of the Church," par. 5
[363] Eusebius, 323, *Church History*, Bk. II, ch. 16, par. 1
[364] Eusebius, *Church History*, Bk. III, ch. 1, par. 1
[365] Eusebius, *Church History*, Bk. III, ch. 36, par. 2

themselves as descendants of Peter. This makes it more important that the bishop of Rome sits in the chair of Peter than that he sits in the seat of Paul. As a result, by Cyprian's time, Paul becomes almost irrelevant to Rome's glory and authority.

Epistle 53(57): Cyprian and Forty Others to Cornelius, c. 253

Cyprian includes forty bishops by name as addressing Cornelius in this letter. He begins by acknowledging that Carthage and Rome had agreed together that those who lapsed needed a "long and full repentance" (par. 1). Now, though, they were seeing omens of a new persecution. Because of this, the bishops in Africa wanted to shorten the time of repentance and admit the lapsed back into the churches to strengthen them for the new persecution.

Cyprian writes, "He cannot be fitted for martyrdom who is not armed for the contest by the Church, and his spirit is deficient which the Eucharist received does not raise and stimulate" (par. 4).

What is important about Cyprian's long argument is the various phrases he uses to make his point:
- "Neither is peace, therefore, to be denied to those who are about to endure martyrdom" (par. 3).
- "Nor let anyone say ..." (par. 4).
- "We have determined by the suggestion of the Holy Spirit and the admonition of the Lord ... to gather within the camp the soldiers of Christ" (par. 5).

These strong assertions are ameliorated by Cyprian's closing words. "And this, we trust, will please you in contemplation of the paternal mercy" and "We ... have laid before you what was on our own mind" (par. 5).

Cyprian is not demanding that Cornelius agree with him and the 40 other bishops, but neither is he requesting permission. He is beginning a discussion as a fellow bishop.

Epistle 54(59): Cyprian to Cornelius, 252

Here Cyprian adds something to his statement that Rome is the chair of Peter (Epistle 51, par. 8). It is also "the chief church from which priestly unity takes its source" (par. 14).

This, too, fits nicely into Cyprian's idea that all bishops have received one succession from Peter and that each is part of the one

episcopate. If Peter is the source of unity as Cyprian argues in "On the Unity of the Church" (par. 4), then the church he led is also the chief source for that unity.

This letter also provides an interesting look at Cyprian's relationship with Cornelius. Cyprian brings up the importance of Rome because Cornelius was facing the same threats from the lapsed, demanding peace, that Cyprian was facing in Carthage. Cyprian, though, worried that Cornelius was being frightened by the threats. He writes:

> I was considerably surprised at observing that you were in some degree disturbed by the threats and terrors of those who had come, when, according to what you wrote, they had attacked and threatened you with the greatest desperation. (par. 2)

The threat was that they would publicly read the letters that confessors had given them readmitting them to the church, and that they would then embarrass Cornelius publicly. Cyprian tells Cornelius that if bishops begin dreading the threats of the unrighteous, then "there is an end to the vigor of the episcopacy, and to the sublime and divine power of governing the Church" (par. 2).

Throughout this letter, Cyprian instructs Cornelius, calling him "dear brother," but also giving firm warnings and instructions about the importance of a bishop leading courageously. The references to Rome in paragraph 14 are to remind Cornelius not to put up with those threats.

Cyprian then uses himself as an example. At the end of paragraph 16, he talks about how open he is to those seeking readmittance so that "I almost sin myself in remitting sins more than I ought." Then he adds, but if anyone comes to him with threats, "against such the church of the Lord stands closed" (par. 17).

By the time Cyprian gets to the end of the letter, he comes just short of commanding Cornelius to make sure the letter is read to everyone:

> And although I know, dearest brother, from the mutual love which we owe and manifest one towards another, that you always read my letters to the very distinguished clergy who preside with you there, and to your very holy and large

congregation, yet now I both warn and ask you to do by my request what at other times you do of your own accord and courtesy. (par. 20)

As I said earlier, Cyprian's letters comfort and cajole the three Roman bishops to which he wrote like a more experienced older brother. There is tender care and instruction in them. His first letter to Stephen is like this, and he must have been shocked to find Stephen threatening to excommunicate him for rebaptizing Novatian converts.

This brings us to some important statements in this letter we should address.

In paragraph 5, Cyprian writes, "Nor do [those who threaten] consider that there is one person for the time priest in the church and for the time judge in the stead of Christ."[366]

What a triumph this would be for Rome's Audacious Claim if this referred to Rome alone! But it does not. Let us look at the rest of the letter.

Cyprian begins by expressing concern that Cornelius is "to some degree disturbed." He then says if bishops are timid, it will "end ... the vigor of the episcopacy" (par. 2).

He then tells Cornelius that no matter where the threat to "a bishop" comes from, he is made glorious by the threats. In the next sentence, he says, "we ought not to consider the mere threats...." In all this, he is speaking of bishops in general (par. 2).

In paragraph 5, he is still speaking generally, mentioning "priestly authority" and those who are "enemies of the priests." Only then, and in this context, does he write:

> For neither have heresies arisen, nor have schisms originated, from any other source than from this, that God's priest is not obeyed; nor do they consider that there is one person for the time priest in the church, and for the time judge in the stead of Christ; whom, if, according to divine teaching, the whole fraternity should obey, no one would stir up anything against the college of priests; no one, after the divine judgment, after the suffrage of the people, after the consent of the co-bishops,

---

[366] Brackets mine

would make himself a judge, not now of the bishop, but of God. (par. 5)

Cyprian continues to mention the "college of priests." His concern is specifically Rome, because Cornelius is showing signs of wavering before the threats of the lapsed. Cyprian reminds him that once a bishop has the consent of his co-bishops, he is established and has authority. Novatian had no right to judge him once he was confirmed in his seat.

I would remind you here that we are talking about Cyprian's view of the authority of a bishop. I am not asking my readers to agree that his view is correct. For the sake of this book, we need to know his view. We already know what his view of the Roman bishop's authority is; he stated it directly in the Seventh Council of Carthage. In these letters, we are establishing that there is nothing in his other writings that contradicts that view.

There is one more passage to acknowledge, found in paragraph 7. Cyprian says, "Peter, upon whom by the same Lord the Church had been built, speaking one for all, and answering with the voice of the Church, says …," and then he cites John 6:68-69. Peter, speaking with the voice of the Church, says only Jesus has the words of life.

Epistle 56(60): Cyprian to Cornelius, 252

We find in this letter that Cornelius has been arrested. Cyprian praises Cornelius that he has become a confessor, leading the church by his bravery and strengthening them through his example. Cornelius sealed his testimony in glorious martyrdom, so the next letter is to a new bishop.

Epistle 57(61): Cyprian to Lucius, 252

Lucius had been arrested and taken away from home after his election (par. 4). This letter celebrates his return with praise and welcome. Interestingly, Cyprian celebrates the fact that Lucius now has the possibility of the victory of martyrdom before the eyes of the church (par. 4). He was martyred within a few months, and there are no more letters to Lucius.

Rome's Audacious Claim

Epistle 66/68: Cyprian to Stephen, 254

As I have said, Cyprian wrote his letters to Cornelius, Lucius, and Stephen in the tone of an older brother. He is giving guidance to a newer bishop. He addresses them as "brother," not "father." In this case, though, he is bristling a bit at a problem, and his older brother tone contains some chiding.

Rome was the nearest apostolic church for North Africa and Gaul (modern France). In this letter, Cyprian appeals to Rome for the dismissal of a bishop in Arles, Gaul. His name was Marcianus, and he had joined the Novatian faction (par. 1).

Cyprian exhorts Stephen with strong words to remove him, saying, "This matter, dearest brother, it is our business to advise for and aid in," (par. 1) and, "It behooves you to write a very copious letter to our fellow-bishops" (par. 2). I was even surprised to find him resorting to the passive aggressive, "He does not yet seem to be excommunicated by us" (par. 2).

It is important to note that although Cyprian regarded it as Stephen's duty to write the letter, the matter was "our business" (par. 1). In Cyprian's eyes, the bishops of the churches were one episcopacy. He reminds Stephen, "Although we are many shepherds, yet we feed one flock" (par. 4).

It is this epistle that let me see how blinding bias can be. John Chapman was a Catholic monk and historian who wrote a book called *Studies on the Early Papacy*.[367] Chapman was thoroughly puzzled as to how Cyprian could recommend the defrocking of Marcianus for disagreeing with Stephen about repentance for the lapsed, but he objected vehemently when Stephen tried to excommunicate him for rebaptizing the Novatians.

> Why should not Marcianus of Arles be as free as Faustinus of Lyons to act as he pleased about the lapsed? There is no answer except that Cyprian happened to agree with Stephen about the lapsed and to disagree with him about baptism.[368]

Faustinus of Lyons is the one who reported to both Cyprian and Stephen that Marcianus had "associated himself with Novatian and has

---

[367] 1928, Ex Fontibus Co.
[368] Chapman, 1928, *Studies on the Early Papacy*, pp. 43-44

Part VI | Chapter 21: Cyprian's Epistles and Treatises

departed from the unity of the Catholic Church" (Epistle 66, par. 2). Chapman completely misses this. He cannot see that Marcianus left the church by joining the Novatians! All he can see is a disagreement with "Pope" Stephen over readmitting the lapsed.

As a result, Chapman cannot understand why Cyprian exhorted Stephen to defrock Marcianus while Cyprian disagreed with Stephen as well. Chapman can see no way out of this, and he repeats his bewilderment several times throughout his discussion of this letter. Finally, he concludes that Cyprian's thought absolutely cannot be systematized.[369]

I am just at bewildered that Chapman could not understand the issue. Marcianus did not just disagree with Stephen—he joined the Novatians! In Cyprian's eyes, he left the Church. He was a heretic! It had nothing to do with disagreeing with Stephen and everything to do with leaving the Church.

Cyprian's concern throughout all his writings was unity. He got in a fierce battle with Stephen over the rebaptism of heretics, but the problem was not the disagreement. The problem was that Stephen tried to excommunicate churches for disagreeing. That is what infuriated Cyprian.

Cyprian's letter clearly states that this is the issue. He writes, "Novatian himself, whom [Marcianus] follows, has formerly been excommunicated and judged as an enemy to the Church" (par. 2). It is not that Marcianus did not want to allow repentance for the lapsed; he had joined an excommunicated enemy of the Church!

Cyprian did not want Marcianus to submit to Stephen. He wanted Marcianus to submit to the one episcopate of all bishops that had excommunicated Novatian. In fact, he must have wondered whether Stephen, who had attacked the unity of the church by his excommunications, ought to face ecclesiastical discipline himself!

In the next letter, we see that Cyprian was indeed wrestling with what to do with Stephen, and he decided to go around Stephen in dealing with the issues in Spain.

---

[369] Chapman, 1928, *Studies on the Early Papacy*, pp. 43-47

Epistle 67(67): Cyprian and Thirty-Six Others to the Clergy and People in Spain, 257

This is a remarkable letter with much to interest Protestants. Clergy and non-clergy from at least three churches had written to Cyprian asking about two bishops, Basilides and Martial, who had purchased a certificate saying they had sacrificed to idols in order to avoid persecution. They had not actually sacrificed to idols, but they had purchased a certificate saying they did. Basilides was now back in office, and the clergy in Spain were not sure what to do about that.

Not just Cyprian, but he and thirty-six others responded to this letter. The reason for this is that they could not get Stephen's support because of their conflict with him. Cyprian said Basilides, who had resigned his post in repentance (par. 6), had "deceived Stephen our colleague" and obtained reinstatement by lies rather than waiting out his time of penance (par. 5). Cyprian absolves Stephen of crime by saying that the one "surprised by fraud" is "not so much to be blamed" as the fraudulent one. On the other hand, "not so much" indicates Cyprian wanted to attribute some fault to Stephen. He points out that Stephen was tricked by "heedlessness" (par. 5). He was not letting the bishop of Rome off the hook entirely.

Besides addressing the conflict with Stephen, this letter brings up another point having to do with the Roman Catholic claim that their bishop is shepherd of the whole Church. What should Christians do when the bishop is corrupt?

Cyprian begins the letter by telling the Spanish churches that "the divine precepts" speak on this, so North African counsel is unnecessary (par. 1). If Scripture speaks on the matter of corrupt bishops, it trumps all other advice.

He then covers several Old Testament passages regarding the purity of priests. He moves from there to Jesus's rejection of the traditions of men in Mark 7 and the cured blind man's statement in John 9:31 that God does not hear sinners (par. 2). With that he concludes that only those God will hear should be chosen for the priesthood. He also warns the church there that they cannot "be free from the contagion of sin while communicating [taking communion] with a priest who is a sinner" (par. 3, brackets mine).

He continues, giving the example of Korah, Dathan, and Abiram. In Numbers 16:26, the congregation is told to separate themselves

Part VI | Chapter 21: Cyprian's Epistles and Treatises

from the tents of those sinful men—because they are about to be swallowed up by the earth! He concludes that "a people obedient to the Lord's precepts ... ought to separate themselves from a sinful prelate and not to associate with the sacrifices of a sacrilegious priest."[370] The reason for this? "They themselves have the power either of choosing worthy priests or of rejecting unworthy ones" (par. 3).

These are strong words, especially since he is writing about a bishop that was reinstated by the bishop of Rome! Though we have no way of knowing from this letter, it would be easy to conclude that Cyprian would have joined Luther, Zwingli, Calvin, and the Anabaptists in leaving the corrupt Roman Catholic hierarchy of the late medieval period. A man who would not eat the bread of communion with a "sinful prelate" might easily find himself without a church in the early 1500s.

> Papal morals, after a temporary improvement, became worse than ever during the years 1492 to 1521.... The writings of contemporary scholars, preachers and satirists are full of complaints and exposures of the ignorance, vulgarity and immorality of priests and monks. Simony and nepotism were shamefully practiced. Celibacy was a foul fountain of unchastity and uncleanness. The bishoprics were monopolized by the youngest sons of princes and nobles without regard to qualification. Geiler of Kaisersberg, a stern preacher of moral reform at Strassburg (d. 1510), charges all Germany with promoting ignorant and worldly men to the chief dignities, simply on account of their high connections.[371]

It is ironic that Cyprian can be cited in defense of the Protestant Reformation. He adds that, "Evil men ... claim ... the episcopate in vain, since it is evident that men of that kind may neither rule over the church of Christ, nor ought to offer sacrifices to God" (par. 6).

We cannot miss, however, that the Protestant Reformation would have broken Cyprian's heart. He fought and battled on behalf of the one Church and its unity. I cannot imagine the despair he might have

---

[370] "Sacrifices" is a reference to the Eucharist (communion), which was considered an offering to God.
[371] Schaff, 1882, History of the Christian Church: Vol. VII, p. 8

felt at the end of the medieval period when his own time was troubling enough to make him think the end of the age was at hand.

> Nor let it disturb you, dearest brethren, if with some, in these last times, either an uncertain faith is wavering, or a fear of God without religion is vacillating, or a peaceable concord does not continue. These things have been foretold as about to happen in the end of the world, and it was predicted by the voice of the Lord and by the testimony of the apostles that now that the world is failing and the Antichrist is drawing near, everything good shall fail, but evil and adverse things shall prosper. (par. 7)

He gives hope to the Spanish, though:

> Evangelical rigor has not so failed in the Church of God, nor the strength of Christian virtue or faith so languished, that there is not left a portion of the priests that in no respect gives way under these ruins of things and wrecks of faith. (par. 8)

Though he gives such encouragement to the Spanish, he speaks of "ruins of things and wrecks of faith." Cyprian felt the hard times deeply. He was a man for his own time. The Church needed a man like him. I could not wish for him to see the rubble of the Church that led to the Reformation.

Epistle 68(66): Cyprian to Florentius Pupianus, 254

This letter is two or three years earlier than the previous one. Pupianus had an objection to Cyprian's appointment from the beginning. Cyprian thought it was cleared up, but now he had received a letter indicating Pupianus's thoughts had not changed.

Cyprian defends himself; the important part of this letter, at least for our purposes, is when Cyprian once again attributes the authority of Peter to himself and all bishops. He cites John 6:67-69, in which Peter tells Jesus that they have to follow him even though the multitude is walking away in offense. He then writes:

> Peter speaks there, on whom the Church was to be built, teaching and showing in the name of the Church, that although a rebellious and arrogant multitude of those who will not hear and obey may depart, yet the Church does not depart from

Christ. They are the church who are a people united to the priest and the flock that adheres to its pastor. From this you ought to know that the bishop is in the church and the church is in the bishop; and if anyone is not with the bishop that he is not in the church.... The Church, which is catholic and one, is not cut nor divided, but is indeed connected and bound together by the cement of priests who cohere with one another. (par. 8)

As we have seen, Cyprian is true to this concept throughout his career and throughout his writings. The Church is united in her bishops.

The end of the letter may not be pertinent, but it is too interesting to leave out. He warns Pupianus: "You have my letter, and I have yours. In the Day of Judgment, before the tribunal of Christ, both will be read."

Epistle 69(70): Cyprian and Thirty-One Bishops to Januarius and Seventeen bishops, 255

This letter defends Cyprian's position on the rebaptism of heretics against Stephen's. I will only point out here that Cyprian mentioned Peter, saying, "Baptism is one, and the Holy Spirit is one, and the Church founded by Christ the Lord upon Peter by a source and principle of unity is one also" (par. 3).

Here Peter and "a source and principle of unity" are mentioned together. Roman Catholics would interpret this as a reference to the pope, but we know that Cyprian believed the unity of the Church to be established on the one episcopate held by all bishops.

Epistle 70(71): Cyprian to Quintus of Mauritania, 255

This is another epistle defending Cyprian's position against Stephen. Quintus had requested Cyprian's opinion (par. 1) because Mauritania is in Carthage's province (Epistle 44, par. 4).

This letter intimates that Stephen was claiming some sort of "primacy" over other churches.

> For neither did Peter, whom the Lord first chose and upon whom he built his Church, when Paul disputed with him afterwards about circumcision, claim anything to himself

insolently nor arrogantly assume anything so as to say that he held the primacy and that he ought to be obeyed by novices.... Nor did he despise Paul because he had previously been a persecutor of the Church, but he admitted the counsel of truth and easily yielded to the lawful reason which Paul asserted. (par. 3)

This complaint is about Stephen, so we know that he was claiming he "held the primacy." Cyprian, too, may well have granted some sort of "primacy" to Stephen, depending on how the word is defined. While he strongly objected to the way Stephen was using the primacy, surely if Irenaeus could call the church in Rome "preeminent," then Cyprian would grant the word "primacy" to the great church of Rome and its bishop.

Primacy to Cyprian, however, could not mean "full, supreme, and universal power over the whole Church." Cyprian did not allow one bishop to be over another. They were one episcopate. In this letter, we learn that even Peter's primacy did not demand obedience from novices.

Stephen, like Victor before him,[372] was trying to use "primacy" to exercise authority over other churches. We do not know the reasons Victor thought he had such authority. We do know that his actions were strongly opposed, the bishops writing letters "sharply rebuking Victor."[373] With Stephen, though, we do know the reason. He based his right to excommunicate other churches on his succession from Peter.

This puts me in an ironic position. The U.S. Conference of Catholic Bishops (USCCB) admitted to the Lutherans that the Roman bishops prior to Pope Leo the Great (ruled 440-461) only "suggested" a correlation between the Roman bishop and Peter.[374] I have to grant an earlier date than the USCCB! Stephen definitely claimed authority based on a succession from Peter.

That said, I do agree with both the USCCB and Roman Catholic scholars that the modern Roman Catholic doctrine of Papal Primacy

---

[372] See chapter 17.
[373] Eusebius, 323, *Church History*, Bk. V, ch. 24, par. 10
[374] United States Conference of Catholic Bishops, 1973, "Differing Attitudes Toward Papal Primacy," par. 18

was first fully expressed by Pope Leo in his address to the Roman Clergy on the second anniversary of his coronation.[375]

Epistle 71(72): "Cyprian and Others" to Stephen, 256

The Seventh Council of Carthage probably sent this epistle prior to its conclusion. They hoped Stephen would give in.

The letter begins respectfully, saying that they want his "gravity and wisdom." They give a few arguments concerning the rebaptism of heretics (par. 1), and then tell Stephen they have attached the letters to Januarius and others in Numidia (Epistle 69) and Quintus in Mauritania (Epistle 70). Both of these provinces are in North Africa and under Carthage's supervision (Epistle 44, par. 4).

They then move on to the subject of elders and deacons who have lapsed or who were ordained among the heretics. Here they make no appeal to Stephen's wisdom, but assert "with common consent and authority" that such men can be received back into the churches, but only as laymen (par. 2).

On the subject of the baptism of heretics, where they knew he would disagree, they write:

> We know that some will not lay aside what they have imbibed and do not easily change their purpose. But, keeping fast the bond of peace and concord among their colleagues, [they] retain certain things peculiar to themselves, which have once been adopted among them. In which behalf we neither do violence to nor impose a law upon anyone, since each prelate has in the administration of the church the exercise of his will free, as he shall give an account of his conduct, to the Lord. (par. 3)

Though Cyprian was in a fierce battle with Stephen, as were the others at the conference, they did not pronounce themselves an authority over Stephen any more than they would allow him to be an authority over them. They grant to bishops who disagreed with them freedom to administrate their church as those who will give account to the Lord, not to Cyprian.

---

[375] Leo I, 442, "Sermons," Sermon III, par. III

This establishes the point I made in the commentary on Epistle 66. Cyprian was not trying to subject Marcianus to Stephen's authority; his concern was unity. Stephen had violated the unity of the Church, and he needed to be called to task. The conflict with Stephen would not have escalated had Stephen not attempted to sever the unity of the Church in order to force his own tradition on others.

Epistle 72/73: Cyprian to Jubaianus, 256

Here we find one more argument against the existence of a one-bishop authority over all the churches. Jubaianus wrote a letter to Cyprian asking him to explain his position. Cyprian answers with a long letter, to which he attaches other letters. He fights with all that is in him to bring Jubaianus to his side.

He answers Stephen's arguments using both Scripture and reason. He gives reasons for rejecting Stephen's appeal to his predecessor's acceptance of Marcion's baptism. He argues over more than 6,000 words; it would take forty minutes to read the letter out loud. Even then, he adds other letters to this letter to Jubaianus.

Yet in all his arguing he never mentions or argues against Stephen's authority. It is not because he cannot. We have seen that he openly rejects any bishop's right to rule over another bishop, yet he does not bring up Stephen's authority to decide on the issue.

Catholic apologist Stephen Ray puts great emphasis on this "argument from silence." He asserts that Cyprian did not argue against Stephen's authority because he agreed that Stephen had the right to decide on this matter.[376] This argument crumbles, though, because the only time Cyprian is silent on Stephen's authority is in this letter. At the Seventh Council of Carthage, he is not silent at all. Neither is he silent in his exchanges with Firmilian, bishop of Caesarea.[377]

Cyprian is silent because there is no reason not to be. Jubaianus did not consider Stephen to be the "full, supreme, and universal power over the whole Church" either. There was no reason to argue against an idea that Jubaianus did not have. When Cyprian and Firmilian bring up Stephen's claim to authority, it is simply in fury that he would dare to excommunicate whole churches.

---

[376] Ray, 2009, *Upon This Rock*, Kindle location 84-88
[377] Cyprian, Epistle 74 (Oxford 75)

Part VI | Chapter 21: Cyprian's Epistles and Treatises

Finally, in a passage we addressed earlier, we see Cyprian apply the promises made by Jesus to Peter to all bishops one more time. He writes:

> The Lord cries aloud that "whoever thirsts should come and drink of the rivers of living water that flowed out of his belly" [Jn. 6:37-38]. To where is he to come who thirsts? Shall he come to the heretics, where there is no fountain and river of living water at all, or to the Church which is one, and is founded upon one who has received the keys of it by the Lord's voice? It is she who holds and possesses alone all the power of her spouse and Lord. In her we preside, for her honor and unity we fight. (par. 11, brackets mine)

This is old news at this point. The Church holds all the power of her spouse and Lord, and in her "we" preside. In Cyprian's eyes, none of the promises of Peter pertain to Rome alone—despite its "primacy"[378] and being the "source of priestly unity"[379]—but rather to all the bishops.

Epistle 73(74): Cyprian to Pompeius, 256

We covered this letter above. Cyprian questions how Stephen will do in the judgment, writing, "Can the account be satisfactory in the Day of Judgment for a priest of God that maintains, approves, and acquiesces in the baptism of blasphemers?" (par. 8).

So then, it should be no surprise that he begins the letter with:

> Since you have desired that what Stephen our brother replied to my letters should be brought to your knowledge, I have sent you a copy of his reply, on the reading of which, you will more and more observe his error in trying to maintain the cause of heretics against Christians and against the Church of God. (par. 1)

I thought it necessary to bring up this passage, but we cannot take Cyprian's disagreement with Stephen too far. Even in the twenty-first century it is permissible to disagree, and even strongly disagree, with the pope. We know Cyprian rejected Papal Primacy because he led a

---

[378] Cyprian, Epistle 70 (Oxford 71), par. 3
[379] Cyprian, Epistle 52 (Oxford 59), par. 14

council saying no bishop can be a bishop over other bishops, not because he disagreed with Stephen.

More important and more relevant is Cyprian's reason for disagreeing with Rome's tradition. He writes:

> Nor ought custom, which had crept in among some, to prevent the truth from prevailing and conquering, for custom without truth is the antiquity of error. (par. 9)

This statement hearkens back to Irenaeus, whose writing are consumed with the preservation of truth. Tradition and succession are important to Irenaeus, but only as tools for the preservation of truth.

Epistle 74(75): Firmilian, Bishop of Caesarea, to Cyprian, 256

We have touched on this letter from Firmilian several times. He was the bishop of Caesarea, far away from Rome, but Stephen had threatened to excommunicate Caesarea and other Cappadocian, Galatian, and Middle Eastern churches.[380]

Roman Catholic apologists cite Stephen's attempt to excommunicate so many churches as though it were proof that he had the right to do so. Stephen did not find support for these excommunications, though, and there were a lot of objections.

No one could have objected more strongly than Firmilian. He calls Stephen's actions "unkindness" and compares them to Judas's betrayal (par. 2); calls them "audacity and pride" (par. 3); says he did them "wickedly" (par. 3); charges him with partaking in Novatian's heresy (par. 5) and defaming Peter and Paul (par. 6); calls his position "absurd" and "ridiculous" (par. 9); speaks of the "greatness of his error" and "depth of his blindness"(par. 16); and announces that he is "justly indignant at this so open and manifest folly" (par. 17).

We have to question whether a bishop would dare to say such things about a man that alone represented the visible unity of the Church or who had "full, supreme, and universal power over the Church."[381]

Firmilian believed exactly what Cyprian believed: that the authority of Peter passed to all the bishops. He wrote:

---

[380] Eusebius, 323, *Church History*, Bk. VII, ch. 5, par. 2, 4
[381] *Catechism of the Catholic Church*, par. 882

Part VI | Chapter 21: Cyprian's Epistles and Treatises

> "... the foundation of the one Church which was once based by Christ upon the rock, may be perceived from this, that Christ said to Peter alone, "Whatever you shall bind on earth shall be bound in heaven, and whatever you shall loose on earth shall be loosed in heaven" [Matt. 16:19]. And again, in the Gospel when Christ breathed on the apostles alone, he said, "Receive the Holy Spirit. Whoever's sins you remit, they are remitted to them, and whoever's sins you retain, they are retained" [Jn. 20:22-23]; therefore, the power of remitting sins was given to the apostles, and to the churches which they ... established and to the bishops who succeeded them by vicarious ordination. (par. 16, brackets mine)

This is exactly the understanding that Cyprian had about this passage. Thus, when Firmilian brings up Stephen's boasting about "the place of his episcopate" and his claim to hold "the succession from Peter," we can properly conclude that Firmilian is granting what Cyprian granted in Epistle 51, par. 8. Stephen's chair was formerly Peter's. He was a direct successor of Peter in a way that no other bishop except the bishop of Antioch was.[382] The heirs of the promises to Peter, however, were neither Stephen nor the bishop of Antioch alone, but all the leaders of the churches. I say "leaders" because Firmilian includes the elders, saying, "All power and grace are established in the Church where the elders preside" (par. 7).

This covers Firmilian's letter thoroughly enough for our purposes, but he has a section on custom (tradition) that we ought to cover. It reminds us of Cyprian's "custom without truth is the antiquity of error" (Epistle 73, par. 9):

> This ... you Africans are able to say against Stephen, that when you knew the truth you forsook the error of custom. But we join custom to truth, and to the Romans' custom we oppose custom, but the custom of truth. We held from the beginning that which was delivered by Christ and the apostles. Nor do we remember that this at any time began among us, since it has always been observed here that we know none but one

---

[382] Eusebius, 323, *Church History*, Bk. III, ch. 36, par. 2

Church of God and accounted no baptism holy except that of the holy Church (par. 19).

In so many words, Firmilian tells Cyprian that it was right to oppose the custom of the Romans, to which the North Africans would normally be subject, because it was in error. The churches in Asia Minor and the Middle East, however, had no such custom and had never accepted the baptism of those outside the one Church. Thus, while Cyprian could only oppose custom with truth from the Scriptures, the church in Caesarea could oppose Roman custom with both Scripture and their own custom.

Firmilian voiced his complaints to Cyprian, but Dionysius the Great, bishop of Alexandria, wrote to Rome directly. He wrote first to Stephen, pointing out that the churches had just become settled and at peace after the problems with the Novatians.[383] He appealed to Rome not to disturb the churches with a new controversy.

After Stephen died, he then wrote Xystus, agreeing with Firmilian that the custom in the Eastern churches was to rebaptize the heretics.

> Truly in the largest synods of the bishops, as I learn, decrees have been passed on this subject, that those coming over from heresies should be instructed, and then should be washed [baptized] and cleansed from the filth of the old and impure leaven.[384]

Dionysius's letter seems gentle, but he has big guns. He says "largest synods," drawing on both the size and the number of these synods. Apparently, the death of Stephen and the election of Xystus in Rome was enough to end the controversy, because Eusebius follows the quotation of Dionysius' letter to Xystus with, "So much in regard to the above-mentioned controversy."[385]

Epistle 74 is the last of Cyprian's letters that we need to cover. We will move on to his various treatises, though the only one pertinent to our subject is "On the Unity of the Church."

---

[383] Eusebius, 323, *Church History*, Bk. VII, ch. 5, par. 1-2
[384] Eusebius, 323, *Church History*, Bk. VII, ch. 5, par. 5; brackets mine
[385] Eusebius, 323, *Church History*, Bk. VII, ch. 5, par. 6

Part VI | Chapter 21: Cyprian's Epistles and Treatises

On the Unity of the Church

Cyprian wrote a treatise called "On the Unity of the Church." In it, he again addresses Jesus's statements to Peter in Matthew 16:

> The Lord speaks to Peter, saying, "I say to you that you are Peter, and upon this rock I will build my Church, and the gates of hell shall not prevail against it. I will give you the keys of the Kingdom of Heaven. Whatever you shall bind on earth shall be bound also in heaven. Whatever you shall loose on earth shall be loosed in heaven" [Matt. 16:18-19] And again to the same [Peter] he says after his resurrection, "Feed my sheep." And although to all the apostles, after his resurrection, he gives an equal power, and says, "As the Father sent me, even so I send you. Receive the Holy Spirit. Whoever's sins you remit, they shall be remitted to him. Whoever's sins you retain, they shall be retained" [Jn. 20:22-23]. Yet, that he might set forth unity, he arranged by his authority the origin of that unity, as beginning from one. Assuredly the rest of the apostles were also the same as was Peter, endowed with a like partnership both of honor and power, but the beginning proceeds from unity.... And this unity we ought firmly to hold and assert, especially those of us that are bishops who preside in the Church, that we may also prove the episcopate to be one and undivided.... The episcopate is one, each part which is held by each one for the whole. (par. 4-5)

The point Cyprian makes here is that God wanted to make sure that everyone understood that there was not just equal authority among the apostles, but that together they held one authority, not twelve authorities. God gave the honor at the beginning to Peter alone so that the authority of the apostles, and later the bishops of the churches, would be one authority, not many authorities that could possibly compete with one another.

The last statement of this passage tells us that each bishop has a part that together constitute a whole. It is this "whole" that has the one authority, not the bishop of Rome.

The Remainder of Cyprian's Treatises

In "On the Dress of Virgins," paragraph 10, Cyprian says that the Lord commended his sheep to Peter to be fed and guarded. If the Roman Catholic apologists want to argue that was Peter was shepherd of the whole Church, this is the passage to use. We must remember, though, that Cyprian regarded all the bishops as heirs of Peter's role. This aligns with what we know of biblical shepherding. All bishops together can watch over all of God's flock, be examples to them, and be accountable for their oversight.

Besides the above, the only pertinent reference in his other treatises is found in "On the Advantage of Patience." In paragraph 9, Cyprian says that the Church was founded on Peter. This, of course, has already been covered.

With that, we end our search into the beliefs of Cyprian, bishop of Carthage. We have covered everything argued by Roman Catholic apologists and much more. There is little else to report until we get to the Council of Nicea. The many writers who wrote during the seventy years between Cyprian's episcopate and the Council of Nicea found little reason to reference Rome or its bishop.

Part VI | Chapter 22: Other Third-Century Writers

Chapter 22: Other Third-Century Writers

We have covered Hippolytus of Rome as well as Origen. We have thoroughly covered Cyprian. This leaves us very little to cover in the third century. Even a thorough read of Jimmy Akin's *The Fathers Know Best* and Stephen Ray's *Upon This Rock* produces only three third-century quotes from anyone other than Cyprian and Origen. Here are the three passages.

Dionysius of Rome Asks a Defense from Dionysius of Alexandria
The first of these quotes is from Stephen Ray's *Upon This Rock*.

> But a charge had been laid by some persons against the Bishop of Alexandria before the Bishop of Rome, as if he had said that the Son was made, and not coessential with the Father. And, the synod at Rome being indignant, the Bishop of Rome expressed their united sentiments in a letter to his namesake. And so the latter [Dionysius of Alexandria], in defence, wrote a book with the title "of Refutation and Defence;" and thus he writes to the other [Dionysius of Rome]:" ... And my Letter, as I said before, owing to present circumstances, I am unable to produce, or I would have sent you the very words I used, or rather a copy of it all; which, if I have an opportunity, I will do still."[386]

This report is from Athanasius, who became bishop of Alexandria in 328. The exchange he is reporting on occurred about 265. Dionysius of Alexandria, Athanasius's predecessor, wrote a letter against the doctrine of Sabellius, who taught that the Father, Son, and Spirit were not three persons, but one. He sent it to Pentapolis, where he had heard that Sabellius's heresy was making headway. Specifically, he sent the letter to Euphranor and Ammonius. While these men did not hold to Sabellianism, they felt Dionysius went too far and made the Son a creation from nothing rather than the eternal Word of God. They did

---

[386] Athanasius, 359, "On the Councils of Ariminum and Seleucia," Part III, par. 43-44, in Ray, 2009, *Upon This Rock*, Kindle location 1607-1613

not take this back to Dionysius but rather went to his namesake in Rome to complain.[387]

In the passage above, Athanasius brings up the Alexandrian Dionysius's letter of defense as part of an argument that all the leaders of the third century believed that the Father and Son are "one in essence," a central theme of the Council of Nicea, which Athanasius was constantly defending.[388]

In another work, he quotes the Roman Dionysius's response for the same purpose. His quotation of Dionysius of Rome is the only portion of the letter we have. After citing it, he writes, "See, we are proving that this view has been transmitted from father to father."[389]

Some party that opposed the Nicene Creed, and there were many, had used the conflict between the two Dionysiuses to argue that not all the fathers before Arius held to the controversial term *homoousios* (one substance). Athanasius, aware of the exchange because he was Dionysius's successor, quoted both letters to argue that *homoousios* was the opinion and teaching of all the fathers prior to Arius.

All Roman Catholic apologists want to turn every reference to the bishop of Rome into an endorsement of his "full, supreme, and universal power." Stephen Ray is no exception. He cites Wladimir D'Ormesson's *The Papacy* to paint a different picture of the Roman Dionysius's role in the matter.

> [The Alexandrians] knew that there existed a sovereign arbiter in disputes which might arise within the Church, and that supreme arbiter was the Bishop of Rome.... [Dionysius of Rome wrote to Alexandria, and] in the following century Athanasius quoted this letter as an unanswerable document.[390]

The first statement in this quote is false. Dionysius of Alexandria's letter was taken to Rome by Euphranor and Ammonius of Pentapolis, not by Alexandrians. The implication in the second statement is unfounded. By "unanswerable document," Ray wants us to conclude that the letter was of supreme authority. The document was

---

[387] Athanasius, 328-373, "Defense of Dionysius," ch. 13
[388] Athanasius, 359, "On the Councils of Ariminum and Seleucia," par. 45
[389] Athanasius, 346-356, "Defense of the Nicene Definition," par. 27
[390] D'Ormesson, 1959, *The Papacy*, pp. 48-49, in Ray, 2009, *Upon This Rock*, Kindle location 5554-5556

Part VI | Chapter 22: Other Third-Century Writers

unanswerable, but only because "this view has been transmitted from father to father." He was not citing the pope as an unanswerable authority.

We need to remember that less than ten years earlier the same Dionysius of Alexandria wrote to Stephen and Xystus to correct Stephen's divisive actions in excommunicating many of the churches in the Eastern empire. The bishops of the empire at that time believed that all the bishops together held the one authoritative and uniting episcopate inherited from Peter. They had not changed their minds just eight years later.

Paul of Samosata

Paul of Samosata was a bishop of Antioch who denied that Jesus existed prior to his birth in Bethlehem. He was ejected from his episcopate and rejected by everyone around him, including the people of Antioch, but he refused to give up the church's house in which he was staying.

Stephen Ray tells us about this incident:

> As Paul had fallen from the episcopate, as well as from the orthodox faith, Domnus, as has been said, became bishop of the church at Antioch. But as Paul refused to surrender the church building, the Emperor Aurelian was petitioned; and he decided the matter most equitably, ordering the building to be given to those to whom the bishops of Italy and of the city of Rome should adjudge it.[391]

Ray got this from Eusebius' *Church History*.[392] There is no more information about this there or anywhere else. Ray argues:

> Antioch is in the East, about 1,330 miles from Rome as a crow flies and only three hundred miles north of Jerusalem. Is it not amazing that even the secular authorities knew who had jurisdiction over the universal Church? Why not give the church building to the bishop of Jerusalem or another nearby patriarch? Why put the church in the hands of the Roman Church? Not only the Church leaders but also the civil

---

[391] Ray, 2009, *Upon This Rock*, Kindle location 1613-1618
[392] Eusebius, 323, *Church History*, Bk. VII, ch. 30

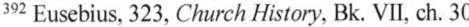

authorities recognized the primacy of Rome's jurisdiction over the universal Church.[393]

Ray draws bold conclusions, but they are not justified. Aurelian devoted his reign (270-275) to taking back sections of the empire that had been captured by barbarians. He would have had little time or care for this trivial Christian matter. It had only been twenty years since major persecutions in the Western empire, and the Great Persecution would begin in thirty years. Aurelian was a pagan emperor, not a Christian one. It is far more likely that turning this over to the bishops of Italy was a simple dismissal of this minor annoyance than an acknowledgment of a non-existent universal jurisdiction of the bishop of Rome.

It is amazing that an emperor was willing to deal with this at all, some forty years before Constantine and Licinius legalized Christianity. It is just as unusual that church leaders would contact the emperor over church property in Antioch at that period of history. Lactantius, who wrote a history of persecutors of the Church, described him as an "outrageous and headstrong" tyrant.[394]

The Letter of Clement to James

Jimmy Akin cites this passage:

> Be it known to you, my lord, that Simon, who, for the sake of the true faith, and the sure foundation of his doctrine, was set apart to be the foundation of the Church, and for this end was, by Jesus himself, with his truthful mouth, named Peter, the first fruits of our Lord, the first of the apostles; to whom the Father first revealed the Son; whom the Christ blessed with good reason; the called, and elect.[395]

This quote is of questionable authorship and dating, as is all the "Clementine" literature. No one knows who wrote it. There is some evidence for an early third-century date, even earlier than the date Akin assigns, but others assign a fourth or fifth-century date.

---

[393] Ray, 2009, *Upon This Rock*, Kindle location 5569-5572
[394] Lactantius, 303-316, "Of the Manner in Which the Persecutors Died," ch. 6
[395] Akin, 2010, *The Fathers Know Best*, Kindle location 2809-2813. Akin assigns this quote to "The Letter of Clement to James" and dates it c. 290.

Part VI | Chapter 22: Other Third-Century Writers

None of this matters, however, because this is one more case of "Peter Syndrome." Roman Catholic apologists assume that anything said about Peter applies to the bishop of Rome. Rome is not mentioned in this quote; neither the church, the bishop, nor the city. Thus, it is pointless to quote this questionable writing in regard to authority of the Roman bishop.

As we saw in the chapter on Cyprian, third-century Christians assigned the promises of Peter and the foundation of unity to the one episcopate of all bishops. They did not apply the promises of Peter to the bishop of Rome. Thus, no matter what is said about Peter in the "Letter of Clement to James," it is irrelevant to Rome's Audacious Claim.

Pseudo-Tertullian: Poem against the Marcionites

Stephen Ray gives this quote in *Upon the Rock*.[396] He got the quote from Jurgens's *The Faith of the Early Fathers*. Jurgens believes the quote to be pre-Nicene (before 325) and the work of an anonymous poet from Gaul.[397] It says:

> In this chair in which he himself had sat, Peter,
> In mighty Rome, commanded Linus, the first elected, to sit down.
> After him, Cletus too accepted the flock of the fold.
> As his successor, Anacletus was elected by lot.
> Clement follows him, well-known to apostolic men.
> After him Evaristus ruled the flock without crime.
> Alexander, sixth in succession, commends the fold to Sixtus.
> After his illustrious times were completed, he passed it on to Telesphorus.
> He was excellent, a faithful martyr.
> After him, learned of the law and a sure teacher ...
> Hyginus, in the ninth place, now accepted the chair.
> Then Pius, after him, whose blood-brother was Hermas,
> An angelic shepherd, because he spoke the words delivered to him;

---

[396] Ray, 2009, *Upon This Rock*, Kindle location 1619-1627
[397] Jurgens, 1970, *Faith of the Holy Fathers*, p. 390

Rome's Audacious Claim

> And Anicetus accepted his lot in pious succession.

This poem gives the same succession that Irenaeus gave a century earlier, and if Jurgens is correct, it is from the same area of Europe. We have already discussed Irenaeus's praise of Rome and the purpose of listing a succession of bishops in Rome.

Conclusion

As said, there is not much to address from the third century apart from Hippolytus, Origen, and Cyprian. Our look at Cyprian's letters and the Seventh Council of Carthage gives a very thorough picture of the view of Roman authority held by the churches of the empire. They believed that Peter was the rock on which the Church was built, but they also believed that Peter's authority had been handed down to all the bishops of the Christian Church. Those bishops inherited the keys of the kingdom together, and they represent the unity of the Christian churches.[398]

The few passages cited by the Roman Catholic apologists in this chapter add nothing to that understanding.

It is in the fourth century that we see the bishop of Rome rise to preeminence himself, rather than just his church.

---

[398] Cyprian, 256, "Epistles of Cyprian," Epistle 72 (Oxford 73), par. 11

Part VII

The Fourth Century and Afterward

Rome's Audacious Claim

Chapter 23: The Fourth Century

Surely the most important event of the fourth century was the Council of Nicea, which was held in 325. There are many myths about the council, and I have addressed them in a book[399] and online.[400] In this chapter, I will forego the mythbusting, and instead tell the story understood and agreed upon by all trustworthy scholars, and explain how the events surrounding the Council of Nicea made the bishop of Rome the go-to bishop for the entire empire.

The Council of Nicea

I will not be giving references for the following short history. The Roman Catholic Church would give the same history, and you can read *The Catholic Encyclopedia*'s history at NewAdvent.org.[401] Two articles there, "The First Council of Nicaea" and "Arianism," should suffice and can be found with a simple search.

Around 318, Arius, an elder of one of the churches of Egypt, told Alexander, the bishop of Alexandria, that there was a time when the Son of God did not exist. He rejected the idea that the Son of God was begotten by God. Instead, Arius argued that God created Jesus from nothing, like everything and everyone else.

Though Alexander spent several years trying to persuade Arius, by 321 the bishops of Egypt convinced Alexander to excommunicate him.

This should have been the end of the story, but Arius fled to Eusebius, the bishop of Nicomedia, for protection and support. This Eusebius is not to be confused with Eusebius the historian, who was bishop of Caesarea. Eusebius of Nicomedia gave his support to Arius and exercised his influence to spread Arius's teaching.

As you might suspect, this led to much controversy among the churches in the Eastern Roman Empire. In 324, the Emperor Constantine won a civil war with his co-emperor Licinius and united the Roman Empire under his dominion. After obtaining control of the empire, he was dismayed to find his empire being torn apart by the very religion he had begun supporting! He demanded the appearance

---

[399] Pavao, 2014, *Decoding Nicea*
[400] Pavao, 2009-2019, "Nicea Myths"
[401] Knight, 2019, The Catholic Encyclopedia

of all the bishops of the empire in the city of Nicea, where he had a palace.

The Council of Nicea met in 325 and condemned the teaching of Arius. Apostolic tradition still held sway, and the bishops made their decision on the basis of apostolic tradition. As Irenaeus, who fought so hard for apostolic tradition more than a century earlier, said, "It does not follow because men are endowed with greater and less degrees of intelligence, that they should therefore change the subject-matter [of the faith] itself."[402] The Nicene bishops did not want to argue points of doctrine, but to determine what had been handed down to them. Famed historian Philip Schaff explains their mindset:

> In this, as in every other of the Seven Ecumenical Councils, the question the Fathers considered was not what they supposed Holy Scripture might mean, nor what they, from à priori arguments, thought would be consistent with the mind of God, but something entirely different, to wit, what they had received. They understood their position to be that of witnesses, not that of exegetes. They recognized but one duty resting upon them in this respect—to hand down to other faithful men that good thing the Church had received according to the command of God. The first requirement was not learning, but honesty. The question they were called upon to answer was not, "What do I think probable, or even certain, from Holy Scripture?" but, "What have I been taught, what has been entrusted to me to hand down to others?"[403]

Schaff says this mindset applied through all seven ecumenical councils. The seventh, the Council of Nicea II, was in 787. It approved the veneration of sacred images. The second Council of Nicea proves there is a limit to the power of apostolic tradition. Irenaeus writes, "[These leaders of the churches], if they discharged their functions honestly, would be a great boon [to the Church], but if they should fall away, the direst calamity."[404] After six centuries, an ecumenical council, representing all the churches of the Roman Empire and

---

[402] c. 185, *Against Heresies*. Bk. I, ch. 10, par. 3
[403] *The Nicene and Post-Nicene Fathers*, 1886-1900; NPNF2, Vol. XIV, section "The First Ecumenical Council," subsection "Historical Introduction"
[404] *Against Heresies*, Bk. III, ch. 3, par. 1; brackets mine

Part VI | Chapter 23: The Fourth Century

Europe, allowed the "veneration" of images. All references to images by the pre-Nicene fathers are negative. They give no hint that they approved bowing to an image under any circumstance. This is, of course, forbidden by the second commandment (Ex. 20:4-5)!

Nicea II's decision was not without controversy. There was a previous Seventh Ecumenical Council, at Hieria in 754, which condemned the veneration of sacred images. This council was condemned at Nicea II. It shows, though, that corruption or time can degrade the best attempts of men, even if they lead churches, to maintain "the faith once for all handed down" without change (Jude 1:3).

The first Council of Nicea, though, did choose the tradition handed down to them. They condemned both Eusebius of Nicomedia and Arius. Constantine, who led the council,[405] expelled them from the empire. By 336 both had returned. Arius died, either from sickness or poison, during a parade that was meant to reinstate him in the church. Eusebius, though, quietly returned to Nicomedia.

When Constantine died in 336, his son Constantius II became emperor in the east. His brothers, Constantine II and Constans, became co-emperors in the West.

Eusebius of Nicomedia was related to the royal household, and he used his influence to persuade Constantius II's household that the teaching of Arius was correct. The emperor became the benefactor of the bishops that opposed Nicea, until his death in 361.

He brought Eusebius from Nicomedia to Constantinople in 341, and Eusebius wasted no time in calling a council to oppose Nicea. They met in Antioch and formed a creed meant to replace the Nicene Creed. While they were at it, they deposed the bishop of Alexandria.

Athanasius had replaced Alexander in Alexandria shortly after the Council of Nicea, but he was no less an opponent of Arius and his doctrines than his predecessor was. When the Council of Antioch deposed him, he made a beeline for Julius in Rome. Julius I was bishop of Rome from 337 to 352, throughout the most active part of the controversy over Nicea.

---

[405] Eusebius, 339, *Life of Constantine*, Bk. III, chs. 10-13

Rome's Audacious Claim

Julius had the support of Constans in the West throughout his episcopate. Emperor Constans's army killed Constantine II in 341, so he was the sole emperor in the Western empire.

Julius, who had nothing to fear from Constantius while Constans held control of the West, sent both Athanasius and Paul, the former bishop of Constantinople, back to their respective sees with a letter reinstating them. It is certain that even if the bishop of Rome had had "full, supreme, and universal power over the whole Church," the Eastern bishops would have disregarded him. If they would not give in to the great Council of Nicea, they were certainly not going to give in to one bishop, even if he were the bishop of the great Roman church.

When Athanasius and Paul returned to their respective sees with their letters, the letters were forwarded to Antioch, because Julius's letters rebuked the participants in the council. They, of course, simply met again and sent back a letter complaining of the indignity with which Julius had treated them. He had no business in their affairs, they said.

Since this is a reference to the way the Arian bishops rejected the authority of Rome, I should include the quote:

> It was not his province, they said, to take cognizance of their decisions in reference to any whom they might wish to expel from their churches; seeing that they had not opposed themselves to him, when Novatus [Novatian] was ejected from the church.[406]

If you read the chapter on Cyprian, then you know that Novatian split the church in Rome in 251, having himself ordained a second bishop in the city. In 251, among the catholic and apostolic churches, division was an unthinkable crime, and the churches across the empire supported Cornelius, the appropriately chosen bishop.

Eusebius of Nicomedia died during this time (and his namesake from Caesarea had died a few years earlier), so the bishops who sent this reply to Julius are unnamed in Socrates Scholasticus's history.[407]

These bishops at Antioch did not need to send Paul or Athanasius back. Constantius took care of that himself. When they returned to

---

[406] Socrates Scholasticus, 439, *Ecclesiastical History*, Bk. II, ch. 15, brackets mine
[407] This Socrates who wrote the church history was not the famous Greek philosopher who lived and died centuries earlier.

Part VI | Chapter 23: The Fourth Century

Rome, Julius appealed to Emperor Constans, who demanded that his brother resolve the controversy he had stirred up. The churches in the West considered the whole Arian controversy, which had primarily taken place in the Eastern churches, to be resolved by the Council of Nicea. Neither they nor Emperor Constans could understand why Constantius had revived the controversy. Constans demanded resolution, and threatened civil war.

The opposers of the Nicene Creed did not want civil war, and they recommended Constantius accept Constans's demand for a council.

The council was to convene in Sardica (which is modern Sofia, Bulgaria), but the Western bishops brought Paul and Athanasius with them. The Eastern bishops refused to meet with them, and they held their own council in Philippopolis. To no one's surprise, the Western bishops in Sardica confirmed the Nicene Creed and reinstated Paul and Athanasius. The Eastern bishops in Philippopolis condemned the term *homoousios* (same substance) that was used in the creed, and they confirmed the removal of the two bishops.

We must stop at this point to cover another argument from the Roman Catholic apologists. Stephen Ray's *Upon this Rock* quotes three canons confirmed at the Council of Sardica.[408]

Canon 3 says that any bishop could appeal a judgment to "Julius, bishop of Rome." Curiously, they did not give this right to just any Roman bishop. Julius, the canon says, would have the right to send arbiters, and the case would be considered again in a "neighboring province." Canon 4 says that if this happens, no one may appoint a replacement bishop until "the bishop of Rome can ... render a judgment." Canon 5 allows the bishop of Rome to "send priests as his personal legates to judge the case."

These canons, of course, are exactly what we would expect from the synod in Sardica. This is especially true of Canon 3, in which Julius himself, rather than the bishops of Rome in general, is given authority to arbitrate the removal of bishops.

The Western bishops were appalled by what they had heard from the East. The emperor was deposing bishops and instituting new ones. Those new ones were rejecting the decisions of a properly held council (Nicea), and in their own partisan councils were deposing bishops who

---

[408] Ray, 2009, *Upon This Rock*, Kindle location 1643-1655

disagreed with them. This was nothing less than a destruction of the unity of the Church.

In times past, the great churches of Antioch, Alexandria, and Rome could have come together to help resolve these tragedies. Eusebius of Nicomedia, with Emperor Constantius's help, had replaced the bishops of Antioch and Alexandria with men who opposed the Nicene Creed. The foxes had taken over the henhouse in the Eastern empire or, to put it biblically, the wolves were in charge of the flocks of God!

It is no wonder, then, that the Council of Sardica enacted such canons. The problem is that the council of Eastern bishops in Philippopolis enacted different canons and would by no means subject themselves to the authority of the Council of Sardica.

The Council of Sardica cannot be used as evidence that the catholic churches agreed that the bishop of Rome had authority to review the appointing of bishops in all churches. The Eastern churches and their puppet bishops rejected the council. The churches even further east or south, in the Persian and Ethiopian empires, likely paid no attention to it at all.

Sardica does, however, show why the bishop of Rome grew in prestige during the fifty-six years of controversy after the Council of Nicea. Constantius had replaced the other patriarchs, who were all in the East.

I will spare you the long story of the devastations of the churches in the Eastern Roman Empire by emperors who opposed Nicea. It went on for another forty years after the divided Councils of Sardica and Philippopolis with several short breaks. In the 350s, Emperor Constans died, and Constantius spread his devastation of the churches to the West. He even forced Liberius, the bishop of Rome, to deny the Nicene Creed.

Constantius died in 361 and was replaced by Julius the Apostate. Julius tried to restore paganism and, for the most part, left the churches to their own affairs. He did remove Athanasius again, because he was converting too many pagans.[409]

By the time the Emperor Theodosius the Great put an end to the controversies in 381-383, the bishop of Rome was well-established as

---

[409] Socrates Scholasticus, 439, *Ecclesiastical History*, Bk. V, ch. 15

Part VI | Chapter 23: The Fourth Century

a solid rock of orthodoxy in the midst of the empire's turmoil. Liberius's recantation in prison was not enough to hurt the prestige of the only apostolic chair unaffected by the decades of heresy.

Interestingly enough, the Vatican itself concedes that the controversies led to the bishop of Rome claiming authority based on Peter's role. This is an admission that such a claim was just beginning to get a foothold even in the West. In 2016, the Roman Catholic Church and Orthodox Church issued a joint statement known as the Chieti Agreement. Chapter 16 of that agreement says:

> In the West, the primacy of the see of Rome was understood, *particularly from the fourth century onwards*, with reference to Peter's role among the Apostles. The primacy of the bishop of Rome among the bishops was gradually interpreted as a prerogative that was his because he was successor of Peter, the first of the apostles. This understanding was not adopted in the East, which had a different interpretation of the Scriptures and the Fathers on this point.[410]

The Chieti Agreement adds that:
- "Appeals regarding disciplinary matters were also made to the see of Constantinople."
- "Appeals to the bishop of Rome from the East expressed the communion of the Church, but the bishop of Rome did not exercise canonical authority over the churches of the East."[411]

Thus, the Vatican itself agrees that the Council of Sardica is not evidence for Papal Primacy. Scott Hahn can appeal to the Council of Sardica because his readers have no idea what that council was. The Vatican, on the other hand, has to contend with the informed objections of the Eastern Orthodox Churches and, therefore, must be more honest than its apologists are.

With that, we conclude our look at the fourth century. It is well-known that the history of the fourth century is more interwoven with

---

[410] Joint International Commission, 2016, "Synodality and Primacy During the First Millennium," par. 16, emphasis mine

[411] Joint International Commission, 2016, "Synodality and Primacy During the First Millennium," par. 19

Rome's Audacious Claim

Athanasius, the bishop of Alexandria, than with the bishop of Rome. As historian Philip Schaff puts it:

> Athanasius is the theological and ecclesiastical centre ... about which the Nicene age resolves.... The personal fortunes of Athanasius are so inseparably interwoven with the history of the Arian controversy that Nicene and Athanasian are equivalent terms.[412]

Athanasius was the center of the Nicene age, but it is Bishop Julius of Rome who enabled him to be. Julius's support and Athanasius's success in the East increased Rome's prestige and helped lead to their crowning moment in the middle of the fifth century.

---

[412] Schaff, 1882, History of the Christian Church, Vol. III, p. 625

Chapter 24: Rome Makes Its Audacious Claim

"Peter has thus spoken through Leo!"[413]

The bishops of the Council of Chalcedon in 451 shouted this after the reading of Leo's letter to Flavian of Constantinople. It is to this Leo that the U.S. Conference of Catholic Bishops grants the first real claim to authority over the whole Church.[414]

Further, the bishops seem to have accepted that claim. "Peter has thus spoken through Leo" is a big admission, but is it an admission that as bishop of Rome, Leo had "full, supreme, and universal power over the whole Church"?

Here is the rest of what the Chalcedonian bishops shouted:

> This is the faith of the fathers, this is the faith of the Apostles. So we all believe, thus the orthodox believe. Anathema to him who does not thus believe. Peter has spoken thus through Leo. So taught the Apostles. Piously and truly did Leo teach, so taught Cyril. Everlasting be the memory of Cyril. Leo and Cyril taught the same thing, anathema to him who does not so believe. This is the true faith. Those of us who are orthodox thus believe. This is the faith of the fathers.[415]

As you can see, the shout of the bishops was not that Leo had authority on his own. Instead, the bishops at Chalcedon shouted his acclaim because they agreed with what he said. Leo's letter, they were announcing, proclaimed the words of the apostles and of Cyril, late bishop of Alexandria, who led the Council of Ephesus in 431. Peter had spoken through Leo based not on the sheer authority of his seat, but based on the truth which the council acknowledged that he spoke.

---

[413] "The Fourth Ecumenical Council," sec. "Extracts from the Acts. Session II. (Continued)." There are two sections with this title; this reference is in the second.
[414] U.S. Conference of Catholic Bishops, 1973, "Differing Attitudes Toward Papal Primacy," par. 18
[415] "The Fourth Ecumenical Council," sec. "Extracts from the Acts. Session II. (Continued)." There are two sections with this section title; this reference is in the second.

Rome's Audacious Claim

This event cannot be the reason that the U.S. Conference of Catholic Bishops puts the first full claim to a primacy of authority over the whole church to Leo. There is no such claim in Leo's letter to Flavian, which was read to the council and prompted the exuberance of the bishops there.

The claim is most clearly stated in Leo's sermon to the bishops of Italy on the anniversary of his ordination. There Leo humbly acknowledged his humanity and unworthiness to hold such a position but, in the process, he fully described the authority he saw in the see of Rome:

> The dispensation of Truth therefore abides, and the blessed Peter persevering in the strength of the Rock, which he has received, has not abandoned the helm of the Church, which he undertook. For he was ordained before the rest in such a way that from his being called the Rock, from his being pronounced the Foundation, from his being constituted the Doorkeeper of the kingdom of heaven, from his being set as the Umpire to bind and to loose, whose judgments shall retain their validity in heaven, from all these mystical titles we might know the nature of his association with Christ. And still today he more fully and effectually performs what is entrusted to him, and carries out every part of his duty and charge in him and with him, through whom he has been glorified. And so if anything is rightly done and rightly decreed by us, if anything is won from the mercy of God by our daily supplications, it is of his work and merits whose power lives and whose authority prevails in his See.[416]

The important parts of this paragraph are the statement that Peter "has not abandoned the helm of the Church" and that his "power lives and whose authority prevails in his See." To this day, the Vatican's preferred term is "The Holy See."

Leo did not invent the claim that Peter is still at the helm of the Church through the bishop of Rome. His wording makes it clear that he is repeating what has been handed down to him. This is no surprise. We saw in the chapter on Cyprian that Stephen felt free to

---

[416] Leo I, 441, "Sermons," Sermon III, ch. 3

Part VI | Chapter 24: Rome Makes its Audacious Claim

excommunicate whole churches based on sitting in Peter's chair. Though that authority was rejected in the 250s, the Roman bishops did not lose this elevated picture of themselves. At the Council of Ephesus in 431, Philip, a presbyter representing Bishop Celestine of Rome, claimed:

> There is no doubt, and in fact it has been known in all ages, that the holy and most blessed Peter, prince ... and head of the Apostles, pillar of the faith, and foundation ... of the Catholic Church, received the keys of the kingdom from our Lord Jesus Christ, the Saviour and Redeemer of the human race, and that to him was given the power of loosing and binding sins: who down even to to-day and forever both lives and judges in his successors. The holy and most blessed pope Coelestine, according to due order, is his successor and holds his place.[417]

Roman Catholic archbishop J. Michael Miller also brings up Siricius, bishop of Rome from 384 to 399. Miller writes:

> "We carry the burden of all who are burdened," [Siricius] wrote. "In fact, the blessed apostle Peter carries these burdens in us, he who, we trust, protects and defends us in everything as the heirs to his office."[418]

That is as early as Miller is willing to go. He gives the origin of the claim of universal jurisdiction to Siricius, saying:

> Siricius was the first pope to apply Paul's "care for all the churches" [2 Cor. 11:28] ... to the apostolic ministry of the bishop of Rome. In theory, if not yet in practice, the popes claimed a jurisdiction extending to all the churches of the Roman Empire.[419]

Throughout the 300s, Rome had been a bastion of orthodox theology, especially under Julius (337-352). The Roman Empire's Eastern churches, meanwhile, and especially the patriarchal centers of Alexandria, Antioch, and Constantinople, thrashed and fought among

---

[417] "The Third Ecumenical Council: The Council of Ephesus," 431, sec. "Extracts from the Acts: Session III"
[418] Miller, 1995, *The Shepherd and the Rock*, p. 84; brackets mine
[419] Miller, 1995, *The Shepherd and the Rock*, p. 84; brackets mine

themselves under the competing sway of Emperor Constantius II and the decisions of the Council of Nicea. Julius's steadfastness only increased the conviction in the Roman church that Peter was holding the Church together through his successors in Rome rather than through all the bishops of the empire. Simple, observable experience testified to it.

In the 400s, the bishops of the East moved from fighting over the relationship between the Father and the Son to fighting over the relationship between the human and divine nature(s) of the Son. Once again, the bishops of Rome proved to be unshakeable and constant. While Cyril of Alexandria was the champion of orthodoxy at the Council of Ephesus in 431, his successor, Dioscorus, was deposed at Chalcedon in 451.

The result of these two councils would be to cut off the truly Eastern churches, those east of the Roman Empire. The churches in the Persian Empire had united as the Church of the East in 410, and the condemnation of Nestorius, bishop of Constantinople, at the Council of Ephesus led to much of Syria uniting with the Church of the East. They remain separated to this day.

The Council of Chalcedon had a similar effect. When Dioscorus was deposed, Egyptian churches separated from communion with the churches of the Roman Empire. The Egyptian churches, known now as the Coptic Orthodox Church, also remain separated to this day. They have united with the Ethiopian Orthodox Church.

Remember that Rome's Audacious Claim is to authority over "the whole Church." As we discuss the reaction of the churches of the Eastern Roman Empire to that claim, remember that the churches of Persia, Syria, Egypt, and Ethiopia not only never agreed to the Roman bishop's authority, but they have been out of communion with him since the fifth century!

With that, let's return to the churches of the Roman Empire. By the fifth century, the barbarian tribes of Europe had as much influence in Rome as the Roman emperor in Constantinople. In 476, the city of Rome was lost to the empire permanently.

The catholic churches of the 250s saw Peter as the source and foundation of unity in the Church. They taught that the manifestation of that unity came through the bishops of all the churches. Only Stephen saw Rome as the one representative of Peter's unity. Other

Part VI | Chapter 24: Rome Makes its Audacious Claim

churches did not agree, and there is no indication that Stephen's predecessors or immediate successors agreed with him, either. Through the fourth century, though, the bishops, at least in the East, proved to be no source of unity at all.

After the conflicts at Ephesus and Chalcedon in the fifth century, every observer could see that Peter speaking through Rome was a much better foundation of unity than Peter speaking through all the bishops of the Roman Empire, at least at that time. (The separated Church of the East and the excommunicated churches of Egypt must be excepted, of course.) In fact, Cyprian could see the unity of the bishops collapsing even in 256, in his letter to bishops in Spain:

> Nor let it disturb you, dearest brethren, if with some, in these last times, either an uncertain faith is wavering, or a fear of God without religion is vacillating, or a peaceable concord does not continue. These things have been foretold as about to happen in the end of the world, and it was predicted by the voice of the Lord and by the testimony of the apostles that now that the world is failing and the Antichrist is drawing near, everything good shall fail, but evil and adverse things shall prosper.[420]

Unity was maintained in the 250s. The bishops came together against Stephen—not against his tradition of accepting the baptism of heretics, but against his authority to excommunicate other churches over Roman tradition—and preserved the unity of the Church.

In the fourth and fifth centuries, though, the unity of the bishops, at least in the East, ceased to exist. Although at one time all churches saw Peter as the source of unity for the whole Church, it was now the Roman bishop carrying that unity, because it was not being provided by the universal college of bishops.

Just as we saw through Cyprian, Firmilian, and others that the churches of the 250s saw a unity based on Peter as essential, so we see that the bishops at Chalcedon wanted the same thing. They were seeing it in Leo.

---

[420] "Epistles of Cyprian," 257, Epistle 67 (Oxford 67), par. 3

Rome's Audacious Claim

For example, when Theodoret, bishop of Cyrrhus in Syria, was condemned prior to the Council of Chalcedon, he appealed to Bishop Leo of Rome through a friend and elder named Renatus:

> That Holy See has precedence over all churches in the world for many reasons, and above all for this, that it is free from all taint of heresy, and that no bishop of heterodox opinion has ever sat upon its throne, but it has kept the grace of the apostles undefiled.[421]

Theodoret does not acknowledge Rome's Audacious Claim here, but instead acknowledges the same adherence to apostolic truth that Irenaeus claimed for Rome. Theodoret was a historian familiar with Eusebius's *Church History* of 323, and he claims orthodoxy for each and every Roman bishop from the beginning. Just as Irenaeus of Lyons concluded that all churches should agree with Rome because of its scrupulous preservation of truth, so Theodoret concluded 250 years later.

In this case, however, Theodoret is not just speaking for himself, but for all the Eastern churches that remained after the Council of Ephesus. Those Eastern churches were condemning Theodoret, but he was confident that approval from Rome would sway the Eastern bishops.

As it turned out, he was wrong. Leo's letter of approval did not help Theodoret against the rabid bishops at Chalcedon. They were eager to condemn him for his support of Nestorius at the Council of Ephesus twenty years earlier. They only approved him after he anathematized Nestorius.[422]

We have now arrived at the time that the bishop of Rome claimed the authority of Peter and expected to be followed by all churches (or at least those not cut off by the Councils of Ephesus and Chalcedon). Stephen's pretensions were rejected in the 250s, but how did the Eastern churches of the Roman Empire react to Celestine's and Leo's claims?

It is to this key question that we must now turn.

---

[421] Theodoret, c. 445-450, "Letters of the the Blessed Theodoret," Letter 116
[422] Baur, 1912, "Theodoret," par. 4

Chapter 25: The Papacy After Leo I

We ended the last chapter by acknowledging that Leo I explicitly stated that the authority of Peter, his place at "the helm of the Church," was exercised through the Roman see.[423] We also acknowledged that this was not his own invention, but was handed down to him by predecessors.

In this chapter we will wrap up the story of the origin of Rome's Audacious Claim. Once it was voiced, what did the rest of the Church do with it?

First, we must remember that large portions of the world had no reaction to Leo I's claim to represent Peter. They were either anathematized at one of the two major councils or were so far away that his claim was irrelevant. As Samuel Moffett, Professor Emeritus at Princeton Theological Seminary, puts it:

> [The Nestorian Controversy's] central figure was Nestorius, the bishop of New Rome, Constantinople, and a man of Antioch. His great antagonist was Cyril, bishop of Alexandria. But its major victor was the bishop of old Rome, Leo I, whose authority both theological and ecclesiastical was strengthened by the acceptance of his guidelines for a theological compromise at the Council of Chalcedon, which, though it reunified the churches in the West, tragically separated them from vast parts of Asia and Africa.[424]

These separated churches agreed neither to Rome's authority nor to the authority of the Councils of Ephesus and Chalcedon. Though there are a few "Roman Rite" churches scattered through the Middle East and Far East in the modern age, the churches outside the empire were lost to both the Roman Catholics and the Eastern Orthodox. The fall of the Western empire left Rome with only the barbarian tribes and kingdoms of Europe. All the other apostolic churches of the New Testament were still in the Roman Empire under the rule of the Roman emperor in Constantine.

---

[423] Leo I, 441, "Sermons," Sermon III, ch. 3
[424] Moffett, 1998, *A History of Christianity in Asia*, Kindle location 4150-4155; brackets mine.

Rome's Audacious Claim

Those churches, now part of the Eastern Orthodox Churches, were the only ones left to deal with Leo's claim. We will turn to them now.

Just as today's Roman Catholic Church descended from the church in Rome, so the Eastern Orthodox Churches descended from the churches in Antioch, Alexandria, Constantinople, and Jerusalem. We all know that the Protestants, in the fifteenth and sixteenth centuries, threw off Rome's Audacious Claim. More significant, though, is the reaction of the Eastern Orthodox Churches that were around throughout the development of Rome's claim to "full, supreme, and universal power over the whole Church."

In the chapter on Cyprian, we learned that third-century bishops believed that Peter, as "the rock," was the foundation of unity for the Church, and the visible expression of that unity was all the bishops of the catholic churches. In the last chapter, we talked about the failure of that system to produce unity and about how the foundation of Rome's claim that the unity based on Peter was better found in Rome's consistently orthodox bishop than in the failing unity of all bishops.

Eastern Orthodox theologian Laurent Cleenewerck explains his predecessors' reaction to the claim of Leo and his successors.

> For many reasons, the Church of Rome was theologically orthodox for the most part of the first millennium ... the East often ended up turning to Rome to resolve its endless controversies.... Rome was orthodox, Rome was the "elder," Rome had the primacy and therefore East and West manifested the same one, holy, catholic and apostolic Church. This does not imply that the Eastern bishops always accepted Rome's view of herself.... The same time, we find St. Maximus the Confessor [d. 662] and St. Theodore the Studite [d. 826] expressing the view that Rome was in unique sense "the Chair of Peter" that would never fall into heresy. This triumph of Roman orthodoxy is an important historical factor. It strengthened the Roman case for being "the See of Peter that can never fail." Thus, Rome's idea of having divine primacy and inerrancy acquired historical support and even found

Part VI | Chapter 25: Papacy After Leo I

sporadic acceptance in the East, notably between 500 and 800.[425]

As Cleenewerck notes, the statements of St. Maximus the Confessor and St. Theodore the Studite do not represent the majority reaction of the Eastern Orthodox Churches. He cites Roman Catholic Cardinal Yves Congar to that effect:

> The East never accepted the regular jurisdiction of Rome, nor did it submit to the judgment of Western bishops. Its appeals to Rome for help were not connected with a recognition of the principle of Roman jurisdiction but were based on the view that Rome had the same truth, the same good. The East jealously protected its autonomous way of life.[426]

Cleenewerck later says it might be better to say that through the first millennium, "the East never overtly condemned Rome for teaching this view."[427] To state the issue in modern terms, the Eastern Orthodox Churches granted Rome a primacy of honor rather than a primacy of authority.

Fortunately for us, this book is being finished in 2019 rather than in 2015 when I started it. The Joint International Commission for Theological Dialogue between the Roman Catholic Church and the Orthodox Church issued a statement in 2016 that can be read on the Vatican website. Because of this, we can let the Roman Catholic and Orthodox Churches speak in agreement on this matter of honor versus authority.

> Between the fourth and the seventh centuries, the order ... of the five patriarchal sees came to be recognised, based on and sanctioned by the ecumenical councils, with the see of Rome occupying the first place, exercising a primacy of honour ... followed by the sees of Constantinople, Alexandria, Antioch and Jerusalem, in that specific order, according to the canonical tradition.

---

[425] Cleenewerck, 2007, *His Broken Body*, p. 225; brackets mine
[426] Congar, 1982, *Diversity and Communion*, pp. 26-27, in Cleenewerck, 2007, *His Broken Body*, pp. 223-24
[427] Cleenewerck, 2007, *His Broken Body*, p. 226

Rome's Audacious Claim

> In the West ... the primacy of the bishop of Rome among the bishops was gradually interpreted as a prerogative that was his because he was successor of Peter, first of the apostles. This understanding was not adopted in the East, which had a different interpretation of the Scriptures and the Fathers on this point.[428]

This is a concession by Rome that the Eastern Orthodox never accepted their claim to a primacy of jurisdiction. It is not yet a retreat from their claim. They have to deal with their infallible council, Vatican I. The Roman Catholic Church held this council from 1869 to 1870. There Pope Pius IX anathematized the Eastern Orthodox Churches for limiting Rome's primacy to one of honor.

> If anyone, therefore, shall say that Blessed Peter the Apostle was not appointed the Prince of all the Apostles and the visible Head of the whole Church Militant; or that the same, directly and immediately, received from the same, Our Lord Jesus Christ, a primacy of honor only, and not of true and proper jurisdiction; let him be anathema.[429]

This "dogmatic" assertion from Vatican I could only have been directed at the Eastern Orthodox, who alone granted a "primacy of honor" during the first millennium. (They would grant it now as well, but they have been divided since 1054.) The Protestants have never conceded any primacy to the pope. The Church of the East and the Oriental Orthodox Churches also do not follow Rome. Only the Eastern Orthodox pay any attention to Rome's Audacious Claim, and they grant a primacy of honor, not jurisdiction.

Further, they do not grant that primacy of honor on Rome's terms. They grant it because of a conglomeration of reasons expressed at the fifth-century Council of Chalcedon, but not because of his succession from Peter or the promises of Matthew 16:

---

[428] Joint International Commission, 2016, "Synodality and Primacy," par. 15-16
[429] Pius IX, 1870, "First Dogmatic Constitution," last paragraph of ch. 1

Part VI | Chapter 25: Papacy After Leo I

> In according Rome a "primacy of honor," the East avoided basing this primacy on the succession and the still living presence of the apostle Peter....[430]

The Eastern Orthodox Churches base Rome's primacy of honor on all the things we discussed earlier: It was the capital of the empire; Peter and Paul both taught there; more martyrs' blood was shed there than anywhere else in the early centuries of the Church; and it was noted for its adherence to the apostolic faith that was handed down to it for almost a millennium. In Eastern Orthodox eyes, though, Peter passed his authority to all the bishops of the churches of the world, not only to Rome. John Meyendorff explains this in an anthology called *The Primacy of Peter*.

> On the other hand, a very clear patristic tradition sees the succession of Peter in the episcopal ministry. The doctrine of St [*sic*] Cyprian of Carthage on the "See of Peter" as being present in every local church, and not only in Rome, is well known. It is also found in the East, among people who certainly never read the *De Unitate ecclesiae* ["On the Unity of the Church"] of Cyprian, but who share its main idea, thus witnessing to it as a part of the catholic tradition of the Church. St Gregory of Nyssa, for example, affirms that Christ "through Peter gave to the bishops the keys of the heavenly honors."[431]

The Eastern Orthodox Churches never surrendered to the idea that the bishop of Rome is the sole representative of Peter on the earth. Instead, they granted Rome the same primacy of honor that Irenaeus gave them as far back as the late second century. They have held steadfastly to the teaching, ubiquitous in Cyprian's time, that all bishops have inherited the office of Peter.

---

[430] Congar, 1982, *Diversity and Communion*, pp. 26-27; in Cleenewerck, 2007, *His Broken Body*, p. 224

431 Meyendorff, 1992, *Primacy of Peter*, pp. 70-71; brackets mine. The quote from Gregory of Nyssa is found in "De Castgatione" ("On Reproof"). It appears this work has not been translated to English. The quote can be found (in Greek and Latin) in J. P. Migne's *Patrologia Graeca*, vol. 47, p. 312.

The Great Schism

The ultimate proof that the Eastern Orthodox Churches rejected Rome's Audacious Claim is the Great Schism. There are many reasons that papal legates and the patriarch of Constantinople excommunicated each other in 1054. Everyone must concede, however, that an excommunication of the pope that has lasted 965 years is certain indication that the Eastern churches did not submit to the "full, supreme, and universal power of the bishop of Rome."

The pope is supposed to be able to exercise that authority "always" and "unhindered."[432] If the Eastern Orthodox Churches believed this, the pope could have resolved the 965-year-old schism by simply telling those churches to submit. That has never happened, of course, because they do not accept Rome's Audacious Claim. It has never been universal.

Conclusion

We have now concluded all pertinent parts of the history of Papal Primacy. I covered the last 1,500 years this briefly because they are irrelevant to our purpose except to establish that there has never been a time when all, or even the majority, of catholic churches have agreed to the "full, supreme, and universal authority" of the bishop of Rome.

I will devote the next chapter to an argument for the divine origin of Rome's Audacious Claim different than that argued at Vatican I, Vatican II, and in the *Catechism of the Catholic Church*. At least one Roman Catholic scholar, Klaus Schatz, rejects the early origin of Papal Primacy, arguing instead for the divinely guided development of the doctrine. We will visit his argument now.

---

[432] *Catechism of the Catholic Church*, 1995, par. 882

Part VI | Chapter 26: Is Papal Primacy
a Divine Development?

Part VIII: Arguments

Rome's Audacious Claim

Chapter 26: Is Papal Primacy a Divine Development?

Klaus Schatz argues that despite the late origin of the Roman church's claim that its bishop has "full, supreme, and universal power over the whole Church," it is nonetheless "instituted by Christ."

> It is clear that Roman primacy was not a given from the outset; it underwent a long process of development whose initial phases extended well into the fifth century. The question is then: Can we reasonable say of this historically developed papacy that it was instituted by Christ and therefore must always continue to exist?[433]

First, I have to point out that Schatz's argument is a *de facto* denial of papal infallibility. As mentioned in chapter 1, all councils defined as "ecumenical" by the Roman Catholic Church are infallible.[434] Vatican I is in the list of ecumenical councils.[435] Vatican I declares:

> If anyone, therefore, shall say that Blessed Peter the Apostle was not appointed the Prince of all the Apostles and the visible Head of the whole Church Militant; or that the same, directly and immediately, received from the same, Our Lord Jesus Christ, a primacy of honor only, and not of true and proper jurisdiction; let him be anathema.[436]

Notice the phrase "directly and immediately." According to the infallible Vatican I Council, Peter—and thus all the Roman bishops—received "direct and immediately ... a primacy of jurisdiction." Thus, if Klaus Schatz is correct, and the pope's primacy of jurisdiction was not conferred by Jesus but divinely developed, then he is anathematized and should not be writing on the subject!

I love the irony of that argument, but the best answer to Dr. Schatz' Audacious Claim is Jude's command to all those "called, beloved in God the Father and kept safe for Jesus Christ" to "contend

---

[433] Schatz, 1996, *Papal Primacy*, p. 36
[434] Catholic Answers, 2018, "Infallibility," sec. "Ecumenical Councils," par. 2
[435] Keating, 1993, "The 21 Ecumenical Councils"
[436] Pius IX, 1870, "First Dogmatic Constitution," last paragraph of ch. 1

for the faith that was once for all handed down to the holy ones" (Jude 1:1, 3).

One simply does not add to the faith. For centuries the churches fought for the faith that came from the apostles and added nothing else. Irenaeus, for example, wrote:

> For the faith being ever one and the same, one who is able at great length to discourse concerning it does not make any addition to it, nor does one who can say but little diminish it. It does not follow that because men are endowed with greater or lesser degrees of intelligence that they should change the content [of the faith] itself.[437]

Tertullian of Carthage wrote:

> Since the Lord Jesus Christ sent the apostles to preach, [our rule is] that no others ought to be received as preachers than those whom Christ appointed.... Nor does the Son seem to have revealed Him to any other than the apostles, whom he sent forth to preach.[438]

Philip Schaff explains this concept as understood by the bishops at the Council of Nicea in 325.

> The question the Fathers considered was not what they supposed Holy Scripture might mean, nor what they, from à priori arguments, thought would be consistent with the mind of God, but something entirely different, to wit, what they had received. They understood their position to be that of witnesses, not that of exegetes. They recognized but one duty resting upon them in this respect—to hand down to other faithful men that good thing the Church had received according to the command of God. The first requirement was not learning, but honesty. The question they were called upon to answer was not, What do I think probable, or even certain,

---

[437] Irenaeus, c. 185, *Against Heresies*, Bk. I, ch. 10, par. 2; brackets in original
[438] Tertullian, 197-208, *Prescription Against Heretics*, ch. 21; brackets in original

Part VI | Chapter 26: Is Papal Primacy a Divine Development?

from Holy Scripture? but, What have I been taught, what has been entrusted to me to hand down to others?[439]

As the councils multiplied over the centuries, adherence to apostolic tradition disappeared, but the idea did not. To this day, even the *Catechism of the Catholic Church* gives lip service to the concept.

> And [Holy] Tradition transmits in its entirety the Word of God which has been entrusted to the apostles by Christ the Lord and the Holy Spirit. It transmits it to the successors of the apostles so that, enlightened by the Spirit of truth, they may faithfully preserve, expound, and spread it abroad by their preaching.[440]

The *Catechism* provides a back door, however, allowing the Roman Catholic Church to add to and change apostolic tradition while claiming to have preserved it.

> Thanks to the assistance of the Holy Spirit, the understanding of both the realities and the words of the heritage of faith is able to grow in the life of the Church:
> —"through the contemplation and study of believers who ponder these things in their hearts"; it is in particular "theological research [which] deepens knowledge of revealed truth."
> —"from the intimate sense of spiritual realities which [believers] experience," the sacred Scriptures "grow with the one who reads them."
> —"from the preaching of those who have received, along with their right of succession in the episcopate, the sure charism of truth."
> "It is clear therefore that, in the supremely wise arrangement of God, sacred Tradition, Sacred Scripture, and the Magisterium of the Church are so connected and associated that one of them cannot stand without the others.

---

[439] Schaff, 1886-1900, *Nicene and Post-Nicene Fathers*, NPNF2, Vol. XIV, "The First Ecumenical Council: The First Council of Nicea," sec. "Historical Introduction," par. 1

[440] *Catechism of the Catholic Church*, 1995, par. 81

Rome's Audacious Claim

Working together, each in its own way, under the action of the one Holy Spirit, they all contribute effectively to the salvation of souls."[441]

The wording is subtle: "The sacred Scriptures 'grow with the one who reads them.'" The result, however, is not so subtle: "sacred Tradition, Sacred Scripture, and the Magisterium of the Church are so connected and associated that one of them cannot stand without the others." As the *Catechism* says of itself, "This catechism will thus contain both the new and the old (cf. *Mt* 13:52), because the faith is always the same yet the source of ever new light."[442]

This kind of thinking has allowed the Roman Catholic Church to add to and change apostolic tradition drastically over the centuries.

Dr. Schatz's book is much like the *Catechism of the Catholic Church*. He acknowledges the authority of apostolic tradition, writing, "When threatened by heresies, the Church learns that it draws its life from the recollection of its apostolic origins." Unfortunately, he makes a concession that undermines the apostles: "In a further process, the Church learns through the experience of schisms that it needs an enduring center of unity."[443]

In both cases, the tradition of the apostles—those teachings, along with Scripture, that we can be reasonably certain were taught by the apostles—is not enough. In addition, we need the bishop of Rome or a "Magisterium of the Church" to be the foundation of unity.[444] The problem is that when they are given equal authority with the Scriptures and apostolic tradition, they spin off ideas like a "treasury of the Church," which contains good works from Mary and other saints. According to the Magisterium, the Church "intervenes in favor of individual Christians and opens for them the treasury of the merits of

---

[441] *Catechism of the Catholic Church*, 1995, par. 94-95; brackets, dashes, and quotation marks in original
[442] *Catechism of the Catholic Church*, 1995, sec. Apostolic Constitution, par. 2, parentheses in original
[443] Schatz, 1996, *Papal Primacy*, p. 37
[444] "By the Magisterium we mean the teaching office of the Church. It consists of the Pope and Bishops." (Most, 1990, "The Magisterium or Teaching Authority of the Church," par. 1)

Part VI | Chapter 26: Is Papal Primacy a Divine Development?

Christ and the saints to obtain from the Father of mercies the remission of the temporal punishments due for their sins."[445]

We saw, in the chapter on the fourth century, that the bishop of Rome did prove a better "center of unity" than the united bishops of the catholic churches. Dr. Schatz spends a great deal of *Papal Primacy* arguing that the progression of history has proven the need for this "enduring center of unity" in Rome. He concludes that unity is so important that …

> … in extreme cases of conflict one cannot orient oneself by some platonic ideal of church unity … but by the unromantic, hard, and conflictual reality of Church communion as the mutual acceptance of sinful human beings.… Even the Petrine office can only be accepted as something that is always sinful as well.[446]

The important thing Dr. Schatz misses here is the uniting authority of the apostles themselves. In the writings of Irenaeus and Tertullian, the bishops and churches are *witnesses* to the teaching of the apostles as written in Scripture and preserved in the churches. Just as the apostles were witnesses to Jesus (Acts 1:8), making Jesus the one foundation (1 Cor. 3:11), so the churches were witnesses to apostolic truth, making that truth the center of unity.

When those churches and bishops stop preserving the truth, it is not logical to remove the authority of the truth and give it to a man or men instead. Perhaps it might be logical to stick to the one bishop preserving the truth if there were one. Dr. Schatz presents the bishop of Rome as that one bishop, but both he and the Roman Catholic Church have forgotten his mission: the preservation of the apostolic preaching unchanged! The *Catechism of the Catholic Church* adds a "Magisterium" of equal authority to apostolic tradition, and Dr. Schatz leaves it out, making the "enduring center of unity" to be "something that is always sinful."[447]

---

[445] *Catechism of the Catholic Church*, 1995, par. 1478; see chapter 28
[446] Schatz, 1996, *Papal Primacy*, p. 37
[447] *Catechism of the Catholic Church*, 1995, par. 96; Schatz, 1996, *Papal Primacy*, p. 37

Rome's Audacious Claim

Schatz's argument replaces apostolic truth with a position filled by sinful men. As Jesus tells us, bad trees always produce bad fruit. They cannot produce good fruit, and Dr. Schatz's "enduring center of unity" has produced the worst of fruit: a permanent schism between the Eastern Orthodox Churches and Europe's Roman Catholicism. By the time of that split, Rome had made itself a prime example of the adage that absolute power corrupts absolutely. The West's "Catholic Church," led by the Roman bishop, was corrupt from top to bottom.[448]

We saw that the Eastern churches of the Roman Empire granted primacy of honor to the Roman bishop and tolerated his claims to a primacy of jurisdiction. This did not lead to an enduring center of unity, but to the Great Schism.[449] As the U.S. Conference of Catholic Bishops acknowledges:

> The particular form of primacy among the Churches exercised by the bishops of Rome has been and remains the chief point of dispute between the Orthodox and Roman Catholic Churches, and their chief obstacle to full ecclesial communion with each other.[450]

Although they admitted this, the U.S. Conference of Catholic Bishops has insisted in their negotiations with Lutheran theologians and Orthodox churches that the universal jurisdiction of the bishop of Rome has served the unity of the Church at times in history.[451] Perhaps this was true from the fourth to the eighth centuries, but, afterward, it has been the source of two of the greatest divisions in Church history: the Great Schism and the Protestant Reformation. The U.S. Conference of Catholic Bishops agrees that Papal Primacy "has been and remains the chief obstacle" to healing those schisms.[452]

---

[448] The state of the Roman Catholic Church at the end of the first millennium and afterward will be given in chapter 27.

[449] Mann, 1925, *The Lives of the Popes: Vol. IV*, p. 6; see chapter 25

[450] United States Conference of Catholic Bishops, 1989, "An Agreed Statement on Conciliarity and Primacy in The Church," par. 7

[451] e.g., United States Conference of Catholic Bishops, 1973, "Differing Attitudes Toward Papal Primacy," sec. "The Setting of the Problem," par. 2b; United States Conference of Catholic Bishops, 1989, "An Agreed Statement on Conciliarity and Primacy in the Church," par. 7b

[452] United States Conference of Catholic Bishops, 1989, "An Agreed Statement on Conciliarity and Primacy in The Church," par. 7

Part VI | Chapter 26: Is Papal Primacy a Divine Development?

With that, we can dismiss Dr. Schatz's argument that the authority of the papacy has been ordained and approved by God by the testimony of history. Rome's Audacious Claim has not proven to be an enduring center of unity. Instead, its claim to "full, supreme, and universal power" has led to "full, supreme, and universal corruption."

In the next chapter, we will let Roman Catholic sources describe that corruption.

Rome's Audacious Claim

Chapter 27: Rome's Corrupt Succession

We talked about "succession" in the chapters on Irenaeus and Tertullian. We saw that this was not merely "succession," but "apostolic succession." It was preserving the truth taught by the apostles in every church from bishop to bishop and from one college of elders to the next.

We saw that the bishop in Rome once had a succession from both Peter and Paul. That succession did not make the bishop of Rome a bishop over other bishops, not even in the days of Rome's greatness, but it did make Rome a "preeminent authority" on apostolic truth.[453] On the two occasions when a Roman bishop tried to exert authority over other bishops, he was repudiated.

After the bishops of Rome faithfully supported the Nicene Creed through the fourth century, they established themselves as "elder,"[454] the rock of orthodoxy when the East was in turmoil. This standard continued through the fifth-century councils, where the patriarchs of the East alienated both the churches of Egypt and those of the Persian Empire. The churches of the Roman Empire would continue to look to Rome for several centuries. The greatness of Rome in the first three centuries became the faithful adherence to orthodoxy into the next five.

What happened afterward, though, was a perfect example, not of a divine stamp of approval, but of absolute power leading to absolute corruption—or, in Rome's case, of "full, supreme, and universal power" leading to "full, supreme, and universal corruption."

There are two issues to address in this chapter: corruption, and the various breaks in the succession of the church in Rome.

Corruption

Jesus said we can recognize true and false prophets by their fruit. "Rotten trees" cannot produce good fruit, and good trees cannot produce bad fruit (Matthew 7:17-20).

"Rotten trees" is excellent wording. At one time, the church in Rome was not only the most respected church in the world, it was also

---

[453] Irenaeus, c. 185, *Against Heresies*, Bk. III, ch. 3, par. 2
[454] Cleenewerck, 2007, *His Broken Body*, p. 225

the most trustworthy. In the fourth century, the Roman church, and in particular Bishop Julius, was a fortress for supporters of the Nicene Creed while the Eastern Roman Empire was disintegrating under the influence of heretical bishops supported by a heretical emperor. When the Eastern bishops found new issues to dispute in the fifth century, the fatherly presence of Leo was there to guide them. But even the best trees can rot.

In 250, the elders of Rome said that to fall from their greatness would be the greatest of crimes.[455] Cyprian decried adhering to a "sinful prelate," saying the people shared in his sin if they communed with him.[456]

The remarkable perversities of the medieval popes of Rome are so famous that modern Rome has resorted to defending the office rather than the men. Horace Mann, whose papal biographies I will quote throughout this chapter, mourned over the papacy of the tenth century, when "the supreme Pontiffs" were "degraded, in part by the treatment to which they were subjected, and in part by the vices of some of those whom brute force thrust into the chair of Peter." He even says that "one might have been tempted to believe that their authority must for ever have come to an end."[457]

Mann found himself required to defend the corruption, saying "Have I not also the assurance of Pope Leo I, the Great, that 'the dignity of Peter is not lost even in an unworthy successor.'"[458]

As said much earlier in this book, Leo would have turned over in his grave if he had seen his anniversary sermon abused in this way. Leo was talking about himself with great humility, acknowledging that even a man like himself, righteous in the eyes of all around him, was unworthy to sit in the chair of Peter.[459] Leo would never have broken bread with the more wayward popes of the tenth century (and later). We would have found him on his knees somewhere, asking God what had become of the church he once knew.

This is what Daniel did in Babylon. He fell on his knees in repentance for the sins of the people (Daniel 9:3-20). Because of those

---

[455] "Epistles of Cyprian," 250, Epistle 30 (Oxford 30), par. 2
[456] Cyprian, 257, Epistle 67 (Oxford 67), par. 3
[457] Mann, 1925, *The Lives of the Popes: Vol. IV*, p. 1
[458] Mann, 1925, *The Lives of the Popes: Vol. IV*, p. viii
[459] Leo I, 443, "Sermons," Sermon III

Part VI | Chapter 27: Rome's Corrupt Succession

sins, Jerusalem had been destroyed, the temple razed, and the people carried captive to Babylon. Dare any of us think that the God who removed kings and eventually sent the kingdoms of Israel and Judah into captivity would overlook the same horrific behavior in Roman bishops? As the writer of Hebrews says:

> Anyone who rejects the law of Moses is put to death without pity on the testimony of two or three witnesses. Do you not think that a much worse punishment is due the one who has contempt for the Son of God, considers unclean the covenant-blood by which he was consecrated, and insults the spirit of grace? (Heb. 10:28-29)

Perhaps Scott Hahn would not have been so hasty to affiliate Peter with a dynasty of stewards if he had paid attention to what happened to those stewards when they were not faithful to God.[460]

Catholic Answers makes a claim, astonishing in its inaccuracy, that "the truly remarkable thing is the great degree of sanctity found in the papacy throughout history; the 'bad popes' stand out precisely because they are so rare."[461]

This is only true if one uses a very generous definition of "rare."

Laurent Cleenewerck, an Orthodox historian, grants Rome theological orthodoxy for "the most part of the first millennium."[462] There is a reason that he has to add "the most part." Let's look at the last tenth of the first millennium and the first tenth of the second millennium.

The Popes of the Tenth and Eleventh Century

I chose Horace Mann's *The Lives of the Popes in the Early Middle Ages: Vol. IV*, published in 1925, for this history. Mann's is the most favorable history of the tenth-century papacy I could find, yet he was reticent even to publish it.[463] He was a Roman Catholic monsignor assigned to write the history of all the popes. Unlike some biographers, he rejects the input of Liudprand, a Lombard historian

---

[460] Hahn, (n.d.), "Scott Hahn on the Papacy," sec. 2, par. 19-27
[461] Catholic Answers, 2018, "Papal Infallibility," sec. "Some Clarifications," par. 4
[462] 2007, *His Broken Body*, p. 225
[463] Mann, 1925, *The Lives of the Popes: Vol. IV*, p. vii

Rome's Audacious Claim

loyal to the German kings Otto, Otto II, and Otto III. Liudprand hated the Romans, and he apparently loved juicy gossip. *The Works of Liudprand of Cremona*[464] provide a much more sordid, but less reliable, history than I will report below.

As the year 900 approached, the papacy had fallen into the control of powerful, competing Italian families. As Mann puts it, "Freedom of election had been lost in the ninth century, and in this dark age the popes and the bishops became the creatures not simply of emperors and kings, but of petty local barons."[465]

The best starting place for our history of the tenth-century popes is the "cadaver synod," led by Pope Stephen VI.[466] He was elected to the "Holy See" in 896. Among his first acts was to exhume the previous pope, Formosus, and put his body on trial in a synod. It should be said that Lambert, the Holy Roman emperor,[467] surely put Stephen up to it. Lambert had been crowned by Pope Formosus, but Formosus turned on him by inviting Arnulf, a descendant of Charlemagne, to invade Italy. Lambert, with "his warlike mother Ageltruda," came to Rome shortly before the bizarre synod.[468]

Stephen appointed a deacon to answer for Formosus's cadaver. The synod found the late Formosus guilty of "performing the functions of a bishop when he had been deposed and for passing from the See of Porto to that of Rome." He was stripped of his papal robes, and the two fingers he used to perform benedictions were cut off. [469]

In 897 Stephen was strangled, and Romanus was chosen in his place. He died four months later, probably taken out by a rival clan. Pope Theodore II replaced him and reigned no more than a month.

---

[464] Wright, 1930, George Routledge & Sons
[465] Mann, 1925, *The Lives of the Popes: Vol. IV*, p. 6
[466] Or Stephen VII. Pope Stephen II was appointed to replace Zachary in 752, but he died before his consecration. Another Stephen replaced him, and later lists differ on whether his replacement was Stephen III because Stephen II was elected or Stephen II because his predecessor never served. To this day, the Stephen that rose to power in 896 is listed as Stephen VI (VII). I will simply refer to him as Stephen VI.
[467] The extent of the Holy Roman Emperor's rule in Europe varied. The title was an attempt to duplicate the combined authority of emperor and pope across Europe that had been achieved by Charlemagne and Pope Leo III in 800. As we progress through these stories, we get a glimpse of how little power some of those emperors had.
[468] Mann, 1925, *The Lives of the Popes: Vol. IV*, p. 80
[469] Mann, 1912, "Pope Stephen (VI) VII"

Part VI | Chapter 27: Rome's Corrupt Succession

The circumstances of his election and death are unknown. John IX replaced him, and he managed to stay alive for two years. A rival faction tried to get Cardinal Sergius on the papal throne, but John was able both to repel and to excommunicate him.

He was followed by Benedict IV in the year 900. Benedict IV seemed to be a decent pope, but he died in the summer of 903. Pope Leo V succeeded Benedict, and a contemporary described him as "of praiseworthy life and holiness."[470] Despite the praise, he was pope only a month before Christopher, a cardinal and priest, overthrew and imprisoned him. The Roman Catholic Church classifies Christopher as an antipope, because he was not duly elected. He reigned for about six months before being overthrown by the same Cardinal Sergius that had opposed John IX.

Cardinal Sergius became Pope Sergius III. In a morbidly humorous historical reference, Eugenius Vulgarius, a contemporary priest from Naples, states that Sergius had both Leo V and Christopher removed from imprisonment and put to death out of pity. Mann comments that "Leo and Christopher could well have done without this" pity. He also mentions that other biographers know nothing of this event.[471]

It had been less than eight years since the ascension of Pope Stephen VI, and five popes and an antipope (Christopher) had sat on Peter's throne.

Christopher managed to remain on the throne for six months, and his successor Sergius III ruled for six years. His ascension brings up an interesting story.

Sergius had been bishop of Caere. He was consecrated to that position by Pope Formosus. The problem is that despite the outrageous and violent ascensions to the papacy, the bishops of Europe were still trying to hold to the ancient canon that says that a bishop cannot move from one see to another.[472] Since the pope is the bishop of Rome, any bishop elected pope was transferring to a new see. To avoid this

---

[470] Mann, 1910, "Pope Leo V"
[471] Mann, 1925, *The Lives of the Popes, Vol. IV*, p. 115
[472] e.g., Canon 15 of the Council of Nicea; see Pavao, 2009-2019, "Canons of the Council of Nicea"

problem, if a bishop had hope of becoming pope, he would sometimes have himself demoted to deacon.[473]

Sergius had done this after serving as bishop for three years. Horace Mann remarks that, "Bishops returning to the rank of deacons to become Popes proves clearly enough that the ambitions of men can scarcely be restrained by regulations."[474]

For our purposes, the most important thing Sergius did was write an epitaph for Stephen VI. In it, he expresses his approval for the "cadaver synod," where Formosus was tried. He also called John IX a "wolf."[475] Since this chapter has to do with the corrupt succession of Roman bishops, it is significant that a pope approved of the posthumous defrocking of a predecessor and described another as a wolf.

It gets worse, though. Sergius got the Roman clergy to rescind all consecrations performed by Formosus, which also meant that all the appointments by these now unconsecrated bishops were also void. "According to Auxilius," he secured the cooperation of the Roman clergy by bribery and threats of exile or violence. Though many bishops, especially those closer to Rome, submitted to reordination, more distant bishops were infuriated.[476]

Another who was infuriated was the said Auxilius. He was probably a deacon in Naples, and he wrote "a series of writings" about Pope Formosus and his successors.[477] Like Cyprian, he did not agree with the idea that it was the office and not the occupant that mattered. He refused reordination by Sergius, yet continued to "perform Mass."[478] In justification of this, he wrote:

---

[473] Apparently, the bishops of the tenth century had forgotten that Canon 15 of the Council of Nicea forbids even deacons to move from church to church (Pavao, 2009-2019, "Canons of the Council of Nicea")
[474] Mann, 1925, *The Lives of the Popes: Vol. IV*, p. 120
[475] Mann, 1925, *The Lives of the Popes: Vol. IV*, p. 121
[476] Mann, 1925, *The Lives of the Popes: Vol. IV*, p. 122
[477] Wikipedia, 2018, "Auxilius of Naples"
[478] By this time, and in fact much earlier, ordination as a "priest" (formerly elder) or bishop was necessary to consecrate the Eucharist, which means to pray the prayer that changes the bread and wine spiritually into the flesh and blood of Christ.

Part VI | Chapter 27: Rome's Corrupt Succession

> "Due honor ... must be paid to the different sees. But if those who occupy them deviate from the right path, they are not to be followed."[479]

Mann defends the honor of Sergius. Sergius was and is still rumored to be the father of a son who would become Pope John XI. Mann denies these rumors,[480] but admits that Sergius III was a "pronounced party-man," meaning a strong defender of his Italian clan. Mann denies also the "revengeful cruelty" and "lust" assigned to him by Vulgarius and Liudprand.[481]

Sergius reigned for seven years, until 911, and was succeeded by two popes about whom we know little. Anastasius III reigned for just over two years, and Pope Lando sat on Peter's throne for a few months.

Lando was followed by John X, of whom *The Catholic Encyclopedia* says, "The real head of this aristocratic faction was the elder Theodora, wife of the Senator Theophylactus."[482] Mann confirms this, writing:

> The faction of Theophylactus and his family were certainly dominant in Rome in the days of Sergius, and of the popes who succeeded him during some sixty years; and if the *Patricians* Crescentii were indeed, as we have supposed, descended directly from Theodora I through her daughter Theodora II, then it may be said that the house of Theophylactus swayed the destinies of Rome until the accession of the German popes.[483]

Theophylactus and Theodora were the parents of Marozia and Theodora II. Marozia was accused by Liudprand of being the mistress of Sergius III. Whether or not this was true, her mother was responsible for the appointing of John X, and John XI and XII were

---

[479] Mann, 1925, *The Lives of the Popes: Vol. IV*, p. 123
[480] Mann, 1912, "Pope Sergius III"
[481] Mann, 1925, *The Lives of the Popes: Vol. IV*, p. 140
[482] Kirsch, 1910, "Pope John X"
[483] Mann, 1925, *The Lives of the Popes: Vol. IV*, p. 138

Rome's Audacious Claim

her son and grandson. That is powerful influence over the papal throne![484]

Marozia's influence over the papacy is almost certainly the foundation for the rumor that there was a Pope Joan, pretending to be a man until she gave birth in public. This rumor is not true, but Marozia's sway over the papacy is.

John X was appointed in 914. Just eighteen years had passed since the ascension of Stephen VI, and eight popes had arisen and been deposed.

John turned out to be a very useful pontiff as far as politics go. He allied King Berengar of Italy, the Italian clans, and the citizens of Rome, and he even secured the aid of Byzantine emperor Leo to drive the Muslim Saracens out of southern Italy. He did this in a few months, and it settled the turmoil of Italy for a decade.

Unfortunately, King Berengar was killed in 924 by assassins from Hungary. Pope John tried to ally himself with King Hugh from Provence (in France), but Marozia, the "senatrix" of Rome, saw that as a challenge to her power. When her husband, Alberic I, died the same year, she married Guy (or Guido), Hugh's half-brother, the marquis of Tuscany. Not long after, Guy made an attack on Rome and had John thrown in prison.

Mann admits it is probable that Marozia chose John's successor, Leo VI.[485] He and Stephen VIII are virtually unknown. Leo reigned a few months and Stephen over two years.

They were followed by John XI, the son of Marozia and either her husband Alberic or of Pope Sergius III, depending on whom you believe. Whoever his father was, John XI was Marozia's son, and she maneuvered him onto the papal throne.

She had less control over her second son, Alberic II. Alberic overthrew his mother and imprisoned her in 932. She was lost to history at that point.

Alberic II took over the secular rule of Rome and made sure his brother, John XI, remained in his role as spiritual leader of Rome, without interfering in the political affairs of the city. Even the book

---

[484] Kirsch, 1910, "Pope John X"
[485] Mann, 1925, *The Lives of the Popes: Vol. IV*, p. 188

Part VI | Chapter 27: Rome's Corrupt Succession

Bad Popes speaks well of the popes elected while Alberic ruled Rome. Chamberlin, author of *Bad Popes*, writes:

> Again, the office of pope had little attraction for the avaricious and the effect upon the characters of the popes was immediate, dramatic and, so long as Alberic ruled, enduring.[486]

Those popes were Leo VII, Stephen VIII, Marinus II, and Agapetus II. They were bishops of Rome from 936 to 955. At that point, Alberic II made the awful mistake of reuniting the secular and spiritual power of Rome. He did this in the person of his son Octavius (grandson of Marozia), who would become both leader of Rome and take the name of Pope John XII.

The papacy of John XII was perhaps the worst thing that ever happened to the Roman church. Even *The Catholic Encyclopedia* say that the Lateran was spoken of as a brothel in his time.[487] Mann writes, "There cannot be a doubt that John XII was anything but what a Pope, the chief pastor of Christendom, should have been."[488]

His story is almost unbelievable.

His father, Alberic II, made the Roman nobles promise that they would elect his son Octavius to succeed Agapetus II as pope. They were true to their word, consecrating him on December 16, 955, as John XII. He also became king of Rome in his father's stead, and he maintained the name "Octavius" when engaging in secular affairs.

In 960, Pope John courted King Otto of Saxony, who had aroused the gratefulness and admiration of Europe by driving the Huns out of Germany. On February 2, 962, John invited him to Rome and crowned him as "Holy Roman Emperor."

This was a huge step. All the kings of Europe longed for the role and the glory of Charlemagne, who was crowned Holy Roman Emperor in 800 by Pope Leo III. Otto now had that glory. Respected by Europe and crowned by the pope, he was Holy Roman Emperor. He enjoyed the support of Pope John XII ... for two weeks.

Apparently, the new emperor made the mistake of giving Pope John a lecture on reforming his life. Even Mann, who carefully

---

[486] Chamberlin, 1969, *Bad Popes*, p. 38
[487] Kirsch, 1910, "Pope John XII"
[488] Mann, 1925, *The Lives of the Popes: Vol. IV*, p. 241

defends these embarrassing popes by finding sources who praise them in opposition to those who vilified them, has to report that John XII could not bear the exhortation to morality and went looking for a new champion.[489] He chose Adalbert, the son of Berengarius, Otto's strongest enemy in Italy.

John tried to stir up Italy to rally with Berengarius and Adalbert against Otto, but Otto got hold of his missives. As he was already engaged in battle, Otto sent representatives to Rome. They came back reporting that female pilgrims were not safe in the city, that the Lateran[490] was a brothel, and that Rome's churches were in ruin. They also reported that John was negotiating with Adalbert, seeking to replace Otto as emperor.

When Otto came back to Rome in November of 963, Pope John and Adalbert fled. Otto held a synod consisting of fifty bishops. They charged John with "sacrilege, simony, perjury, murder, adultery, and incest."[491]

Liudprand, the bitter biographer of Marozia and the Roman popes, was with Otto, so in this case he was an eyewitness to these events. He recorded every testimony of the synod carefully. Each person, no matter his rank, had his name and testimony written by Liudprand. This was to ensure that the trial run by an emperor would not be rejected by the inhabitants of Rome. The emperor had no authority there, and Liudprand wanted to ensure the inhabitants of Rome would not see the trial as an inappropriate intervention by a secular emperor. But his careful record-keeping backfired.[492]

Otto and the synod appointed a new pope, Leo VIII, who is recognized as a pope by the Roman Catholic Church today.[493] He was unable to stay in power. In February of 964, just three months after Otto's synod, John XII returned with the support of the Roman populace. Leo VIII fled to Otto. Apparently, a pope appointed by a German emperor did not please the citizens of Rome.

John called another synod that declared the previous one invalid. At that council he avenged himself on those who had testified against

---

[489] Mann, *The Lives of the Popes: Vol. IV*, p. 254
[490] The pope's dwelling place in Rome.
[491] Kirsch, 1910, "Pope John XII"
[492] Chamberlin, 1969, *Bad Popes*, p. 56
[493] *The Catholic Encyclopedia*, 1911, "The List of Popes"

Part VI | Chapter 27: Rome's Corrupt Succession

him. *The Bad Popes* reports, probably on the witness of Liudprand, that John tore out the tongue of one witness, scourged another, and severed the hand of a third.[494] Mann reports that John "severely punish[ed] some of his enemies by mutilation or death."[495]

Otto considered returning, but there was no need, as John died in May. Rumor had it that John had been caught in adultery and killed by the angry husband. The story is probably not true, but it does indicate the Roman estimation of Pope John's character.[496]

I could go on from pope to pope, showing that their elections, appointments, and deaths had little or nothing to do with anything Christian.

We will jump forward a few decades to address another set of sibling popes who were driven from their thrones by their nephew, who also held the name of Theophylact and was from Tusculum. The city of Tusculum held the papacy in its grip for more than a century, from the ascension of Sergius III in 904 through the multiple reigns of Benedict IX from 1032 to 1048.

Benedict VIII and John XIX were sons of Count Gregory I of Tusculum, and their nephew, Benedict IX, was his grandson.

Benedict's story is interesting even on the surface, so we will let Horace Mann's article in *The Catholic Encyclopedia* tell it:

> [Benedict IX] was a disgrace to the Chair of Peter. Regarding it as a sort of heirloom, his father Alberic placed him upon it when a mere youth ... of about twenty (October, 1032)....
>
> Taking advantage of the dissolute life he was leading, one of the factions in the city drove him from it (1044) amid the greatest disorder, and elected an antipope (Sylvester III) in the person of John, Bishop of Sabina.... Benedict, however, succeeded in expelling Sylvester the same year.[497]

Not satisfied with demeaning the papacy with profligate living, Benedict *sold* the episcopacy of Rome for "a large sum."[498] *The Bad*

---

[494] Chamberlin, 1969, *Bad Popes*, p. 60
[495] Mann, 1969, *The Lives of the Popes*, p. 262
[496] Hemans, 1869, *History of Medieval Christianity*, p. 22
[497] Mann, 1907, "Pope Benedict IX"; brackets mine, parentheses in original
[498] Mann, 1907, "Pope Benedict IX"

Rome's Audacious Claim

Popes says this sum was 1,500 pounds of gold, but it gives no source for this figure.[499]

The buyer of the papacy was Giovanni Gratiano, archpriest of St. John in Rome. All sources agree that Gratiano was just trying to rid the papal throne of its unworthy occupant. Gratiano was officially elected, and he became Gregory VI.

Benedict changed his mind, however, and he returned to Rome to get his chair back. Henry III, king of Italy (and Germany and Burgundy) intervened. He arranged a council in Sutri (about thirty miles from Rome), which ousted Benedict, Sylvester, and Gregory. A German bishop was elected as Clement II in 1046.

Clement turned out to be another decent person, but Horace Mann's introduction to him highlights the papal problem of the tenth and eleventh centuries:

> The second German whom the arbitrary power of the princes of his country had placed on the chair of Peter, he was a credit to the king who selected him, and a man of very different character to some of those whom the local magnates of Rome had thrust into the Holy See.[500]

Ironically, Mann's praise of Clement II as a decent person condemned at least some of his 150 years of his predecessors as "of very different character."

The succession of Roman bishops in the tenth and eleventh centuries was in no way like the one described by Irenaeus, in which a bishop and his elders carefully preserved the teachings of the apostles in order to pass them on to God's people. If the Roman Catholic Church and its apologists are going to appeal to Irenaeus and Tertullian for support of Rome's Audacious Claim, they will need to explain just how Irenaeus' description of apostolic succession justifies the succession we have just read about.

To be clear, though, the problems did not end with Clement II. We cannot continue describing all the immoral or unspiritual popes. This is not a history of the papacy from Peter to the present. Horace Mann and others have written that history. This is an examination of Rome's

---

[499] Chamberlin, 1969, *Bad Popes*, p. 70
[500] Mann, *The Lives of the Popes: Vol. V*, p. 270

Part VI | Chapter 27: Rome's Corrupt Succession

Audacious Claim, and it is time to move on to a different problem with Rome's succession.

Breaks in the Succession

Almost 250 years after Clement II, the Roman Catholic Church found a new way to mar their claimed succession. I do not think it is necessary to go much into detail here. The events are so famous they have names: "the Babylonian Captivity of the Church" and "the Great Western Schism."

The Babylonian Captivity of the Church is also called the "Avignon Papacy." It began in 1305 with the election of Pope Clement V.

Due to political conflict in France and Italy, King Philip IV of France got an Italian family to kidnap Pope Boniface VIII from Rome. When Boniface refused to resign, his captors publicly shamed him, and he died not long after.

Philip then gathered cardinals in France, who elected Clement V. Clement served in Avignon rather than Rome, and so did six other popes after him. For seventy-three years, not one pope set foot in Rome.

I remind my readers that "pope" is just English for the Latin word "*papa*." It means "father." "Pope" is not his position; it's a title, and one (among several) banned for spiritual leaders by Jesus (Matt. 23:8-10). The pope's *position* is bishop of Rome. Surely one cannot be bishop of a city that is 595 miles away.

Worse, once the Italian cardinals managed to elect a "bishop of Rome" in Rome after seventy-three years, they did not like him! Urban VI wanted too many reforms. The most unwelcome reform was the elimination of simony.[501] Since most of the cardinals had purchased their positions, it is easy to see why his papacy failed.

The Italian cardinals turned on him, going to the Avignon cardinals to complain that Urban had forced them to elect him. The French cardinals responded by electing Clement VII. There were now two duly elected popes!

This event began the Great Western Schism. Four popes served in Rome and two in Avignon from 1378 to 1409.

---

[501] The purchase of clerical offices.

Rome's Audacious Claim

In 1409, a council was held in Pisa that tried to appoint a pope to replace Gregory XII (Rome) and Benedict XIII (Avignon). They appointed Peter Philarges as Alexander V. But neither Gregory nor Benedict agreed to resign, so now there were three popes!

Alexander died a year later and was replaced by another participant in the Council of Pisa, who became John XXIII.

In October 1413, King Sigismund of Germany convinced John XXIII to convene a council and invite both of the other popes. The council convened in November 1414 in Constance.[502] The council rejected all three popes and appointed Martin V in their place. King Sigismund enforced the decision, and the papal throne again had one occupant.

This morass of competitors for the papal throne that Rome calls a succession bears no resemblance to the careful preservation of apostolic truth described by Irenaeus and Tertullian. Because of this, we have to ask whether Rome was able to preserve apostolic truth with a corrupt and divided succession. It is to that question we will now turn our attention.

---

[502] Now Konstanz, Germany.

Part VI | Chapter 28: Apostolic Tradition Preserved in Rome?

Chapter 28: Apostolic Tradition Preserved in Rome?

> For [the apostles] were desirous that these men should be very perfect and blameless in all things, whom also they were leaving behind as their successors, delivering up their own place of government to these men; which men, if they discharged their functions honestly, would be a great boon (to the Church), but if they should fall away, the direst calamity.[503]

We have seen that the leaders of the church of Rome did fall away. They were not "perfect and blameless," and they did not "discharge their functions honestly." The elders of Rome called this a "great crime,"[504] and, in the quote above, Irenaeus called it "the direst calamity."

We saw a portion of that calamity in the last chapter in the corruption of the papal throne itself, which became a political tool, and in the corruption of the popes themselves. The primary purpose of succession, however, was to preserve apostolic truth.

We will now look at that "direst calamity" in the area of apostolic tradition. How well did Rome preserve it?

True Roman Catholic Doctrines

In the second chapter of this book, we discussed the difference between scholarly and apologetic works. Scholarly works are held to a higher standard. Though I do not have the educational qualifications to arouse the review of scholars or to publish in Christian journals, my goal is to meet scholarly standards in this book.

Before I challenge the worst of Roman Catholic doctrines, I need to address some doctrines that are not false. I do not want anyone to assume that I consider all Roman Catholic doctrines false or all Protestant doctrines true.

---

[503] Irenaeus, c. 185, *Against Heresies*, Bk. III, ch. 3, par. 1; brackets mine, parentheses in original
[504] "Epistles of Cyprian," 250, Epistle 30 (Oxford 30), par. 2

Rome's Audacious Claim

Baptismal regeneration is not a false doctrine. It was the universal teaching of the Church from the beginning. In the middle of the second century, Justin Martyr wrote, "As many as are persuaded and believe that what we teach and say is true ... are brought by us where there is water, and they are regenerated in the same manner in which we were ourselves regenerated."[505] Thirty years later, Irenaeus wrote, "This class of men [i.e., the gnostics] has been instigated by Satan to a denial of that baptism which is regeneration to God."[506]

You will find nothing to contradict this in any of the pre-Nicene fathers, and even Protestants know that the Roman Catholic and Orthodox Churches taught baptismal regeneration after Nicea.

Biblically, the idea that conversion and rebirth happen at baptism is so clear that the strongest argument for it is to list all the verses that mention baptism or water in the New Testament.[507] As Paul wrote to Titus:

> "Not by works of righteousness which we did ourselves, but according to his mercy, he saved us through the washing of regeneration and renewing by the Holy Spirit. (Tit. 3:5)

Anyone familiar with Church history will have an almost impossible time denying that Paul meant baptism when he wrote "the washing of regeneration."

That said, baptism is not magical. It is the action taken by someone who wants to follow Jesus and join his kingdom. It is an act of faith and commitment. Infant baptism is a very early practice in the apostolic churches, but not so early that it qualifies as apostolic tradition.[508]

That works are required to go to heaven is not a false doctrine. While we are initially justified and saved apart from works (Rom. 3:28; Eph. 2:8-9), even Christians will be judged by their works. Our works are the product of grace and the new birth (Eph. 2:8-10), the power of the Spirit (Gal. 6:8-9), the teaching of Scripture (2 Tim. 3:16-17), and the help of our brothers and sisters (Heb. 3:12-13;

---

[505] Justin Martyr, 150-160, *First Apology*, ch. 61
[506] Irenaeus, c. 185, *Against Heresies*, Bk. I, ch. 21, par. 1
[507] e.g., Mark 16:16; Jn. 3:5; Acts 2:38; Acts 22:16; Rom. 6:3; Gal. 3:27; Col. 2:12; Tit. 3:5; 1 Pet. 3:21
[508] Pavao, 2009-2019, "FAQ: Infant Baptism"

Part VI | Chapter 28: Apostolic Tradition Preserved in Rome?

10:24-25), but we will still be judged by them (Matt. 25:31-46; 2 Cor. 5:10-11; 1 Pet. 1:17; Rev. 3:4-5). Just as a trip through early Church history undoes Rome's Audacious Claim, so the same trip undoes many treasured Protestant traditions.

That we are mystically eating the flesh and blood of the Lord Jesus Christ at communion is not a false doctrine. While I cannot argue for the "real presence" of Christ in the Eucharist (i.e., communion) from Scripture, the earliest church fathers universally taught it. Thus, it has a strong, almost undeniable, claim to apostolic origin. Ignatius, bishop of the apostle Paul's home church of Antioch in the early second century, called the bread and wine of communion "the medicine of immortality, the antidote which prevents us from dying, and a cleansing remedy driving away evil."[509]

Justin Martyr, who lived in Rome in the mid second century, wrote:

> Not as common bread and common drink do we receive these, but in the same way as Jesus Christ our Savior, having been made flesh by the Word of God, had both flesh and blood for our salvation, so likewise have we been taught that the food which is blessed by the prayer of his word, and from which our blood and flesh by transmutation are nourished, is the flesh and blood of that Jesus who was made flesh.[510]

The "transmutation" mentioned here is digestion, not transubstantiation. I reject transubstantiation—the idea that the Eucharist is no longer bread and wine but actual flesh and blood[511]—as a carnal interpretation of what Jesus himself called spiritual words (Jn. 6:63). "Real presence," however—the idea that the flesh and blood is mystically present in the Eucharist—is almost certainly of apostolic origin.

That said, I can now address the more awful doctrines that the church in Rome has proffered over the centuries.

---

[509] Ignatius, 107 or 116, "Epistle to the Ephesians," ch. 20
[510] Justin, 150-160, *First Apology*, ch. 66
[511] *Catechism of the Catholic Church*, 1995, par. 1375

The Papacy

We have spent this whole book showing that the papacy has no foundation in Scripture, no foundation in the first few centuries of Christian history, and has produced bad fruit. This doctrine split the apostolic churches of the Roman Empire and led to the Protestant Reformation.

A New Priesthood

Bishops and elders, who are the same people in Scripture,[512] are not called priests in the Bible. Neither are they called priests in the fathers until they began writing in Latin.[513]

While the Roman Catholic Church does not deny the priesthood of all believers, it has has made the clergy another class of priests. In Hebrews 7:12, we read, "When there is a change of priesthood, there is necessarily a change of law as well." It is one thing for Jesus the Messiah to take the priesthood of Melchizedek and bring the law of Moses to its fullness; it is quite another for anyone else to establish a new priesthood.[514]

Indulgences

This doctrine directly led to the Protestant Reformation, and to this day it is an embarrassment to the Roman Catholic Church; yet it has not been eliminated.

The Roman Catholic Church distinguishes between "grave sin" that makes a person "incapable of eternal life" and other sins which "must be purified here on earth, or after death in the state called purgatory."[515] We can be forgiven of these sins, but "temporal punishments" to purify the sinner are experienced in "sufferings and trials." "Works of mercy," "charity," "prayer," and "practices of penance" are also ways God gives temporal punishments that purify the Christian.[516]

---

[512] Acts 28:17,28; Tit. 1:5-7; 1 Pet. 5:1-4; see also ch. 6
[513] Jenkins, 2017, "Inventing the Christian Priesthood." Tertullian and Cyprian, mentioned in this article, both wrote in Latin.
[514] Heb. 7:11-26; Matt. 5:17
[515] *Catechism of the Catholic Church*, 1995, par. 1472
[516] *Catechism of the Catholic Church*, 1995, par. 1471, 1473

Part VI | Chapter 28: Apostolic Tradition Preserved in Rome?

An indulgence is the granting, by the Church, of relief from these temporal punishments.[517]

This doctrine cannot be found in Scripture nor in the first thousand years of Church writings. Indulgences themselves, however, are not nearly as shocking to common sense and Christian doctrine as the foundation on which they lie: the "Church's treasury."

The Church's treasury, according to the Roman Catholic Church, is "the infinite value, which can never be exhausted, which Christ's merits have before God." This is an inoffensive start, but it leads to a terrible ending:

> "This treasury includes as well the prayers and good works of the Virgin Mary. They are truly immense, unfathomable, and even pristine in their value before God. In the treasury, too, are the prayers and good works of all the saints, all those who have followed in the footsteps of Christ the Lord and by his grace have made their lives holy and carried out the mission the Father entrusted to them. In this way they attained their own salvation and at the same time cooperated in saving their brothers in the unity of the mystical body."[518]

Leaving aside the point that the apostles called all Christians saints,[519] this treasury of the Church is bizarre on the surface. Even if such a treasury existed, nothing could justify adding anything to the "infinite value" of the merits of Christ. God gives his glory to "no other" (Is. 42:8). In the ages to come, God will show "the immeasurable riches of his grace in his kindness to us in Christ Jesus" (Eph. 2:7). God agrees that the grace Jesus bought with his blood is infinite ("immeasurable"), and he will not display any other merit in the ages to come, nor in this age, but that which comes from Jesus.

Perhaps the Roman Catholic Church should look back to the apostle whom they claim to represent and read that even the righteous are "barely saved" (1 Pet. 4:18). They have no "extra" merit or works to add to a treasury of the merit of Jesus.

---

[517] *Catechism of the Catholic Church*, 1995, par. 1471
[518] *Catechism of the Catholic Church*, 1995, par. 1477
[519] Sixty times in the New Testament, always referring to ordinary Christians.

Rome's Audacious Claim

Nor is there anything in Scripture remotely justifying the overzealous praise of Mary, that her prayers and deeds are "truly immense, unfathomable, and even pristine in their value before God." There is no problem with "pristine," but "immense" and "unfathomable" are words better left to the praise of God. Such words are not based on apostolic tradition, but on the idolization and deification of Mary, which we will discuss in the next section.

The doctrine of indulgences was the match that lit the fire of the Protestant Reformation. The ninety-five theses that Martin Luther wrote in 1517 and (probably) nailed to the door of the Wittenberg cathedral were all in response to the sale of indulgences in Germany.[520] Luther felt that poor Germans were being extorted out of what little money they had by the promise of the instant release of their deceased relatives from the fires of purgatory. Luther launched his crusade against indulgences with the ninety-five theses, which were published all over Germany. When he would not back down, the pope excommunicated him with a "papal bull," which backfired when German nobles backed Luther rather than the pope.[521]

The bishops of Rome fought for full authority over the apostolic churches of the Roman Empire and wound up alienating them enough to produce a schism that continues to this day. The false doctrines invented by the Magisterium and the horrific behavior of their clergy lost the Roman Catholic Church the control of Europe as well.[522]

While the Roman Catholic Church has officially stopped selling indulgences, the doctrine has not gone away. As you just saw, the *Catechism of the Catholic Church* still espouses it.

Rome justifies indulgences by appealing to the power of binding and loosing. We learned earlier[523] that "binding and loosing" means churches have the right to retain or remit sins. Indulgences, however, and the "treasury of the Church" are a strange caricature of the authority Jesus gave to the apostles, foreign to both the Scriptures and church history.

---

[520] Luther, 1517, "95 Theses"
[521] A papal bull is any edict issued directly by the pope.
[522] Pope Leo X, 1520, *Exsurge Domine*
[523] Chapter 4

Part VI | Chapter 28: Apostolic Tradition Preserved in Rome?

Foreign Language Bibles and Liturgies

For centuries, in Roman Catholic masses[524], the liturgy and Scripture were spoken and read in Latin to congregations who did not speak the language! It was only at Vatican II, in the 1960s, that the Roman Catholic Church allowed the liturgy to be spoken in the language of the hearers.[525]

Throughout much of the late medieval period, the Roman Catholic Church did not allow their congregants access to the Scriptures at all, claiming that laypeople cannot understand Scripture, so they need it explained to them. *A Catholic Dictionary* from 1887 says:

> In early times, the Bible was read freely by the lay people, and the Fathers constantly encourage them to do so, although they also insist on the obscurity of the sacred text. No prohibitions were issued against the popular reading of the Bible. New dangers came during the Middle Ages. When the heresy of the Albigenses arose there was a danger from corrupt translations, and also from the fact that the heretics tried to make the faithful judge the Church by their own interpretation of the Bible. To meet these evils, the Council of Toulouse (1229) and Tarragona (1234) forbade the laity to read the vernacular translations of the Bible. Pius IV [1559-1565] required the bishops to refuse lay persons leave to read even Catholic versions of the Scripture, unless their confessors or parish priests judged that such readings was likely to prove beneficial.[526]

First, it is not true that the fathers, at least not any that I have read, "insist on the obscurity of the sacred text." Peter said there are "some things" in Paul's letters that are hard to understand, but he was appealing to those letters as support for his own. He was not insisting

---

[524] The Roman Catholic Church calls their church service "mass," from the Latin phrase "*Ite missa est*," which the priests have used to dismiss services for many centuries (Pohle, 1911, "Sacrifice of the Mass," par. 4).
[525] Tufano, 2010, "When Did We Start Celebrating Mass in Latin"
[526] Addis & Arnold, 1887, *A Catholic Dictionary*, p. 82; parentheses in original, brackets mine

on the obscurity of Paul's letters; he was encouraging his readers to read Paul as well. Reading his letters would help them correct or refute the "ignorant and unstable" who distort Paul's letters "to their own destruction" (2 Pet. 3:15-16). The book of Acts commends Berean Jews for being open enough to Paul's preaching to examine the Scriptures to verify the things he said (Acts 17:11). Paul rejoiced that Timothy had learned the Scriptures "from infancy" (2 Tim. 3:15) and commanded him to "attend to" the public reading of Scripture (1 Tim. 4:13).[527]

Second, notice that *A Catholic Dictionary* calls the judging of the Roman Catholic Church by the Scriptures an evil. It is not just the supposedly corrupt translations of the Albigenses that were evil in the eyes of the Councils of Toulouse and Tarragona—it was also judging the Church by one's own interpretation of the Bible. Rather than defending their interpretation of the Scriptures like the early Christian apologists did,[528] the Roman Catholic Church responded to the Albigenses by refusing the Scriptures to their own members!

Today the Roman Catholic Church encourages their members to know and read Scripture, but this has been entirely the result of their interaction with the Protestants.

State Churches

This charge of deviation from apostolic doctrine applies to almost everyone. Protestants, Roman Catholics, and almost every branch of Orthodoxy have formed alliances with secular governments, then persecuted dissenters from the official faith with violence and even death. The Assyrian Church of the East may be the one exception to this. They have thrived under persecution from Islamic rule for almost a thousand years.

This is a horrific departure from the teachings of Jesus and the apostles, and it has been the consistent practice of popes and the

---

[527] The NABRE footnote on 1 Timothy 4:13 says, "The Greek word ... probably designates the public reading of Scripture in the Christian assembly." Many translations, such as the New International Version, the New American Standard Bible, and the English Standard Version translate the word as "public reading of Scripture."

[528] See chapter 14.

Part VI | Chapter 28: Apostolic Tradition Preserved in Rome?

Roman Catholic hierarchy from at least from the tenth century through the time of the Reformation.

Many branches of Christianity used the state to persecute dissenters, but only the Roman Catholic Church continues to claim supreme authority over you, me, and the churches of which we are a part.

Most people believe the Inquisition is a simply a long-ago time period, but it is actually an office of the Roman Catholic Church that began in the thirteenth century and continues to this day. It is now called the "Congregation for the Doctrine of the Faith."[529]

The concept behind the office is that it would combat heresies. Combatting heresies is not a problem if the combat is limited to words, but the Inquisition did not limit itself to words.

Today, Roman Catholic apologists try to downplay the horrors of the Inquisition, suggesting that the numbers were much smaller than their opponents claim. No matter what the numbers are, anyone who reads any of the more than 4,000 accounts of torture and killing in *Martyrs Mirror* will reject all excuses or defenses of the tortures that the Roman church devised for dissidents. The two that leap to my memory are Michael Sattler, who had his tongue ripped out and his body torn with red-hot tongs,[530] and "Geylen the shoemaker," who was hung by his right thumb with weights on his ankles, burned with candles, and scourged, before being burned at the stake.[531]

In addition to these horrors, there are the Crusades. On the surface, the Crusades were an attempt to wrest the Holy Land from Muslim hands and put them back in Christian control. This is a normal course of action for a king or emperor. We have detailed enough horrors that it is not necessary to recount those that occurred during the various Crusades. For this book, it is enough to note that the papacy became a political throne with political motives and not spiritual ones. It lost all resemblance to the greatness which the apostle Paul assigned to the

---

[529] The Holy See, n.d., "Congregation for the Doctrine of the Faith"
[530] Van Braght, 1660, *Martyr's Mirror*, Kindle location 16983
[531] Van Braght, 1660, *Martyr's Mirror*, Kindle location 38549-38562

church in Rome, and from which the Roman elders of the 250s were afraid to fall.[532]

Idolatry and the Ten Commandments

No one can testify to the idolatry in the Roman Catholic Church like those who were raised in it. When I was at Dominican Elementary School in Taipei, Taiwan, our teacher led my whole class, one by one, to a statue of Mary to kiss her feet. I have seen ladies gathered around the statues in the sanctuaries of cathedrals, weeping before one saint or another. It is impossible to reconcile this behavior with the second of the Ten Commandments:

> You shall not make for yourself an idol or a likeness of anything in the heavens above or on the earth below or in the waters beneath the earth; you shall not bow down before them or serve them. (Ex. 20:4-5)

The teachers and nuns in my school did not have to explain why we were kissing the feet of a statue even though the Ten Commandments forbid bowing down to images. They simply taught us a version of the Ten Commandments that did not include that command!

Almost everyone knows that the Roman Catholic Church, alone of all branches of Christianity, makes statues and encourages their members to bow down in front of them, kiss their feet, and pray to the persons the figures represent. What few know is that the Roman Catholic Church has changed the Ten Commandments! The command not to make or bow down to graven images is not in their list.

Instead of the second commandment, they have split the tenth commandment into two. While all other branches of Christianity list "you shalt not covet" as the tenth commandment, the Roman Catholic Church breaks this in two and makes, "You shall not covet your neighbor's wife," the ninth commandment and, "You shall not covet your neighbor's goods," the tenth commandment.[533]

The apologetic website Catholic Answers gives arguments for their version of the Ten Commandments. They appeal to the list of the

---

[532] See chapter 21, discussion on Epistle 30.
[533] Wensing, 2004, "The True Ten Commandments"

Part VI | Chapter 28: Apostolic Tradition Preserved in Rome?

Ten Commandments given by Augustine, which comes from Deuteronomy 5.[534] They argue that the Protestants, led by John Calvin, changed the way the Ten Commandments are listed in the sixteenth century as part of their crusade against Catholic statues.[535] There are three problems with this argument.

First, all branches of the Orthodox Churches list the Ten Commandments the way the Protestants do.[536] Augustine did not influence the Eastern Orthodox Churches as much as he influenced the Roman Catholics (and the Protestants who descended from them). The charge that the Protestants changed the Ten Commandments is hard to uphold when the Eastern and Oriental Orthodox Churches and the Church of the East, which are all as ancient as the Roman church, listed the Ten Commandments the same way as the Jews from the very beginning.

Second, that John Calvin tried to shut down idolatry was a good thing–the prohibition against making images and bowing down to them is in the Bible! Roman Catholics do not typically read their Bibles, and during medieval times, Bible reading was often forbidden. Instead, they memorized a short version of the Ten Commandments, like I did when I was a child, a list which did not have the commandment against bowing down to images. That the Protestants would restore a more accurate short list of the Ten Commandments to expose a violation of them is to be commended, not condemned!

Third, while the Ten Commandments in Deuteronomy 5 can be broken down the Roman Catholic way, one cannot break down the Ten Commandments in Exodus 20 the same way. Exodus 20:17 does not allow for the commandment not to covet to be broken into coveting a wife and coveting goods. "Wife" is in the middle of the things not to be coveted in Exodus 20's tenth commandment.

---

[534] Wensing, 2004, "The True Ten Commandments," par. 10 (counting each list of commandments as one paragraph).
[535] Wensing, 2004, "The True Ten Commandments," par. 11 (counting each list of commandments as one paragraph).
[536] See Russian Orthodox Cathedral of St. John the Baptist, n.d., "Ten Commandments"; Antiochian Orthodox Christian Archdiocese of North America, 2018, "The Ten Commandments"; Mastrantonis, 1985, "The Ten Commandments"

Rome's Audacious Claim

This reflects on Augustine as well. Augustine was a master of the Scriptures. That he did not compare Deuteronomy 5 with Exodus 20 and produce the same list of Ten Commandments as his peers and the Jews reflects badly on his motives as well. He became bishop of Hippo in 396, decades after the influx of pagans into the churches that happened under Emperor Constantine. That influx is the most likely origin of venerating images. Those who appeal to the church fathers in defense of the veneration of images are forced to appeal exclusively to post-Constantinian writings.[537] The apologetic website Catholic Answers seems not to know that Roman Catholics do not just venerate statues, but also bow down to and pray in front of them.[538] They do quote pre-Constantinian fathers, but only against the use of images![539]

The Roman Catholic Church does not deny that the Ten Commandments forbid both the making of images and bowing down to them. They simply found a creative way to hide that prohibition from their members: just change the short version that your congregants are memorizing and reciting.

The Orthodox Churches, with one exception, also make images, though only two-dimensional images.[540] They claim to "venerate" them, which they distinguish from "worship" without biblical justification.[541] The writings of the Church from before Nicea do not justify any use of images in worship. In the fourth century, there was a massive influx of pagans into the Church as Constantine supported Christianity more and more. Only after this influx do we find

---

[537] For example, a blogger giving his name only as "Brian" devoted 3,700 hours to scouring the thirty-eight volumes of *The Ante-Nicene Fathers* and *The Nicene and Post-Nicene Fathers* series. The first reference to honoring images he can find is from Basil the Great in 360, more than twenty years after Constantine's death (Brian, 2013, "Early Church Fathers on Relics, Statues, and Images"). I, on the other hand, had no problem finding many prohibitions against honoring images from before Constantine in my spare time (Pavao, 2009-2019, "Quotes About Religious Icons").

[538] e.g., Broussard, 2017, "Why Veneration Isn't Idol Worship"; Catholic Answers Staff, 2011, "Is Veneration of Relics Condemned by the Bible?"; Catholic Answers, 2018, "Saint Worship?"

[539] Fortescue, n.d., "Veneration of Images," sec. IV ("Enemies of Image-Worship Before Iconoclasm")

[540] The Church of the East (with the affiliated Assyrian Church of the East) does not venerate images. It has been separated from the churches of the Roman Empire since the fifth century.

[541] I address this topic at Pavao, 2009-2019, "The Orthodox Church and Icons."

Part VI | Chapter 28: Apostolic Tradition Preserved in Rome?

references to Christians venerating images; this is a suspect beginning at best.

Bowing down to images was a symptom of a much greater problem, at least during the Reformation in Europe. John Calvin gave a description of the sixteenth-century Roman Catholic behaviors that drove him away from Rome. These words are from a letter to a Roman Catholic cardinal, but Calvin wrote them as a prayer to God.

> Those who were regarded as the leaders of faith, neither understood Thy Word, nor greatly cared for it.... Among the people themselves, the highest veneration paid to Thy Word was to revere it at a distance, as a thing inaccessible, and abstain from all investigation of it.
>
> Owing to this supine state of the pastors, and this stupidity of the people, every place was filled with pernicious errors, falsehoods, and superstition.... They ... had for themselves as many gods as they had saints, whom they chose to worship. Thy Christ was indeed worshipped as God, and retained the name of Saviour; but where He ought to have been honored, He was left almost without honor.... He passed unnoticed among the crowd of saints, like one of the meanest of them. There was none who duly considered that one sacrifice which He offered on the cross, and by which He reconciled us to Thyself—none who ever dreamed of thinking of His eternal priesthood, and the intercession depending upon it; none who trusted in His righteousness only. That confident hope of salvation which is both enjoined by Thy Word, and founded upon it, had almost vanished.[542]

This description by John Calvin gives insight into just how much Roman Catholics had lost their vision of Jesus and turned their saints into idols. This was the fruit of Rome's Audacious Claim before the Protestant Reformation forced them to clean up their act ... a little.

---

[542] Schaff, 1903, *History of the Christian Church*, Vol. VII, p. 406

The Peak of Idolatry: The Virgin Mary

The idolization of Mary began in the second century. A "Gospel of James," eventually rejected by the Church, taught Mary's perpetual virginity.[543] Origen cites this Gospel in the third century, but even the apologist site Catholic Answers can find nothing else until Athanasius and Hilary of Poitiers in the mid-fourth century.[544]

Mary's perpetual virginity has scarce support in the fathers, and Matthew 1:25 states, "He had no relations with her until she bore a son," which is plenty of reason to reject the claim. It is, however, a small error. There is nothing divine about remaining a virgin throughout one's lifetime. That small beginning, though, was a stepping stone for increasing deification within the Roman Catholic Church.

I will skip a lot of development in Mariology over the centuries and jump straight to modern times. In 1854, Pope Pius IX, in a papal bull named *Ineffabilis Deus*, dogmatically declared that Mary was born free of original sin.[545] In 1943, in an encyclical called *Mystici Corporis Christi*, Pope Pius XII held that she was "free from all sin, original or personal."[546] In 1950, he declared she was assumed bodily into heaven.[547] The only possible source of such additions to the apostolic tradition are the imaginations of men; the only possible goal is to exalt her to a status nearly equivalent to Jesus.

Worst of all, though, was to assign her the titles of "Advocate," "Helper," and "Mediatrix."[548] At that point, the Roman Catholic Church has given her titles that belong to the Holy Spirit and to Jesus (Jn. 14:16, 26; 1 Tim. 2:5; 1 Jn. 2:1). With these titles they have made an idol of her, whether or not they bow down to her statue.

Pope Pius XII wrote that his "studies and investigations have brought out into even clearer light the fact that the dogma of the Virgin Mary's assumption into heaven is contained in the deposit of

---

[543] Also called "Protoevangelium of James."
[544] Catholic Answers, 1996-2019, "Mary: Ever Virgin"
[545] *Catechism of the Catholic Church*, 1995, par. 491
[546] Pope Pius XII, 1943, *Mystici Corporis Christi*, par. 110
[547] Pope Pius XII, 1950, "Apostolic Constitution of Pope Pius XII"
[548] *Catechism of the Catholic Church*, 1995, par. 969. It seems worse, somehow, that the *Catechism* capitalizes these words in reference to Mary

Part VI | Chapter 28: Apostolic Tradition Preserved in Rome?

Christian faith entrusted to the Church."[549] If he means the faith for which Jude exhorts his readers to contend, he is mistaken. That idea cannot be found at all during the three centuries before "converted" pagans began bowing down to images.

Conclusion: The Fruit of Papal Primacy

I suspect that, except for the hiding of the second commandment, none of the issues in this chapter were new to you. You may not agree that all these doctrines are blatantly false, but none of them belong to "the faith that was once for all handed down to the holy ones" (Jude 1:3).

We have looked at the fruit of Rome's Audacious Claim, and we have seen that it has produced doctrines and practices that have created the two largest schisms in Christian history. It has produced wicked, political, and ambitious popes, and even bishops of Rome who reigned from other countries. Above all, no matter what the numbers are, it has produced the torture and murder of those who dared to disagree with the bishop of Rome. It has turned the great church of Rome into a political machine responsible for wars, coups, oppression, and cruel persecution.

It is apparent that we must reject Rome's Audacious Claim. This leaves us with a problem, though. If the Roman Catholic Church is not "The Church," then what is?

---

[549] Pope Pius XII, 1950, "Apostolic Constitution of Pope Pius XII"

Rome's Audacious Claim

Chapter 29: A Call to Action

I own several websites for various purposes. As a result, I have subscribed to several newsletters that give advice to webmasters. One tip I read recently was to ensure my websites have a call to action.

I have several calls to action for this book.

Obviously, one of them is to reject Rome's Audacious Claim. Jesus Christ is alive, well, seated at the right hand of God, and working on earth through the Holy Spirit. He is the "full, supreme, and universal power over the whole Church," and he is well able to carry out his role as Head of the Church (Eph. 1:22) and Chief Shepherd (1 Pet. 5:4). Grow into him (Eph. 4:15)! Hold closely to him (Col. 2:19)!

I also call you to contend for the faith that was once for all handed down to the holy ones (Jude 1:3). Do not accept additions to it! This is commanded by Scripture! Irenaeus and Tertullian give you the same call. Do not let anyone call you to anything that the apostles did not teach!

Because of that second call to action, I cannot call you to leave the Roman Catholic Church. That may be surprising, but I do not have "full, supreme, and universal power" over you any more than the pope does. More importantly, I do not know which other church to send you to.

You may assume that because I wrote a book revealing the errors and deception of Roman Catholic apologists, I must support Protestant doctrines. I do not. I am a follower of Jesus Christ doing my best to adhere to apostolic tradition and to teach others to do the same.

I want to call you to reject Protestant tradition every bit as much as Roman Catholic tradition. Traditions of men are traditions of men, no matter what denomination created them. Only the apostles get to create tradition, as they were those who were sent and commissioned by Christ to do so. Along with Paul, Jude, Irenaeus, and Tertullian, I urge you to follow only the traditions of the apostles.

Build on the Right Rock

Jesus wants to build his Church on the confession that Jesus is the Christ, the Son of the living God (Matt. 16:18). If you want to have life through his name, you need to believe that (Jn. 20:31). Throughout

Acts, the apostles preached the resurrection to prove that Jesus was Lord and Christ (Acts 2:36) and Judge (Acts 10:42; 17:31). They were not building churches on the atonement; they were building on the confession that Jesus is Christ, Son of God, and Judge of the living and the dead. This is why they were called to be witnesses of the resurrection rather than witnesses of the atonement (Acts 1:22; 2:32; 3:15; 4:33; 5:32; 10:41-42; 13:30-31).

The apostles did teach the churches that Jesus died for our sins. That teaching can be found throughout the letters to the churches. They did not preach this to the lost, as proven by their preaching recorded in the book of Acts.

Most Protestant churches are built on the atonement, not on the revelation that Jesus is Christ, Lord, Judge of the living and the dead, and the Son of God. This is a terrible flaw, and it is the first reason so many Protestants fall away from the faith or live nominal Christian lives.

Salvation by Faith Alone

Equally bad is the Protestant idea that a person goes to heaven by faith alone. The New Testament verses that teach faith apart from works universally address our entrance into the faith, not our final entrance into the eternal kingdom of God. I was very excited when famed Protestant teacher John Piper realized this.[550] He has been castigated for this, of course, because the traditions of men hold much more sway among Protestants (and Roman Catholics) than the traditions of the apostles.[551]

Despite the castigation, it is not difficult to see in Scripture that Piper is correct. The simplest beginning is to point out that those who are immoral, impure, or greedy have no inheritance in the kingdom of God and of Christ, which is said three times (Eph. 5:5; Gal. 5:19-21; 1 Cor. 6:9-11). We can add that those who "grow tired of doing good" will not reap eternal life (Gal. 6:8-9). Doing good is the fruit of walking in the Spirit (Gal. 6:8-9; Rom. 8:2-4), of the new birth (Eph. 2:10), of studying the Scriptures (2 Tim. 3:16-17), of grace (Rom.

---

[550] Piper, 2017, "Does God Really Save Us by Faith Alone?"
[551] As a reminder, the idea of apostolic tradition is not just found in the writings of Irenaeus and Tertullian, but also in the writings of the apostle Paul (1 Cor. 11:2; 2 Thes. 2:15).

Part VI | Chapter 29: A Call to Action

6:14; Tit. 2:11-12), and of Jesus's death (Tit. 2:13-14), but it is necessary nonetheless. God works in us to desire and to work (Php. 2:13), but it is also true that we must work out our salvation with fear and trembling (Php. 2:12).

Contrary to a common Protestant proverb, we not only should "add to our faith," but we should do so diligently, or we will not gain an abundant entrance into the kingdom of Jesus, our Lord and Savior (2 Pet. 1:5-11).

Jesus gives a standard by which we will be judged when he sits on his "glorious throne" (Matt. 25:31). We will not be judged by the sacraments we kept, nor will we be judged by our faith in Jesus's blood. We will be judged by how we loved others (Matt. 25:32-46).

I will never forget the day in 1992 when I was driving through Tyler, Texas, listening to an appeal from a local food bank on the radio. One of the hosts brought up the judgment of the sheep and the goats in Matthew 25. His co-host, in his zeal to get donations for the food bank, pointed out that the only difference between the sheep and the goats was what they did.

There was a pregnant pause, then he burst into an impromptu retraction. He did not want to take back what he said, but he also knew that his Protestant tradition demands that deeds have nothing to do with going to heaven. In the end, he could not believe the Word of God in Matthew 25:31-46 because of his Protestant tradition.

Songsmith, pianist, and singer Keith Green was much bolder. Towards the end of the song he says, "Friends, the only difference between the sheep and the goats, according to the Scripture," then he pauses and, pounding on the keys of his piano, bursts out with, "is what they did and didn't do!"[552]

The Final Judgment

This error is entwined with the errors we have just covered. Protestants have pulled one verse out of context to teach that God's standard of judgment is sinlessness (Jas. 2:10). They ignore more direct statements about the judgment. A sacrificial lamb had to be flawless (Ex. 12:5), and the Lamb Who Was Slain from the Foundation of the World was sinless (Rev. 5:5; 13:8), but sinlessness

---

[552] Green, 1981, "The Sheep and the Goats," 7:35-7:50

is not the standard by which we will be judged. God himself describes just judgment in Ezekiel 18:20-30. Even the wicked, if they turn from their wickedness and do righteousness, will live because of the righteousness they are now doing. In fact, all their wickedness will be forgotten (v. 22), not because of sacrifice, but because they repented. Further, the righteousness of which God speaks in Ezekiel 18 cannot be sinless perfection. The Scriptures teach that none but Jesus has ever met that standard (1 Kings 8:46; Eccl. 7:20; Jas. 3:2; 1 Jn. 1:8).

Even in the Gospel of John, which is full of statements about eternal life in return for faith, the judgment is described as a resurrection of life for those who have done good deeds and a resurrection of condemnation for those who have done wicked deeds (Jn. 5:28-29).

It has amazed me throughout my Christian life that Protestants, or at least evangelicals, who are a subset of Protestants, cite 1 John 5:13 to give assurance of eternal life to new Christians. It reads, "I write these things to you so you may know that you have eternal life, you who believe in the name of the Son of God." Somehow, evangelicals have managed to divorce 1 John 5:13 from 1 John 1:1 through 5:12. There are a lot of verses leading up to chapter 5 and verse 13 of the First Epistle of John. One of them says that if you claim to know God, but do not keep his commandments, then you are a liar and the truth is not in you (1 Jn. 2:4)! Another says that if you are sinning on an ongoing basis,[553] you are not born of God (1 Jn. 3:9)! John wrote 1 John 2:4 and 3:9 to those who were believing in the name of the Son of God so that they could determine whether they had eternal life (1 Jn. 5:13).

If you want to assure a Christian of his or her salvation, it would be far better to use an actual assurance verse. 1 John 3:16-19 says:

> The way we came to know love was that he laid down his life for us; so we ought to lay down our lives for our brothers. If someone who has worldly means sees a brother in need and

---

[553] It is unfortunate, but true, that if you want to understand John's Gospel and letters, you have to learn one facet of Greek grammar. The Greek present tense conveys not just time (the present), but also ongoing action. Thus, 1 John 3:9 should always be translated, "No one who is begotten by God is committing sin." In other words, sinning is not an ongoing thing in their lives.

refuses him compassion, how can the love of God remain in him? Children, let us love not in word or speech but in deed and truth. This is how we shall know that we belong to the truth and reassure our hearts before him.[554]

We can assure our hearts before God, but it is by loving in deed and truth. The example given is showing compassion to a brother in need, which makes sense, given that Jesus will judge us based on our compassion to the needy (Matt. 25:31-46).

The things the Scriptures teach about the judgment are difficult to bear if we do not remember that God is merciful. If we repent, he will forget all the wickedness we have ever done (e.g., Ezek. 18:21-23; Acts 11:18; 26:20). If we are walking in the light, the blood of Jesus will give us fellowship with one another and cleanse us from all sin (1 Jn. 1:7). Thus, the promise of God is that if we will do our part, walking in the light, then God will do his part and ensure that we arrive at the throne of God unblemished (Jude 1:24). Remember, though, we are "righteous, just as he is righteous" only as long as we act in righteousness (1 Jn. 3:7).[555]

Everything I have written in this chapter is not only from Scripture, but mostly quotes of Scripture. Though I used the Roman Catholic NABRE, you will find Protestant versions translate them similarly. Across the board, both the Old and New Testaments teach that we will be judged by our deeds. Unfortunately, Protestants have a hard time with these passages. This is largely because of their misunderstanding of the atonement.

---

[554] I left out the "[now]" that the NABRE version added to the beginning of the last sentence, because it is unnecessary. Brackets like that one indicate the word is not in the Greek from which the English was translated. Most other translations, such as the New American Standard, use italics to show words the added. Sometimes this is necessary, but it can also change the meaning of a verse based on the bias of the translator.

[555] Remember once again that "acts in righteousness" in 1 John 3:7 is in the Greek present tense. It means the ongoing practice of righteousness, not perfection. Perfect righteousness, or blamelessness, is what is bestowed when we walk in the light and act righteously.

The Atonement

Protestants often teach that Jesus paid for our sins in the sense that he took the penalty for all sins that have ever been done and ever will be done by mankind.

This cannot be true. The letters to the churches in the New Testament are full of penalties for sin. These include corruption (Gal. 6:8), death (Rom. 8:12), being worse off than before we were saved (2 Pet. 2:20-21), and being spit out of his mouth (Rev. 3:16). Those are not only penalties—they are severe penalties.

Jesus died not only so that past sins could be forgiven (2 Pet. 1:9), but also to release us from slavery to sin. God has always been willing to forgive the sins of those who turn from wickedness to righteousness, as Ezekiel 18:20-30 and many other Old Testament passages testify. The problem is that humans, as a whole, are incapable of continuing in the righteousness that brings eternal life (Ezek. 18:21-22; Rom. 2:6-7). Paul devotes two chapters of his letter to the Romans (3 and 7) to this problem, and then says that the sacrifice of Jesus resolves the problem (Rom. 8:2-4; cf. Gal. 6:8-9).

The penalty that Jesus took care of was our slavery to sin. When Protestants say Jesus "paid the price," they mean that he took away the penalties for sin. This is wrong. As we have seen, the penalties for sin still exist, even for Christians. When the Bible says Jesus paid a price, the price is for us. He bought us out of slavery to sin (e.g., 1 Cor. 6:20).

The words "redemption" (Eph. 1:7) and "ransom" (Matt. 20:28) are purchase words. To redeem is to "buy back," and to ransom is a payment to release from captivity. The Bible is even more clear than this, though, saying, "Do you not know that ... you are not your own? For you have been purchased at a price" (1 Cor. 6:19-20).

There is a critical verse in Romans 5:19. It says:

> For just as through the disobedience of one person the many were made sinners, so through the obedience of one the many will be made righteous.

We are not guilty of Adam's sin. Instead, we inherited death and slavery to sin from Adam (Rom. 5:12-14; Eph. 2:1-3). Romans 5:19 tells us that "just as" we were all made sinners by Adam, we will be made righteous by Jesus. Adam did not give us "wrong standing" with

Part VI | Chapter 29: A Call to Action

God. He gave us death and a propensity to sin. "Just as" Adam did this, so Jesus gave us more than "right standing" with God. He gave us life, and a propensity to do righteousness.

This is why the apostle John was so bold as to say that only those who practice righteousness are righteous as Jesus is righteous (1 Jn. 3:7). He knew that practicing righteousness is the normal behavior of someone who has been bought with a price by Jesus.

Titus 2:11-14 is an excellent description of the purpose of Jesus' death.

> For the grace of God has appeared, saving all and training us to reject godless ways and worldly desires and to live temperately, justly, and devoutly in this age, as we await the blessed hope, the appearance of the glory of the great God and of our savior Jesus Christ, who gave himself for us to deliver us from all lawlessness and to cleanse for himself a people as his own, eager to do what is good.

Protestants often confuse grace and mercy. Mercy is God forgiving us of our sins. Grace, God's favor, brings us the power of the Holy Spirit so we are no longer under the power of sin (Rom. 6:14; Gal. 5:16). Grace is the foundation of spiritual gifts as well (1 Pet. 4:10-11). Grace means "favor," but that favor teaches us to "reject godless ways and worldly desires."

This passage also teaches us that one purpose of Jesus's death was to have a people he owned who are eager to do what is good. Protestant translations, such as the New American Standard Bible, say we are a "people for his own possession," who are "zealous for good deeds."

Romans 14:9 says he died (and rose) so that he might be Lord of the living and the dead. 2 Corinthians 5:15 says he died for all so we would not live for ourselves any longer, but for him.

The Scriptures say that we have "redemption through his blood, the forgiveness of our trespasses" (Eph. 1:7). 1 Corinthians 15:3 tells us that he "died for our sins." Neither of these statements can mean that he paid the penalty for all sins of mankind, whether past, present, or future. As pointed out, there are a lot of penalties for sin threatened in letters to Christian churches.

Rome's Audacious Claim

"Forgiveness" or "remission" in the Bible is a very interesting word. There are four Greek words that are translated with some form of the word "forgive" in the Bible: *aphesis, aphiemi, apoluo*, and *charizomai*. Almost any time forgiveness is associated with the death of Jesus, and every time the word "remission" is used (at least in the King James and New King James Versions), the Greek word is *aphesis*.

Aphesis has a grand history in the Old Testament. In the Greek translation of the Hebrew Scriptures (called the Septuagint or LXX), *aphesis* translates the release from debts that occurred every seven years (Deut. 15:1-10), "Jubilee" (Lev. 25:10-12), and most importantly, the "scapegoat," the goat that was released with a red cord around its neck every year on the Day of Atonement (Lev. 16:26). Isaiah 61:1 prophesies that the Messiah will proclaim *aphesis* to the captives.

While "forgiveness" is not a wrong translation of *aphesis*, it means much more than that. Its primary meaning is "release." Thus, the scapegoat represents the "release" or sending away of Israel's sins. The year of Jubilee is the "release" of land back to its original owners, and every seven years all debts are "released." Jesus quotes Isaiah 61:1 in reference to himself and uses *aphesis* to mean the "release" of both the captive and the oppressed.

What Jesus bought for us with his blood was *aphesis* (Eph. 1:7). According to Hebrews 9:22, without the shedding of blood, there is no *aphesis*. God shows mercy for sin even without blood, as Psalm 51:18-19 and Ezekiel 18:20-30 tell us. The release from captivity to sin, however, can only be bought with blood; specifically, with the blood of the unblemished Lamb of God, Jesus. Thus, when he held up the cup and said, "This is my blood," he also said it was shed for the *aphesis* of sins (Matt. 26:28).

Jesus paid the price for us. He did not pay the penalty of sin. This is why he can still punish sin, as he threatens to do throughout the letters to the churches in Revelation, chapters 2 and 3. All our previous sins are washed away in baptism (Acts 2:38; 22:16), and we are born again, saved, put in right standing with God, and delivered from the power of sin (Rom. 6:14). We are no longer sinners (Rom. 5:19). In fact, we have escaped the corruption that is in the world through lust

Part VI | Chapter 29: A Call to Action

(2 Pet. 1:3) and are warned not to become entangled in that corruption again (2 Pet. 2:19-21).

You can see how important and central these things are. Jesus paid the price for "a people for his own possession, zealous for good deeds" (Tit. 2:14). Paul told Titus to "speak and exhort and reprove with all authority" about these things (Tit. 2:15).

Because Protestant traditions leave these things out, I do not want to send you to a Protestant church any more than to a Roman Catholic one. Both Roman Catholics and Protestants reject many important apostolic traditions. Instead, no matter what church you attend, my call to action is that you do what Paul told Timothy, "Pursue righteousness, faith, love, and peace along with those who call on the Lord with purity of heart" (2 Tim. 2:22). "God's solid foundation" has an insignia on it that says, "Let everyone who calls upon the name of the Lord avoid evil" (2 Tim. 2:19). Without those things, "no one will see the Lord" (Heb. 12:14).

We all need help with these things. "Encourage yourselves daily while it is still 'today,' so that none of you may grow hardened by the deceit of sin" (Heb. 3:13).

Encouraging or exhorting one another is the main purpose of our gathering together. Protestants all know that the Bible says not to forsake the assembling of ourselves together, but no one seems to know what the Bible says to do when we assemble. The passage reads like this:

> We must consider how to rouse one another to love and good works. We should not stay away from our assembly, as is the custom of some, but encourage one another, and this all the more as you see the day drawing near. (Heb. 10:24-25)

The word "encourage" in this passage and in Hebrews 3:13 is not a very good translation, though what word to use instead is hard to determine. "Help" may be a better word. The Greek word is *parakaleo*, and the noun form is used to describe both the Holy Spirit (Jn. 14:26) and Jesus (1 Jn. 2:1). Thayer's Lexicon gives "call for," "speak to," "admonish," "exhort," "beg," "entreat," "console," "comfort," "encourage," "strengthen," "instruct," and more as possible translations for the word.

Rome's Audacious Claim

I like to use 1 Thessalonians 5:14 to define *parakaleo*. There the apostle Paul tells us to "admonish the idle, cheer the fainthearted, support the weak, be patient with all." These things all fall within the definition of *parakaleo*, and if we want to obey the biblical command not to forsake the assembling of ourselves, then we need to "consider" how to *parakaleo* each other so we can rouse each other to love and good works.

This is biblical Christianity. The reason I say all these things so boldly is not only because these things are clear in Scripture, as I have shown you, but also because they are taught by the churches the apostles started. Irenaeus and Tertullian did not only argue that the churches in their day had carefully preserved apostolic tradition, but they explained apostolic tradition as well. Though we cannot "have recourse to the most ancient Churches with which the apostles held constant intercourse,"[556] we can read Rome's letter to Corinth from the year 95 or 96, Irenaeus's *Proof of the Apostolic Preaching*, and many other writings from that "one holy, catholic, and apostolic Church" of the second century.

We cannot be Jesus's disciples if we do not deny ourselves, take up our cross, and follow him (Luke 9:23). His words are even more breathtaking in Luke 14:26-33. You can see how the church in Jerusalem obeyed Jesus's words in the first few chapters of Acts. You can see how the apostolic churches obeyed his words in the second century in passages like these:

c. 150:

> We who formerly delighted in fornication now embrace chastity alone.... We who valued above all things the acquisition of wealth and possessions now bring what we have into a common stock and share with everyone in need. We who hated and destroyed one another and would not live with men of a different tribe because of their different customs now, since the coming of Christ, share the same fire with them. We pray for our enemies and endeavor to persuade

---

[556] Irenaeus, c. 185, *Against Heresies*, Bk. III, ch. 4, par. 1

Part VI | Chapter 29: A Call to Action

those who hate us unjustly to live conformably to the good precepts of Christ.[557]

175-180:

Among us you will find uneducated persons, craftsmen, and old women, who, if they are unable in words to prove the benefit of our doctrine, yet by their deeds exhibit the benefit arising from their persuasion of its truth. They do not rehearse speeches, but exhibit good works; when struck, they do not strike again; when robbed, they do not go to law; they give to those that ask of them, and love their neighbors as themselves.[558]

198-217:

It is mainly the deeds of a love so noble that lead many to label us. "See," they say, "How they love one another!" For themselves are animated by mutual hatred. "How they are ready even to die for one another!" For they themselves will sooner put to death.... The family possessions, which generally destroy brotherhood among you, create fraternal bonds among us. One in mind and soul, we do not hesitate to share our earthly goods with one another. All things are common among us but our wives.[559]

160-250:

We despise the bent brows of the philosophers, whom we know to be corrupters, and adulterers, and tyrants, and ever eloquent against their own vices. We who bear wisdom not in our dress, but in our mind, we do not speak great things, but we live them; we boast that we have attained what they have sought for with the utmost eagerness, and have not been able to find.[560]

---

[557] Justin, 150-160, *First Apology*, ch. 14
[558] Athenagoras, 175-180, *A Plea for the Christians*, ch. 11
[559] Tertullian, 198-217, *Apology*, ch. 39
[560] Minucius Felix, 160-250, *The Octavius*, ch. 38

Rome's Audacious Claim

This is the Christianity I long to see in the earth again, the faith taught by the true "full, supreme, and universal power over the whole Church," our Lord Jesus, the Christ of God. The Scriptures give us a method: "pursue righteousness, faith, love, and peace along with those who call on the Lord with purity of heart" (2 Tim. 2:22), and "*Parakeleo* yourselves daily while it is still 'today,' so that none of you may grow hardened by the deceitfulness of sin" (Heb. 3:13). Do the same every time you assemble (Heb. 10:24-25).

Our Father, may your kingdom come and your will be done; as in heaven, so on earth. Amen.

Bibliography:

Addis, W. E. & Arnold, T. (1887). *A Catholic Dictionary: Containing Some Account of the Doctrine, Disciplines, Rites, Ceremonies, Councils, and Religious Orders of the Catholic Church.* New York: The Catholic Publications Society Co. p. 82. In Mizzi, J. Dr. (2011). "The Bible Forbidden to the Laity." Web. Just for Catholics. Retrieved March 13, 2019 from http://www.justforcatholics.org/a198.htm

Allert, C. (2007). *A High View of Scripture?: The Authority of the Bible and the Formation of the New Testament Canon.* Paper. Grand Rapids, MI: Baker Academic.

Akin, J. (2010). *The Fathers Know Best: Your Essential Guide to the Teachings of the Early Church.* Kindle. San Diego, CA: Catholic Answers.

Akin, J. (2017). "What Is the Evidence for Papal Primacy?" YouTube Video. Catholic.com. Retrieved March 25, 2019 from https://www.youtube.com/watch?v=JvI4IaMDpJk&t=522s

Amazon.com, inc. (1996-2019). "Rome Sweet Home: Our Journey to Catholicism." Web. Retrieved March 2, 2019 from https://www.amazon.com/Rome-Sweet-Home-Journey-Catholicism/dp/0898704782/

Amazon.com, inc. (1996-2019). "The Complete Bible Answer Book (Answer Book Series)." Web. Retrieved March 2, 2019 from https://www.amazon.com/Complete-Bible-Answer-Book/dp/0718032497/

Andrews, J. (2017.) Facebook comment made on the page "Patristics for Protestants" on August 28, 2017 in response to my request for the original text of Tertullian's *Prescription of Heretics*.

Anonymous. (50-120). "The Teaching of the Twelve Apostles" or *Didache*.
   See *Ante-Nicene Father*. Vol. VII.

Ante-Nicene Fathers, The. (1867-1873). This 10-volume set, originally published in Edinburg, Scotland and edited by Alexander Roberts and James Donaldson. An American edition of the series was edited by A. Cleveland Coxe and published in 1886. I used the

PDF copy released by the Christian Classics Ethereal Library (2002-2006, http://www.ccel.org/fathers) for this book.

The list below is the list of fathers sorted into the volumes in which they are found. The dates are the father's writing career. Some writings have more exact dates.

ANF, Vol. I:
- Anonymous. A.D. 50-120.
  - "Epistle of Mathetes to Diognetus." 50-120.
- Athenagoras. A.D. 175-180.
  - *A Plea for the Christians.* 175-180.
- Clement of Rome. A.D. 81-96.
  - *1 Clement.* 81-96.
- Ignatius of Antioch. A.D. 107 or 116.
  - "Epistle to the Ephesians." 107 or 116.
  - "Epistle to the Magnesians." 107 or 116.
  - "Epistle to the Philadelphians." 107 or 116.
  - "Epistle to the Romans." 107 or 116.
  - "Epistle to the Smyrneans." 107 or 116.
  - "Epistle to the Trallians." 107 or 116.
  - "The Martyrdom of Ignatius." 107 or 116.
- Irenaeus of Lyons. c. A.D. 185.
  - "Introductory Note to Irenaeus Against Heresies." 1886-1887.
  - *Against Heresies.* 185.
- Justin. A.D. 150-160.
  - *First Apology.* 150-160.
- Polycarp. A.D. 107-165.
  - "Epistle of Polycarp to the Phillipians." 110-150.
  - "The Martyrdom of Polycarp." 155-165.

ANF, Vol. II:
- Clement of Alexandria. A.D. 182-202.
  - "Who Is the Rich Man Who Must Be Saved?" 182-202.

ANF, Vol. III:
- Tertullian. A.D. 197-220.
  - *Against Marcion.* 207.
  - *Against Praxeas.* 208-220.
  - *Apology.* 198-217.

Bibliography

De Corona. 204.
"On Monogamy." 208-217.
"On Modesty." 208-220.
Scorpiace. c. 205.
Prescription Against Heretics. 197-208.

ANF, Vol. IV:
    Felix, M. A.D. 160-250.
        The Octavius. 160-250.
    Origen, A.D. 217-250
        De Principiis. 217-230.

ANF, Vol. V:
    Cyprian. A.D. 249-258.
        "Epistles of Cyprian." 250-258.
        "On the Unity of the Church." 251.
        "Seventh Council of Carthage." 256-258.
    Hippolytus. A.D. 218-235
        Discourse on the Holy Theophany. 218-235.
        Refutation of All Heresies. 223-235.

ANF, Vol. VI:
    Peter of Alexandria. A.D. 300-311.
        "The Canonical Epistle, with the Commentaries of Theodore Balsamon and John Zonaras." 300-311.

ANF, Vol. VII:
    Anonymous. A.D. 50-120
        "The Teaching of the Twelve Apostles" or *Didache*. 50-120.
    Lactantius. A.D. 303-316.
        Of the Manner in Which the Persecutors Died. 303-316.

ANF, Vol. XIII:
    Pseudo-James. c. A.D. 145.
        "Protoevangelium of James." c. 145.

ANF, Vol. IX:
    Origen. A.D. 217-250.
        Commentary on Matthew. 246-248.

Antiochian Orthodox Christian Archdiocese of North America. (2018). "The Ten Commandments." Web. Retrieved February 27, 2019 from http://ww1.antiochian.org/ten-commandments

Archive.org. (n.d.). "Full text of 'The epistles of S. Cyprian, Bishop of Carthage and martyr : with the Council of Carthage on the baptism of heretics ; to which are added the extant works of S. Pacian, Bishop of Barcelona.'" Web. Retrieved August 23, 2018 from https://archive.org/stream/a566175002cypruoft/a566175002cypruoft_djvu.txt

Armstrong, Dave. (2013). *Catholic Church Fathers: Patristic and Scholarly Proofs*. Kindle. Published by Dave Armstrong.

Athanasius. (328-373).
See *Nicene and Post-Nicene Fathers*. NPNF2, Vol. IV.

Athenagoras. (175-180).
See *Ante-Nicene Fathers*. ANF, Vol. I.

Baur, C. (1912). "Theodoret." Web. *Catholic Encyclopedia*. New York: Robert Appleton Co. Retrieved May 16, 2019 from New Advent: http://www.newadvent.org/cathen/14574b.htm

Bible Hub. (2004-2018). "Matthew 16:19." Web. Retrieved April 6, 2019 from https://biblehub.com/commentaries/matthew/16-19.htm

Bible Hub. (2004-2018). "Revelation 1:20." Web. Retrieved April 22, 2019 from https://biblehub.com/commentaries/revelation/1-20.htm

bibleinfo.com. (2012). "Bible facts and trivia." Web. Retrieved March 28, 2017 from http://www.bibleinfo.com/en/questions/bible-trivia-facts

Bock, D.L., Ph.D. (2006). *The Missing Gospels*. Paperback. Nashville, TN: Thomas Nelson.

Brian. 2013. "Early Church Fathers on Relics, Statues, Images." Web. Blogger.com. Retrieved June 8, 2019 from http://practicalapologetics.blogspot.com/2013/07/early-church-fathers-on-relics-statues.html

British Library Board. (n.d.). "Codex Alexandrinus." Retrieved February 21, 2017 from http://www.bl.uk/onlinegallery/sacredtexts/codexalex.html

Broadbent, E.H. (1931). *The Pilgrim Church*. PDF. London: Pickering & Inglis LTD. Retrieved June 7, 2019 from https://jesus.org.uk/wp-content/uploads/2015/05/the-pilgrim-church.pdf

Bibliography

Broussard, K. (2017). "Why Veneration Isn't Idol Worship." Web. Catholic Answers. 1996-2019. Retrieved June 8, 2019 from https://www.catholic.com/qa/why-veneration-isnt-idol-worship

Butler, B.C. (2016). "The Need for Vatican II." Web. Vatican II—Voice of the Church. Retrieved April 24, 2017 from http://vatican2voice.org/2need/need.htm

Butler, S., Dahlgren, N. & Hess, D. (1996). *Jesus, Peter, & the Keys: A Scriptural Handbook on the Papacy*. Santa Barbara, CA: Queenship Publishing Co.

canonlawmadeeasy. (2012). "Was theologian Hans Küng Ever Excommunicated?" Web. Caridi, C. 2007-2018. *Canon Law Made Easy*. Retrieved October 23, 2018 from http://canonlawmadeeasy.com/2012/11/08/was-theologian-hans-kung-ever-excommunicated/

Catechism of the Catholic Church: With Modifications from the Editio Typica. (1995). Second Edition. Kindle. New York, NY: Doubleday.

Catholic Answers. (2017). "What Is the Evidence for Papal Primacy." Video. YouTube. Retrieved February 16, 2017 from https://youtu.be/JvI4IaMDpJk

Catholic Answers. (2018). "Papal Infallibility." Web. Retrieved March 8, 2019 from https://www.catholic.com/tract/papal-infallibility

Catholic Answers. (2018). "Infallibility: Treatment of the Role of Infallibility in the Church." Web. Catholic Answers. Retrieved March 8, 2019 from https://www.catholic.com/encyclopedia/infallibility

Catholic Answers. (2018). "Saint Worship?" Web. Catholic Answers. Retrieved June 8, 2019 from https://www.catholic.com/tract/saint-worship

Catholic Answers Staff. (2011). "Is Veneration of Relics Condemned by the Bible?" Web. Catholic Answers. 1996-2019. Retrieved June 8, 2019 from https://www.catholic.com/qa/is-veneration-of-relics-condemned-by-the-bible

Catholic Apologetics. (n.d.). "Vatican II: Renewal or a New Religion?." Web. Retrieved June 28, 2019 from http://www.catholicapologetics.info/modernproblems/vatican2/renew2.html

The Catholic Encylopedia. 1911. "The List of Popes." Web. *The Catholic Encyclopedia*. Retrieved February 16, 2019 from http://www.newadvent.org/cathen/12272b.htm

Catholicism.org. (2005). "The Infallibility of the Pope—Basic Facts About an Essential Dogma." Web. (2001-2017). Richmond, NH: Saint Benedict Center. Retrieved April 23, 2019 from https://catholicism.org/apologetics-infallibility.html

Catholics Come Home, inc. (2008-2019). "Catholics Come Home." Web. Retrieved March 2, 2019 from https://www.catholicscomehome.org/

Chamberlin, E.R. (1969). *The Bad Popes*. Hardback. 1998 edition. Barnes & Nobel Books.

Chapman, J. (1909). "Evodius." In *The Catholic Encyclopedia*. New York: Robert Appleton Company. Web. Retrieved April 23, 2019 from http://www.newadvent.org/cathen/05653a.htm

Chapman, J. (1911). "Montanists." In *The Catholic Encyclopedia*. New York: Robert Appleton Company. Web. Retrieved March 31, 2018 from http://www.newadvent.org/cathen/10521a.htm

Chapman, J. (1911). "Novatian and Novatianism." In *The Catholic Encyclopedia*. New York: Robert Appleton Company. Web Article. Retrieved March 31, 2018 from http://www.newadvent.org/cathen/11138a.htm

Chapman, J. (1928). *Studies on the Early Papacy*. Ed. 2015 Reprint. Ex Fontibus Co.

Cleenewerck, L. (2007). *His Broken Body: Understanding and Healing the Schism Between the Roman Catholic and Eastern Orthodox Churches*. Kindle Edition. CreateSpace. (Originally published by Euclid University Press, Washington, D.C.)

Clement of Alexandria.
   See *Ante-Nicene Fathers*. ANF, Vol. II.

Clement of Rome.
   See *Ante-Nicene Fathers*. ANF, Vol. I.

Congar, Y. (1982). *Diversity and Communion*. Mystic, CT: Twenty-Third. Cited by Cleenewerck, L. (2007). *His Broken Body: Understanding and Healing the Schism Between the Roman Catholic and Eastern Orthodox Churches*. Kindle Edition. CreateSpace. pp. 223-224.

Bibliography

Congar, Y. (1998). *Tradition and Traditions.* San Diego: Basilica Press. Cited by Madrid, P. 2016. *Pope Fiction: Answers to 30 Myths and Misconceptions about the Papacy.* Huntington Beach, CA: Basilica Press. Kindle locations 1033-1035.

Conte, R.L., Jr. (n.d.). "First Vatican Council: 1869 to 1870 A.D. under Pope Blessed Pius IX." Web. Catholic Planet. Retrieved March 2, 2019 from http://www.catholicplanet.org/councils/20-Pastor-Aeternus.htm

Continuing Witness Training: *Apprentice Manual.* (1982). Alpharetta, GA: Home Mission Board of the Southern Baptist Convention

Council of Chalcedon.
   See *Nicene and Post-Nicene Fathers: NPNF2, Vol. XIV*

Coxe, A. C., ed. (1886). "Introductory Note to Irenaeus Against Heresies." In Schaff, Philip. *ANF01. The Apostolic Fathers with Justin Martyr and Irenaeus.* PDF. Christian Classics Ethereal Library, 2004. URL: http://www.ccel.org/ccel/schaff/anf01.html. Also can be seen at Plantings, H. (1993-2015). Christian Classics Ethereal Library. Web. Retrieved September 11, 2017 from http://www.ccel.org/ccel/schaff/anf01.ix.i.html

Cunningham, L. & Editors of Encylopaedia Brittanica. (2017). "The Church Since Vatican II." Web. Encyclopaedia Brittanica, inc. Retrieved April 24, 2017 from https://www.britannica.com/topic/Roman-Catholicism/The-church-since-Vatican-II

Cyprian.
   See *Ante-Nicene Fathers.* ANF05.

d'Ormesson, W. 1959. *Papacy.* Burns & Oates. London: Burns & Oates. In Ray, S.K., Dr. (2009). *Upon This Rock.* Modern Apologetics Library. Kindle. Ignatius Press.

Damick, A.S. (2015). "One Quote from Ignatius Converted This Guy to Catholicism?." Web. Ancient Faith Ministries. Retrieved July 10, 2019 from https://blogs.ancientfaith.com/orthodoxyandheterodoxy/2015/09/11/one-quote-from-st-ignatius-converted-this-guy-to-catholicism/

Department of Christian Education of the Orthodox Church of America. (n.d.). "Martyrs and Confessors." Web Article. Retrieved April 13, 2018 from

http://dce.oca.org/assets/templates/bulletin.cfm?mode=html&id=85

EmersonKent.com. (2016). "Map of Asia Minor under the Greeks and Romans." Web. Retrieved Feb. 15, 2017 from http://www.emersonkent.com/map_archive/asia_minor_4th_cent.htm.

Eternal Word Television Network. (n.d.). "Questions and Answers." Web. Eternal Word Television Network. Retrieved June 24, 2019 from https://www.ewtn.com/library/ANSWERS/CONTRAD.HTM

Eusebius of Caesarea.
See *Nicene and Post-Nicene Fathers:* NPNF2, Vol. I.

Evans, E. (ed.). (1972). *Tertullian: Adversus Marcionem.* IV:5. In Pearse, R. (2002). The Tertullian Project. Retrieved November 4, 2019 from http://tertullian.org/articles/evans_marc/evans_marc_09book4.htm

Felix, M.
See *Ante-Nicene Fathers*. ANF, Vol. IV.

"The First Ecumenical Council: The First Council of Nice." A.D. 325.
See *Nicene and Post-Nicene Fathers*. NPNF2, Vol. XIV.

"The Fourth Ecumenical Council. The Council of Chalcedon." A.D. 451.
See *Nicene and Post-Nicene Fathers*. NPNF2, Vol. XIV.

Firmilian
See *Ante-Nicene Fathers*. ANF, Vol. V. "Epistles of Cyprian."

Fortescue, A. (n.d.). "Veneration of Images." Web. Catholic Answers. 1996-2019. Retrieved June 8, 2019 from https://www.catholic.com/encyclopedia/veneration-of-images

Franciscan Media.org. (n.d.). "Solemnity of the Assumption of Mary." Web. Franciscan Media. Retrieved April 27, 2019 from https://www.franciscanmedia.org/solemnity-of-the-assumption-of-mary/

Frend, W.H.C. 2018. "St. Cyprian: Christian Theologian and Bishop [Died 258]." Web. 2019. Encyclopedia Britannica. Retrieved May 3, 2019 from https://www.britannica.com/biography/Saint-Cyprian-Christian-bishop

Bibliography

Glimm, F. (trans.) & Schopp, L. (ed.). (1947). *The Apostolic Fathers*. Fathers of the Church, Vol. I. Catholic University of America Press.

Green, K. (1981). "The Sheep and the Goats." Web Video. User: possiblyfake. (2012). YouTube. Retrieved June 7, 2019 from https://www.youtube.com/watch?v=kBkNzb283-U

Guardian, The. (2016). "Every Pope ever: the full list." Web. Retrieved August 28, 2017 from https://www.theguardian.com/news/datablog/2013/feb/13/popes-full-list

Hahn, S. (n.d.). "Scott Hahn on the Papacy," Web. Catholic-Pages.com. 1996-2007. Retrieved February 15, 2017 from http://www.catholic-pages.com/pope/hahn.asp

Hahn, S. (2007). *Reasons to Believe: How to Understand, Explain, and Defend the Catholic Faith*. Kindle. New York: Doubleday Press

Harper, D. (2001-2019). "Bishop." Online Etymology Dictionary. Web. Retrieved May 26, 2017 from http://www.etymonline.com/index.php?term=bishop

Harper, D. (2001-2019). "Easter." Online Etymology Dictionary. Web. Retrieved May 1, 2019 from https://www.etymonline.com/search?q=easter

Hefele, K.J. (1871). *A History of the Councils of the Church: To the Close of the Council of Nicea, A.D. 325*. Edinburgh: T&T Clark.

Hemans, C. I. (1869). *A History of Medieval Christianity and Sacred Art in Italy*. Web Archive. London: Williams & Norgate. Retrieved February 16, 2019 from https://archive.org/details/historyofmediaev01hema/page/22

Hill, J. (2003). *History of Christian Thought*. Kindle. Lion Books.

Hippolytus
    See *Ante-Nicene Fathers*. ANF, Vol. 5

Holy See, The. (n.d.). "The Holy See." Web. Retrieved May 16, 2019 from http://w2.vatican.va/content/vatican/en.html

Holy See, The. (n.d.). "Congregation for the Doctrine of the Faith." Web. Retrieved March 13, 2019 from http://www.vatican.va/roman_curia/congregations/cfaith/storia/do

cuments/rc_con_cfaith_storia_20150319_promuovere-custodire-fede_en.html

Horn, T. (2017). *The Case for Catholicism: Answers to Classic and Contemporary Protestant Objections.* Kindle edition. Ignatius Press.

Horn, T. (2017). *Why We're Catholic: Our Reasons for Faith, Hope, and Love.* Kindle Edition. El Cajon, CA: Catholic Answers, Inc.

Ignatius of Antioch. A.D. 107 or 116.
   See *Ante-Nicene Fathers.* ANF, Vol. I.

Irenaeus. (c. 185).
   See *Ante-Nicene Fathers.* ANF, Vol. I.

Irenaeus. (c. 180). *The Demonstration of the Apostolic Preaching.* PDF. Translated by Robinson, A., D.D. 1920. London: The MacMillan Co. This edition can be obtained in various formats from http://www.ccel.org/node/3084

Jenkins, P. (2017). "Inventing the Christian Priesthood." Web. Patheos. Retrieved June 7, 2019 from https://www.patheos.com/blogs/anxiousbench/2017/11/christian-clergy-became-priests/

Joint International Commission for Theological Dialogue between the Roman Catholic Church and the Orthodox Church. (2016). "Synodality and Primacy During the First Millennium: Towards a Common Understanding in Service to the Unity of the Church." Web. The Holy See. Retrieved March 15, 2018 from http://www.vatican.va/roman_curia/pontifical_councils/chrstuni/ch_orthodox_docs/rc_pc_chrstuni_doc_20160921_sinodality-primacy_en.html

Jurgens, W.A. (1970). *The Faith of the Early Fathers: Volume I.* Collegeville, MN: Liturgical Press.

Justin. (150-160).
   See *Ante-Nicene Fathers.* ANF, Vol. I.

Keating, K. (1993). "The 21 Ecumenical Councils." Web. Catholic Answers. Retrieved March 15, 2019 from https://www.catholic.com/magazine/print-edition/the-21-ecumenical-councils

Kennedy, D.J., Dr. (1996). *Evangelism Explosion.* Fourth Ed. Carol Stream, IL:Tyndale House Publishers, Inc.

Bibliography

Kennedy, J.W. (1983). *The Torch and the Testimony*. Christian Books Publishing House.

Kirby, P. (2019). *Early Christian Writings*. Web. Early Christian Writings. Retrieved April 27, 2019 from http://earlychristianwritings.com/

Kirby, P. (2001-2019). "Ignatius to the Romans." Web. Early Christian Writings. Retrieved April 24, 2019 from http://earlychristianwritings.com/text/ignatius-romans-lightfoot.html

Kirsch, J.P. (1910). "Pope John XII." In Knight, K. 2017. *The Catholic Encyclopedia*. Web. New York: Robert Appleton Company. Retrieved February 7, 2019 from http://www.newadvent.org/cathen/08426b.htm

Kirsch, J.P. (1910). "St. Hippolytus of Rome." In *The Catholic Encyclopedia*. Web. New York: Robert Appleton Company. Retrieved April 3, 2019 from http://www.newadvent.org/cathen/07360c.htm

Knight, K. (2019). *The Catholic Encyclopedia*. Web. Retrieved April 26, 2017 from http://newadvent.com/cathen/

Küng, H. (2001). *The Catholic Church: A Short History*. New York: Random House, Inc.

Lactantius. (303-316).
See *Ante-Nicene Fathers*. ANF, Vol. VII.

Leo I (the Great). 440-461.
See *Nicene and Post-Nicene Fathers: NPNF2, Vol. VI.*

Liang, J. (2014). "5 Things to Know About Montanism." Web article. Western Seminary. Retrieved September 11, 2017 from https://www.westernseminary.edu/transformedblog/2014/01/07/5-things-to-know-about-montanism/

Libreria Editrice Vaticana. (2002). "New American Bible": Revelation chapter 1. Note 19[20]. Web. Retrieved February 15, 2017 from http://www.vatican.va/archive/ENG0839/__P12K.HTM

Luther, M. (1517). "95 Theses." Web. 1997. KDG Wittenberg. Retrieved May 31, 2019 from https://www.luther.de/en/95thesen.html

Madrid, P. 2016. *Pope Fiction: Answers to 30 Myths and Misconceptions about the Papacy*. Huntington Beach, CA: Basilica Press.

Mann, H.K. (1907). "Pope Benedict IX." In Knight, K. 2017. *The Catholic Encyclopedia*. Web. New York: Robert Appleton Company. Retrieved February 7, 2019 from http://www.newadvent.org/cathen/02429a.htm

Mann, H. K. (1910). *The Lives of the Popes in the Early Middle Ages: Vol. V: The Popes in the Days of Feudal Anarchy*. London: Kegan, Paul, Trench, Trubner & Co., Ltd. Page numbers given are those printed on the pages rather than the number given by my PDF reader.

Mann, H.K. (1910). "Pope Leo V." In Knight, K. 2017. *The Catholic Encyclopedia*. Web. New York: Robert Appleton Company. Retrieved February 7, 2019 from http://www.newadvent.org/cathen/09159b.htm

Mann, H.K. (1912). "Pope Sergius III." In Knight, K. 2017. *The Catholic Encyclopedia*. Web. New York: Robert Appleton Company. Retrieved February 16, 2019 from http://www.newadvent.org/cathen/13729a.htm

Mann, H.K. (1912). "Pope Stephen (VI) VII." In Knight, K. 2017. *The Catholic Encyclopedia*. Web. New York: Robert Appleton Company. Retrieved February 7, 2019 from http://www.newadvent.org/cathen/14289d.htm

Mann, H. K. (1925). *The Lives of the Popes in the Early Middle Ages; Vol. IV: The Popes in the Days of Feudal Anarchy*. Second Edition. London: Kegan, Paul, Trench, Trubner & Co., Ltd. 2016 PDF by Forgotten Books & Co., Ltd. Page numbers given are those printed on the pages rather than the number given by my PDF reader.

Martyrdom of Ignatius. (107 or 116).
    See *Ante-Nicene Fathers*. ANF, Vol. I.

Martyrdom of Polycarp. (155-165).
    See *Ante-Nicene Fathers*. ANF, Vol. I.

Mastrantonis, G. (1985). "The Ten Commandments." Web. Greek Orthodox Archdiocese of America. Retrieved February 27, 2019 from https://www.goarch.org/-/the-ten-commandments

Bibliography

Matthews, J.F.; Nicol, D.M. (2018). "Constantine I: Roman Emperor." Encyclopædia Britannica, Inc. Web. Retrieved June 19, 2018 from https://www.britannica.com/biography/Constantine-I-Roman-emperor

McElwee, J.J. (2014). "Francis and Bartholomew issue resounding, historic calls for church unification." National Catholic Reporter. Web. Retrieved on January 6, 2017 from https://www.ncronline.org/news/global/francis-and-bartholomew-issue-resounding-historic-calls-church-reunification

McBrien, Fr. R. (2008). *The Church: The Evolution of Catholicism*. Paperback. New York, NY: HarperOne.

McBrien, Fr. R. P. (2016). "The Papacy." In Phan, P.C. (2016). *The Gift of the Church: A Textbook on Ecclesiology*. Kindle. Collegeville, MN: Liturgical Press.

McGuire, Brendan (Ph.D.). (n.d.). "The Medieval Papacy": Part One. Institute of Catholic Culture. Audio. Retrieved on January 6, 2017 from https://instituteofcatholicculture.org/talk/the-medieval-papacy/

Meyendorff, J. (1992). *Primacy of Peter*. Paper. zzz

Meyendorff, J. (2019). "Eastern Orthodoxy." Web. Encyclopedia Britannica. Retrieved September 1, 2019 from https://www.britannica.com/topic/Eastern-Orthodoxy

Miller, J.M. (1995). *The Shepherd and the Rock: Origin, Development, and Mission of the Papacy*. Hardback. Huntington, IN: Our Sunday Visitor Publishing Division.

Moffett, S.H. (1998). *A History of Christianity in Asia, Volume I: Beginnings to 1500*. Kindle. Maryknoll, NY: Orbis Books

Most, W.G. (1990). "The Magisterium or Teaching Authority of the Church." Web. EWTNews. Retrieved July 10, 2019 from https://www.ewtn.com/faith/teachings/chura4.htm

Most Holy Family Monastery. (2014). "Was Vatican II Infallible?." Web. 2019. Most Holy Family Monastery. Retrieved June 24, 2019 from https://www.mostholyfamilymonastery.com/catholicchurch/vatican-ii-infallible/#.XRDqrOhKhPY

National Catholic Reporter. (2015). "Fr. Richard McBrien, theologian and church expert, dies at 78. Web. Retrieved February 7, 2017

from https://www.ncronline.org/news/people/fr-richard-mcbrien-theologian-has-died

Nicene and Post-Nicene Fathers (NPNF). (1886-1900). Series 1 (NPNF1) was edited by Philip Schaff, and Series II (NFNF2) was edited by Philip Schaff & Henry Wace.

The list below is the list of fathers sorted into the volumes in which they are found. The dates are the father's writing career. Some writings have more exact dates.

NPNF2, Vol. I.
- Eusebius of Caesaria. A.D. 300-340.
  - *The Church History of Eusebius.* 323.
  - *Life of Constantine.* 339.

NPNF2, Vol. II.
- Socrates Scholasticus. c. A.D. 439.
  - *The Ecclesiastical History of Socrates Scholasticus.* c. 439.

NPNF2, Vol. III.
- Theodoret. d. A.D. 458-466
  - "Letters of the Blessed Theodoret, Bishop of Cyrus." c. 445-450.

NPNF2, Vol. IV.
- Athanasius. A.D. 328-373.
  - "Defense of Dionysius" or *De Sententia Dionysii.* 328-373.
  - "Defense of the Nicene Definition" or *De Decretis.* 346-356.
  - "On the Councils of Ariminum and Seleucia" or *De Synodis.* 359.

NPNF2, Vol. VI.
- Leo I (the Great). A.D. 440-461.
  - "Sermons." 440-461.

NPNF2, Vol. XIV.
- "The First Ecumenical Council: The First Council of Nice." A.D. 325
- "The Fourth Ecumenical Council: The Council of Chalcedon." A.D. 451.
- "The Third Ecumenical Council: The Council of Ephesus." A.D. 431.

Bibliography

"The XXX Canons of the Holy and Fourth Synods, of Chalcedon." A.D. 451.

Numen: The Latin Lexicon. (n.d.). "Definition of Principalitas." Retrieved April 26, 2017 from http://latinlexicon.org/definition.php?p1=2047679

Origen. 217-250.
   See *Ante-Nicene Fathers*. ANF, Vol. V and IX

Pavao, P.F. (2013). *The Apostles Gospel: Should Paul's Letters to Christians Be the Guide to Converting the Lost?* Selmer, TN: Yachad LLC.

Pavao, P.F. (2014). *Decoding Nicea: Constantine Changed Christianity and Christianity Changed the World.* Selmer, TN: Greatest Stories Ever Told.

Pavao, P.F. (2009-2019). "The Canons of the Council of Nicea." Web. Christian History for Everyman. Retrieved June 23, 2017 from http://www.christian-history.org/council-of-nicea-canons.html

Pavao, P.F. (2009-2019). "Christian History for Everyman." Web. Retrieved May 28, 2019 from https://www.christian-history.org/index.html

Pavao, P.F. (2009-2019). "FAQ: Infant Baptism." Web. Retrieved May 28, 2019 from https://www.christian-history.org/faq-infant-baptism.html

Pavao, P.F. (2009-2019). "Gnosticism." Web. Christian History for Everyman. Retrieved May 7, 2017 from http://www.christian-history.org/gnosticism.html

Pavao, P.F. (2009-2019). "Nicea Myths: Common Fables About the Council of Nicea and Constantine." Web. Christian History for Everyman. Retrieved October 15, 2018 from https://www.christian-history.org/nicea-myths.html

Pavao, P.F. (2009-2019). "The Orthodox Church and Icons." Web. Christian History for Everyman. Retrieved June 7, 2019 from https://www.christian-history.org/orthodox-church-icons.html

Pavao, P.F. (2009-2019). "Quotes About Religious Icons." Web. Christian History for Everyman. Retrieved June 8, 2019 from https://www.christian-history.org/religious-icons-quotes.html

Pearse, R. (2001). *Tertulliani Liber De Praescriptione Haereticorum.* The Tertullian Project. Web. Retrieved August 28, 2017 from http://www.tertullian.org/latin/de_praescriptione_haereticorum.htm

Peter of Alexandria. (300-311).
    See *Ante-Nicene Fathers*. ANF, vol. VI.

PewResearchCenter. (2011). "Leaving Catholicism." Web. Retrieved December 8, 2016 from http://www.pewforum.org/2009/04/27/faith-in-flux3/

PewResearchCenter. (2011). "Changing Within Protestantism." Web. Retrieved December 8, 2016 from http://www.pewforum.org/2009/04/27/faith-in-flux4/

Pohle, J. (1911). "Sacrifice of the Mass." In Knight, K. 2017. *The Catholic Encyclopedia*. Web. New York: Robert Appleton Company. Retrieved June 8, 2019 from http://www.newadvent.org/cathen/10006a.htm

Pontifical Gregorian University. (2000). "The Pontifical Gregorian University." Web. Retrieved May 25, 2017 from https://www.unigre.it/Univ/chi_siamo_en.php

Polycarp.
    See *Ante-Nicene Fathers*. ANF, Vol. I.

Pope John XXIII. (1962). "Speeches 1962." Web. The Holy See. Retrieved June 24, 2019 from https://w2.vatican.va/content/john-xxiii/en/speeches/1962.index.html

Pope Leo X. (1520). *Exsurge Domine*. Web. 2000-2017. Papal Encyclicals Online. Retrieved May 31, 2019 from http://www.papalencyclicals.net/Leo10/l10exdom.htm

Pope Paul VI. (1964). "Dogmatic Constitution on the Church. *Lumen Gentium*. Solemnly Propagated by His Holiness Pope Paul VI on November 21, 1964." Web. The Holy See. Retrieved November 5, 2016 from http://www.vatican.va/archive/hist_councils/ii_vatican_council/documents/vat-ii_const_19641121_lumen-gentium_en.html

Pope Pius IX. (1870). "First Dogmatic Constitution on the Church of Christ." Web. Catholic Planet. (n.d.). Retrieved January 11, 2019 from http://www.catholicplanet.org/councils/20-Pastor-Aeternus.htm

Pope Pius XII. (1943). *Mystici Corporis Christi*. Web. The Holy See. Retrieved July 6, 2019 from http://w2.vatican.va/content/pius-

Bibliography

xii/en/encyclicals/documents/hf_p-xii_enc_29061943_mystici-corporis-christi.html

Pope Pius XII. (1950). "Apostolic Constitution of Pope Pius XII." Web. Libreria Editrice Vaticana. Retrieved February 28, 2019 from http://w2.vatican.va/content/pius-xii/en/apost_constitutions/documents/hf_p-xii_apc_19501101_munificentissimus-deus.html

"Protoevangelium of James." c. 145. See *Ante-Nicene Fathers*. ANF, Vol. VIII.

Ray, S.K., Dr. (2009). *Upon This Rock*. Modern Apologetics Library. Kindle. Ignatius Press.

Roberts, S. (2015). "Rev. Richard McBrien, Dissenting Catholic Theologian, Dies at 78." Web. New York Times, January 28, 2015. Retrieved May 25, 2017 from https://www.nytimes.com/2015/01/29/us/rev-richard-mcbrien-catholic-firebrand-dies-at-78.html

Robinson, A, D.D. (Ed.). (n.d.). *The Demonstration of the Apostolic Preaching*. PDF. The Macmillan Co.

Russian Orthodox Cathedral of St. John the Baptist. (n.d.). "Ten Commandments." Web. Retrieved February 27, 2019 from https://stjohndc.org/en/orthodoxy-foundation/ten-commandments

Schaff, P. (1882). *History of the Church, Volume II: Ante-Nicene Christianity*. PDF. Grand Rapids, MI: Christian Classics Ethereal Library.

Schaff, P. (1882). *History of the Church, Volume III: Nicene and Post-Nicene Christianity*. PDF. Grand Rapids, MI: Christian Classics Ethereal Library.

Schaff, P. (1882). *History of the Christian Church, Volume VII: Modern Christianity. The German Reformation*. PDF. Grand Rapids, MI: Christian Classics Ethereal Library.

Schaff, P. (1901). *History of the Christian Church*, Vol. 2. New York: Charles Scribner's Sons. p. 158. Cited by Horn, T. (2017). *The Case for Catholicism: Answers to Classic and Contemporary Protestant Objections*. Kindle edition. Ignatius Press. Kindle locations 1663-1671.

Schaff, P. (1903). *History of the Christian Church, Volume VII-2: Modern Christianity: The Swiss Reformation*. Fourth edition, revised. New York: Charles Scribner's Sons

Schatz, K. Dr. (1996). *Papal Primacy: From Its Origins to the Present*. Paperback. Collegeville, MN: Liturgical Press.

"Seventh Council of Carthage." A.D. 256.
 See *Ante-Nicene Fathers*. ANF, Vol. VIII.

Society of St. Pius X. 2003. "The Errors of Vatican II: Part I." Web. Retrieved June 24, 2019 from https://sspxasia.com/Documents/SiSiNoNo/2003_January/errors_of_vatican_II.htm

Socrates Scholasticus.
 See *Nicene and Post-Nicene Fathers: NPNF2, Vol. II*.

Tertullian. A.D. 197-220.
 See *Ante-Nicene Fathers*. ANF, Vol. III.

Tertullian Project. (n.d.). *Adversus Marcionem (Against Marcion)*. Web. Retrieved July 4, 2019 from http://tertullian.org/works/adversus_marcionem.htm

Theodoret.
 See *Nicene and Post-Nicene Fathers*. NPNF2, Vol. III.

"The Third Ecumenical Council: The Council of Ephesus." A.D. 431.
 See *Nicene and Post-Nicene Fathers*. NPNF2, Vol. XIV.

Tixeront, J., D.D. (1920). *Handbook of Patrology*. In Kirby, P. (2001-2019). "Handbook of Patrology. Web. Early Christian Writings. Retrieved June 27, 2019 from http://earlychristianwritings.com/tixeront/section1-1.html

Trigillo, Fr. John. (2018). "What is Papal Primacy?." Legatus Magazine. Web. Legatus Magazine. Retrieved December 8, 2016 from http://legatus.org/what-is-papal-primacy/

Trinity Communications. (2019). "Catholic Dictionary: Cardinal." Web. Retrieved July 4, 2019 from https://www.catholicculture.org/culture/library/dictionary/index.cfm?id=32332

Tufano, V.M. (2010). "When Did We Start Celebrating Mass in Latin." Web. U.S. Catholic. Retrieved March 13, 2019 from http://www.uscatholic.org/church/2010/06/when-did-we-start-celebrating-mass-latin

Bibliography

Unitatis Redintegratio. (1964). "Decree on Ecumenism." Web. The Holy See. Retrieved April 24, 2017 from http://www.vatican.va/archive/hist_councils/ii_vatican_council/documents/vat-ii_decree_19641121_unitatis-redintegratio_en.html

United States Council of Catholic Bishops (USCCB). (1973). "Differing Attitudes Toward Papal Primacy." Web. Retrieved January 30, 2019 from http://www.usccb.org/beliefs-and-teachings/ecumenical-and-interreligious/ecumenical/lutheran/attitudes-papal-primacy.cfm

United States Conference of Catholic Bishops (USCCB). (1989). "An Agreed Statement on Conciliarity and Primacy in The Church." Web. Retrieved January 30, 2019 from http://www.usccb.org/beliefs-and-teachings/ecumenical-and-interreligious/ecumenical/orthodox/conciliarity-and-primacy.cfm

United States Conference of Catholic Bishops (USCCB). (2017). "New American Bible Revised Edition." Web. *United States Conference of Catholic Bishops*. 2018. Retrieved on January 6, 2017 from http://www.usccb.org/beliefs-and-teachings/ecumenical-and-interreligious/ecumenical/lutheran/attitudes-papal-primacy.cfm

United States Conference of Catholic Bishops (USCCB). (2019). "Acts, Chapter 15." Web. Retrieved April 14, 2019 from http://www.usccb.org/bible/acts/15

Van Braght, T.J. (1660). *The Bloody Theater or Martyr's Mirror of the Defenseless Christians*. Kindle, second English edition; twenty-seventh printing, 2006.

Wace, H. (n.d.). *A Dictionary of Christian Biography and Literature to the End of the Sixth Century A.D., with an Account of the Principal Sects and Heresies*. PDF. Grand Rapids, MI: Christian Classics Ethereal Library.

Weidenkopf, S. (2014). "The Antipope Who Became a Saint." Web. Catholic Answers. Retrieved May 9, 2017 from https://www.catholic.com/magazine/online-edition/the-antipope-who-became-a-saint

Wensing, Michael, S.T.L. (2004). "The True Ten Commandments." Web. Catholic Answers. 1996-2018. Retrieved February 27, 2019

from https://www.catholic.com/magazine/print-edition/the-true-ten-commandments

White, J. (2013). "The Great Debate III – Papacy – Pacwa." Youtube video. Alpha & Omega Ministries. Retrieved May 10, 2018 from https://www.youtube.com/watch?v=WefaXKQYUv4

Wikipedia. (2018). "Auxilius of Naples." Web. Wikipedia Foundation, Inc. Retrieved May 3, 2019 from https://en.wikipedia.org/wiki/Auxilius_of_Naples

Wikipedia. (2019). "List of Popes." Web. Wikipedia Foundation, Inc. Retrieved May 3, 2019 from https://en.wikipedia.org/wiki/List_of_popes

Wright, F.A. (trans.). (1930). *The Works of Liudprand of Cremona.* London: George Routledge & Sons, LTD. This translation can be read online at https://archive.org/details/in.ernet.dli.2015.168391/page/n6. (Retrieved May 27, 2019).

"XXX Canons of the Holy and Fourth Synods, of Chalcedon, The." See *Nicene and Post-Nicene Fathers*. NPNF2, Vol. XIV.

Index

1 Clement, 18, 71, 76, 82, 99
1 Peter 5
    1-4, 18, 43, 49-50, 59, 65, 85, 246, 259
Acts 15
    Council of Jerusalem, 18, 37, 41, 62
Against Heresies by Irenaeus, 19, 38, 72, 74, 79, 97-98, 101-106, 108, 110-112, 120, 131, 141-142, 145, 147-148, 200, 222, 229, 243-244, 268
Against Marcion by Tertullian, 81, 113, 114, 116
Akin, Jimmy (Catholic apologist), 14, 29, 33-34, 44, 118, 119, 137-139, 152, 191, 194
antipopes, 131, 233, 239
antiquity of error, 186-187
Apologists, the, 93-95
apologists, see scholars vs. apologists
Apostles
    authority of 54-55, 101-102, 105, 229
    churches founded by, 34, 53-56, 101-102, 115, 141-142
apostolic succession, 14, 17, 33, 42, 54, 55, 94, 102-106, 108, 110, 112, 126, 131, 144, 150, 162, 171-172, 182, 186-187, 195-196, 205, 216-217, 223, 229, 234, 240-243
apostolic tradition, see tradition, apostolic
arguments from silence, 33, 38, 40, 67-68, 184
Arian Controversy, 20, 147, 192, 199-201
Armenian Orthodox Church, 52

Armstrong, Dave (Catholic apologist), 9-12, 152
Athanasius, bishop of Alexander, 191-192, 201-204, 206, 256
atonement, 164, 260, 263
Avignon Papacy, 241-242
Babylonian Captivity of the Church, 241
baptismal regeneration, 152, 244
Benedict IX, Pope
    sold office 239-240
Bible, the
    forbidden by Rome, 249-250
binding and loosing, 17, 32, 34, 37, 40-43, 117, 138, 248
bishop
    monarchial, 15, 72-75, 78-82, 88-90, 104, 108
bishop of bishops, 146, 150
Cathari, see Novatian
catholic
    definiton of 53-54
Catholic Answers, apologetic ministry, 6, 29, 131, 161-162, 221, 231, 252, 254, 256
chair of Peter, 143, 154, 170-172, 230, 240
Chapman, John (Catholic apologist), 19, 35, 79, 147, 176-177
chief shepherd, 17, 44, 88, 259
Chieti Agreement, 13-14, 17, 23, 205, 216
Church's treasury, 224, 247-248
Cleenewerck, Laurent, 15, 214-215, 217, 229, 231
Clement of Alexandria, 60, 73, 80-81, 93
Clement of Rome, 71-78
college of elders, 18, 49-51, 72, 75, 78-82, 89-90, 104, 108, 229

communing with corrupt priests, 178-179, 230
Congar, Yves 39, 215, 217
Constantine I (the Great), Emperor, 20-22, 194, 199, 201-202, 213, 254
Constantinople
    bishop of, 22, 52, 202, 210
Constantius II, Emperor, 21, 201-204, 210
Cornelius, bishop of Rome, 19, 63, 104, 142, 146-147, 159, 165-176, 202
Council of Carthage, A.D. 256, 20, 145-152, 156, 171, 175, 183
Council of Chalcedon, A.D. 451, 21, 52-54, 125, 207, 210-213, 216
Council of Constantinople, A.D. 381, 125
Council of Ephesus, A.D. 431, 53, 207-213
Council of Jerusalem (Acts 15), 37, 41
    leader of 18, 61-62
Council of Nicea, A.D. 325, 10-11, 20-21, 34, 38-39, 51-52, 86, 125, 147, 190, 192, 195, 199-204, 210, 222-223, 233-234
Council of Sardica, A.D. 343, 203-205
Crusades, the, 251
Cyprian of Carthage, 20, 38, 40, 86, 97, 104, 140-196, 202, 208, 211, 214, 217, 230, 234, 243, 246
    misuse of his writings, 145-146, 151-155
    one episcopate only, 143-146, 151, 155, 171-173, 177, 181-182, 185, 195
    questions salvation of Stephen I, 153-154
    unity, 20, 143-144, 147, 170-171, 176-177, 181-182, 189, 195, 210-211, 214
definition of terms, 49-54, 56-57

Dionysius (the Great), bishop of Alexandria, 77, 152-153, 188, 191-193
Dionysius, bishop of Corinth, 77.......
Dionysius, bishop of Rome, 191-192
dynastic stewardship, 33
Eastern Orthodox Churches, 7, 9, 22, 125, 205, 213-218, 226, 253
Eleutherius, bishop of Rome, 107
    embraces heresy, 120-121
    Gaul's letter to,, 120-121
Ephesus, church in, 10, 50, 54, 73, 76, 80-83, 85, 106, 109-110, 113, 116, 124, 142
Eusebius of Caesarea (historian), Bishop, 9-11, 18-21, 32, 76-77, 116, 120-126, 150, 153, 169, 171, 182, 186-188, 193, 199, 212
Eusebius of Nicomedia, Bishop, 20, 199, 201-202, 204
evangelicals, 163, 167
Faith of the Early Fathers by William Jurgens, 136, 138, 155, 195
Father Knows Best, The by Jimmy Akin, 33, 119, 137-139, 152, 191, 194
Firmilian, bishop of Caesarea, 145-146, 148, 150-151, 184, 186-188, 211
first among equals (see also papal primacy), 22
Formosus, Pope, 232-234
    posthumously tried, 232-234
foster churches, St. John's, 81-82, 113
gates of Hades, 27, 29-30, 134, 161
gnostics and gnosticism, 18, 33-34, 103-106, 110, 148, 244
Gratiano, Giovanni (Pope Gregory VI)
    bought pope's office, 240
great crime,, 162, 243
Great Schism, The, 23, 52, 218, 226
Great Western Schism, 241

Index

Gregory the Great, Pope,
  servant of the servants of God, 22
Hahn, Scott (Catholic apologist), 3, 14, 31-33, 36, 40-42, 76, 87, 137-138, 205, 231
Hippolytus, antipope, 19, 93, 131-132, 191, 196
Holy Roman Emperor, 232, 237
  description of, 237
Horn, Trent (Catholic apologist), 76, 152-155, 168
idolatry, 30, 252,-253
Ignatius of Antioch, 15, 79-89, 99-100, 245
  Epistle to the Romans, 84-88
images
  veneration of, 200-201, 252-255, 257
indulgences, 248
Inquisition, the, 251
Irenaeus, 11, 18-19, 38-39, 53, 72, 74-75, 7- 79, 93, 95, 97-126, 131, 141-142, 144-145, 147-148, 155, 161, 171, 182, 186, 196, 200, 212, 217, 222, 225, 229, 240, 242-244, 25- 260, 268
Isaiah 22
  15-25, 31-33, 38
James the apostle, 18, 61-67, 194-195, 256
John 20:22-23; 17, 29, 42, 151, 187, 189, 259
John 21:15-17; 17, 27, 42, 43, 44, 49, 94, 95, 157, 160
John the apostle, 60, 73, 76, 79-82, 85, 88, 110, 114, 123-124, 265
John XII, Pope, 56, 95, 237-238
Joint International Commission for Dialogue Between the Roman Catholic Church and the Orthodox Church
  see Chieti Agreement
Julius, bishop of Rome, 21, 201-204, 206, 209, 230

Jurgens, W.A. (author), 136, 138, 155, 195, 196
Justin Martyr, 93, 244, 245, 269
keys of the kingdom, 15, 17, 27-28, 30-39, 42, 61, 67, 86, 95, 115-119, 134, 139, 143, 185, 189, 196, 209, 217, 261
Küng, Hans (Catholic theologian), 13
lapsed Christians, 142-144, 154, 158-160, 163-165, 172-173, 175-177, 183
Leo I (the Great), Pope, 14, 21, 56, 182-183, 207-208, 211-214, 230, 232-233, 236-238, 248
Liberius, bishop of Rome, 21, 204-205
Licinius, Emperor, 20, 194, 199
Linus I, bishop of Rome
  first pope?, 17, 75, 107, 195
Liudprand of Cremona (papal biographer), 231, 235, 238-239
Madrid, Patrick, 14
Madrid, Patrick (Catholic apologist), 14
magisterium, 27, 30
Mann, Horace (papal biographer), 36, 56, 226, 230-240
Marcianus, bishop of Arles, 39, 176-177, 184
Marcion, heretic, 109, 147-148, 153, 184
Marozia, senatrix of Rome, 235238
Mary and mariology, 73, 85, 94, 105, 224, 247-248, 252, 256
Matthew 16; 17, 27-30, 32, 37-39, 41-42, 49, 78, 93-95, 105, 115, 117, 133-138, 140-146, 151, 156-157, 159, 165, 189, 216
Matthew 18; 17-18, 32, 42, 137, 138
McBrien, Richard (Catholic theologian), 5, 12, 30, 35, 72, 75, 88, 98, 101, 118, 126, 144, 155,

180-181, 185, 216, 226, 247, 254, 257
messenger
   office of, 73-75, 108
Miller, Michael (Catholic theologian), 15, 21-22, 75, 209
monarchial leadership, 15, 72-75, 78-82, 88-90, 104, 108
   in Rome, 72-75, 108
   origin of, 80-82
Montanus and the Montanists, 34-35, 116-121
Nestorius, condemned bishop of Constantinople, 52, 210, 212-213
Novatian and Novatians, 19, 142, 143, 146-147, 165-170, 174-177, 186, 202
Office of the Inquisition, 251
Oriental Orthodox Church, 216, 253
Origen, 37, 132-139, 142, 163, 191, 196, 256
Orthodox Churches, Eastern, 13, 15, 23, 52-54, 102, 205, 210, 214-216, 244, 253-254
papal primacy
   caused division, 226
   first claim, 207-209
   Orthodox Church reactions, 213-218
   primacy of honor, 22, 215-217, 221
   primacy of jurisdiction, 22, 216, 221
Passover, see Quartodeciman Controversy
Pastor of Hermas, 74, 195
patriarchs, 49, 51-54, 56, 193, 204, 218, 229
Paul of Samosata, 193
Peter
   and James, 61-64
   chair of, 143, 154, 170-72, 230, 240

Peter's confession, 17, 29, 33, 37, 39, 119, 132, 137, 140, 163-164, 259
   leader of the apostles, 17, 44
   as presbyter, 69-71
   the rock, 17, 28-29, 132, 134, 137, 151, 155, 161, 163, 165, 187, 195-196, 208, 214, 229
   shepherd of whole Church, 43-44, 88
Peter Syndrome, 34, 119, 136, 143, 171, 195
Polycarp of Smyrna, 79, 80, 82-85, 89, 98, 109-110, 123-124, 126
Polycrates, bishop of Ephesus opposed Rome, 10, 124, 125
pope
   corrupt popes, 55-56, 162-163, 229-240
   definition of, 53
   multiple popes, 241-242
   office sold, 239-240
   Peter's successor, 14-19, 21, 105, 144-145, 170-173, 186-187, 195-196, 205, 214-216, 230
Pope Fiction by Patrick Madrid, 14
preeminent authority, 19, 38, 97-98, 106, 112, 161, 229
presbyter, see college of elders
presbytery, see college of elders
priests and priesthood, 49, 51, 53, 57, 124, 153, 170, 174-175, 178-179, 180-181, 185, 203, 233, 234, 246, 249, 255
Proof of the Apostolic Preaching, The by Irenaeus, 38, 268
Protestant Gospel, 163-164
Protestant Reformation, 23, 179-180, 226, 246, 248, 251, 255
Protestants, 4, 28, 32, 51, 54, 82, 163, 178, 214, 216, 244, 250, 253, 260-267
Quartodeciman Controversy, 10-11, 19, 121, 123, 125-127

Index

Ray, Stephen, 14, 15, 40, 87, 119, 136-137, 140, 150, 152, 168, 184, 191-195, 203
real presence, 245
rebaptism of heretics, 147-150
Reasons to Believe by Scott Hahn, 14, 40, 76
rebaptism of heretics, 150, 153, 159, 177, 181, 183
rock, the, see Peter, the rock
Rome, church of
    breaks in succession, 241-242
    chief source of Church unity, 144-145, 154, 172-173, 181
    corruption of succession, 229-241
    greatness of, 18, 40, 67, 77-78, 97-98, 106, 112, 154, 161-163, 182, 204, 257
    preeminent authority, 19, 38, 97-98, 106, 112, 161, 229
    roll of bishops, 107-108, 195-196
    true doctrines, 243-245
root and mother of the Church, 166, 168
saints, 113-114, 124, 247,
salvation by faith alone, 260-263
Schaff, Philip (historian), 76, 82, 179, 200, 206, 222-223, 255
Schatz, Klaus (Catholic theologian), 12, 40, 53, 218, 221, 224-226, 227
scholars vs. apologists, 9, 11-15, 17, 75, 123
second commandment, 253-255
Second Council of Nicea, A.D. 787, 200
see images, 252-254
servants of the servants of God (see also Gregory the Great), 22
shepherd, true role, 18, 43-44
Shepherd and the Rock, The, 15, 22, 75, 209
Shepherd of Hermas, see *Pastor of Hermas*
Sigismund, King, united the papacy, 242
simony, 238, 241
sola scriptura, 149-150
soulish, the, 34, 116
state Churches, 250-252
Stephen I, bishop of Rome, 19- 20, 77, 142-143, 145-148, 150-155, 159, 167, 174, 176-178, 181,-188, 193, 208-212
steward, Peter as, 32-33, 37, 42
Studies on the Early Papacy by John Chapman, 176-177
succession, spiritual, 54-56
Tertullian of Carthage, 13, 18, 33-38, 40-42, 54-55, 81, 93, 95, 99, 101-102, 112-121, 124, 127, 141, 144, 148-149, 155, 195, 222, 225, 229, 240, 242, 246, 259-260, 268, 269
The Bad Popes by E.R. Chamberlin, 239-240
Theodora, mother of Marozia, 235
Theodoret, historian, 212
throne of Peter, see chair of Peter
tradition,
    apostolic, 11, 18-19, 38, 94-95, 97-112, 115, 123, 125, 145, 148-150, 185, 187-188, 200-201, 211, 217, 223-226, 242-244, 248, 259-260, 268
    of men, 12, 148-149
    of Rome, 20-21, 77, 121, 148-149, 183-185, 187-188, 211, 223-224, 242-257
    Protestant, 259-263, 268
transubstantiation, 245
treasury of the Church, 224, 247-248
truth vs. men, 108-110, 225-227
United States Conference of Catholic Bishops, 9, 13-15, 17-

18, 27, 41, 68, 97, 182, 207-208, 226
unity as evidence of truth, 114-115
universal bishop, 22
Upon This Rock by Stephen Ray, 14-15, 87, 119, 136-137, 140, 152, 168, 184, 191-195, 203
Urban VI, Pope, 241
Vatican I Council, 3-6, 12, 13, 15, 17, 27, 39, 94, 216, 218, 221, 249
Vatican II Council, 4-6, 12, 13, 15-17, 27, 39, 94, 218, 249
Vatican, the, 6, 9, 13-15, 17, 22, 27, 68, 97, 205, 208, 215
vicar of Christ, 3, 5, 93-94
Victor I, bishop of Rome, 9-11, 19, 121, 123-126, 182
White, James (Protestant apologist), 34, 171
Xystus, bishop of Rome, 77, 152-153, 188, 193

Greatest Stories Ever Told
P.O. Box 307
Selmer, TN 38375
731-645-0106
admin@christian-history.org
https://www.RebuildingtheFoundations.org

Other books published by Greatest Stories Ever Told®:

Slavery During the Revolutionary War (April 2013)
The Apostles' Gospel (June 2013)
Forgotten Gospel (December, 2014)
The Promise (November 2014)
Decoding Nicea (May 2014)

Rome's Audacious Claim

www.ingramcontent.com/pod-product-compliance
Lightning Source LLC
Chambersburg PA
CBHW070532010526
44118CB00012B/1111